Viceroys,
Vicars,
and Vergers

British English for Readers

Bill Harvey

2nd Edition

San Francisco

ISBN: 979-8-9888182-1-2

Sunset Boulevard Press
775 Post #210
San Francisco, CA 94109

INTRODUCTION:

✻

England and America are "two nations divided by a common language."
   Oscar Wilde
   G. B Shaw
   (Take your pick –it's been attributed to both.)

Books don't usually come with instructions. This one does. Think of this as a concise dictionary that translates British English into American English. Have it at hand when you pick up Shakespeare, or Agatha Christy, Douglas Adams, or even Harry Potter. Hit a confusing part or come across a word you have heard, but don't really know what it means to the Brits, look it up! If you are a little more curious, read the stuff that follows. If you really get curious –or are still confused- do the see *also.*

There are some subjects that are too interesting or too complicated to nail down in a short definition. You will find longer natterings sprinkled throughout listed alphabetically and titled more or less with the words a reader might use to look up a broad or nebulous subject.

Some of these longer offerings include:
- Accent, the English
- Americans, How the English feel about
- Architecture
- Clergy
- Cocktails
- Divisions (Regions, Counties, Parishes etc.)
- Food
- Government
- Homes & houses
- Knights & the knighthood

- Military (The Army, Navy, RAF, & regiments)
- Monarchy, the
- Money
- Peerage, the
- Schools
- Servants / Domestics
- Women

Do not be frightened of the bits on English History. Some things all but require a little historic perspective for an non English person to get a grip on. (Some of them are so confusing that not even the Brits really understand them.) I offer a few takes on the subject of history, none of which would satisfy a history professor, but would serve as a nice refresher to those who have forgotten it all after some class back in school. If this isn't enough, I suggest Winston Churchill's <u>A History of the English-Speaking Peoples</u>. I haven't read it myself. It took him 20 years to write. (WWII was a distraction.) It's four volumes long and the Dorset Press version totals 1708 pages.

NOTE / DISCLAIMER:
"England' is only one part of the United Kingdom and to dwell just on the "English" is to give short shrift to the Scots, Welsh, and Irish. Not at all politically correct. None the less, they are to be called the "English" or "Brits,"and the place where they all live "England" Deal with it.
Then read the bit about *divisions, political.*

*Two lions (the king of the beasts) show up on Plantagenet family arms in about 1180. Richard the Lionhearted added another lion in 1198 and about 1340 it started getting complicated with the addition of the French fleurs-de-lis. Thereafter it was off to the races. Today the royal family's crests all have a third lion, a unicorn, and variously the Scottish thistle, the Irish shamrock, the crosses of three different saints, and assorted crowns, coronets, scrolls and whatnot.

The letter *a* is the third most common letter in English, after *e* & *t*. It comes to us  from ancient Egypt where it got its start as an ox's head. The Phoenicians turned it sideways, and the Semites finished turning it upside-down for the Greeks and so it remains. There are a very few words in English that use the double *a* as in aardvark, but other languages are rather more keen on *a*'s -double or otherwise. Spanish, for example, uses the letter fully twice as often as does English. BTW, the two ways to write it are called *single-story* and *double-story.*

A   -the designation for a highway. It is typically a paved two-way road but some have as many as three lanes each direction. What Yanks would think of as a freeway, the Brits call a *motorway* abbreviated with an M. The A's that tend to show up in literature start in London and run as follows:

A1 -north as far as Edinburgh   A12 -northeast
A2 -to Dover   A20 -southeast
A3 -to South Hampden   A23 -south to Gatwick Airport and
A5 -northwest to Wales   on to Brighton
A6 -northeast to Manchester   A40 -northwest to Oxford
A10 -to the east coast

Some of the A's have grown up to become *M*s

AA -Automobile Association

abbey   -either a religious community, or after Henry VIII did away with the pope etc., it was a large manorial home that had once been part of an abbey, for example *Westminster Abbey.*

AC -Assistant Commissioner   (of police)

AA -Automobile Association

abbey   -either a religious community, or after Henry VIII did away with the pope etc., it was a large manorial home that had once been part of an abbey, for example *Westminster Abbey.*

AC -Assistant Commissioner   (of police)

Accent, the English   This is an utterly hopeless subject in general, made all the more so by the limitations of the written word. Here are a few thoughts that might help Americans understand just a little of what English writers are trying to convey:
- Accents are only about pronunciation. The grammar and vocabulary do not change -unless the author deliberately uses misspelled words and bad grammar to tell the reader something about the speaker; probably that the character is of a lower class.
- Accents may indicate where the speaker is from as well as his or her social status and education. America certainly has regional accents, probably as many–or even more than the English–but accent does not indicate social or educational level in America as much as it does in England. American writing uses grammar and vocabulary to indicate regionalism. To put it in other words, in England people from the same region might have different accents over and above vocabulary and grammar differences. In America, grammar and vocabulary will differentiate the educated rich from the lower classes, but the accent probably will not. (It's all about the American ideas of equality and what-not.)
- The English can probably tell a more about a person from hearing them speak than an American can tell about another American.
- The English language (and the American language too) is a mixture of Latin, Germanic Anglo-Saxon, and French, with some small bits of Celtic remaining.
- Welsh, Scottish, and Irish (Gaelic) are all derived from the original Celtic, but are not mutually understandable.

There are a couple of interesting ideas that the academic people kick around. One suggests that the way the Brits speak English is a consequence of these three different Germanic tribes that came to Britannia about 1500 years ago. It is, however, doubtful that anyone but the English can interpret these subtitle distinctions in speech. When this idea taken even further and to America, the same professorial types say that America has northern and southern accents because the north was settled by people from eastern England, -the Angles & Jutes, while the south was settled by people from the west side of England, the Saxons. Maybe. Sort of.

These academics categorize accents into two broad categories, the MLE -Multicultural London English which is a mix of cockney and other ethnic accents / languages. The other is RP or *Received Pronunciation* or what is commonly called the BBC accent. There are also distinctive accents for Ireland, Scotland, and Wales and even these may be subdivided into northern, southern, eastern, western, urban, rural etc. Pretty meaningless to any but an English language academic weeny.

Another of the tweed jacket and elbow patch crowd insist that America's southern drawl is nothing more than a proper English accent slowed way down, and is in fact the only place outside of England where proper English is still spoken at all!. I leave it to the reader to decide for this themselves. The whole issue gets real interesting, but real complicated and real quick when you stir in the New York Dutch, the French in New Orleans, the Irish in Boston, and Germans in Pennsylvania. Mercifully, we are considering just the English now.

According to Hoyle   -according to the rules of the game from the highest authority. Edmund Hoyle (1672 – 1769), was a lawyer and big fan of card games. He wrote <u>A Short Treatise on the Game of Whist</u> wherein he listed both the rules of the game along with some how-to. (The ***Marquis of Queensbury*** rules apply to boxing.)

accumulator   -a car's battery. It *accumulates* electricity. In horse racing, it is a series of cumulative bets.

Admiral   In Henry's Navy and onward, an Admiral was the commander of a fleet. They come in four flavors and in order of authority they run: Admiral of the Fleet, Admiral, Vice Admiral, and Rear Admiral. see ***military, Navy***

Admiralty   Much the same as America's old Department of the Navy. It goes back to 1832 and has been under the Department of Defense since 1965.

afters   -desert. see ***pudding***

air host / hostess   -a flight attendant -what Americans used to call stewards or stewardess.

Air Ministry   -the flying equivalent of the Admiralty and like the Admiralty, now a part of the Ministry (Department) of Defense.

Alderman   -either the head of a guild, or someone appointed by the king for some specific purpose. They are no longer appointed by the monarch, and may be elected like American aldermen or city councilman etc. In smaller boroughs, their role is like a America mayor. see ***divisions***

ale   -stronger and sweeter than ordinary beer. Even before it was rediscovered by today's trendy brew-snobs, it was more expensive.

A-levels   -voluntary Advanced Level Exams. Much like America's SAT or ACT exams used for college admission, but unlike the general American exams, the A-levels are subject specific, so a student might usually take two or three and the over-achiever might take any number of exams at various levels at various times in his or her school career. Students who have no plans to go on to college also take these tests to include their scores in their resumes. Students are required to stay in school only till age 16.

AELFREDUS
MAGNUS

Alfred the Great (849 – 899) The Saxon king crowned in 871. Alfred beat the Vikings, at least temporarily, and was thought of as an educated and merciful king. He improved the legal system, military, and quality of life for the people. see ***monarchy***

alley   -a narrow garden path. What Americans think of as an *alley* behind the house, the Brits call a ***mews***.

All Saints Day   -November 1. This is a somber religious thing to contemplate both the saints and martyrs. The previous day, October 31, is Halloween or *All Hallows Eve* and this is party time. The Brits go in for costumes and parties, but with pagan roots going much back farther even than Christianity. Dead people came back to life on this night so you had to dress up in an equally frightening manner for your own protection if you had to go out after dark. This business of going around town begging for candy also has religious roots, but it has a confusing conflation of alms for the poor, apple bobbing, bobbing women to see if they were witches, cracking nuts as treats, thumping doors to scare kids when the living-dead were out and about, and finally carving frightening lanterns out of pumpkins and gourds for protection against the dead. The candy thing is one of those rare instances when something uniquely American had been adopted by the Brits. (***All Fool's Day*** is much like America's April Fools Day.)

Americans   *"To be snooty about Americans while slavishly admiring them; this is another crucial characteristic of being British."* The Economist

There are some historic facts that can be pinned down between the Americans and the English, but it's hard to get a grip on their feelings about the Yanks. Objectivity goes out the window. Clearly between 1776 and 1812 Americans were not high on the English hit-parade. However there are some historic facts that American's tend to have forgotten about the English. First, the crown spent a lot of money protecting the colonists from the French and Indians between 1754 and 1763. Then, a whole twelve years later when the Crown wanted a little money to pay for it all, the colonists allied themselves with the French *against* the Brits.

The whole time, there were Brits back home who felt America was a lost cause and not worth the effort. Some even thought it was simply the right and moral thing to do, aside from the cost. In the view of most English at the time that the important fight was with the French. In 1812 the English needed sailors to blockade the French ports. They solved a serious personnel problem by taking Americans off of any American merchant (non-combatant) ship they happened across on the high seas. Magically, these men were transformed into English sailors to man the British Navy's cannons. This lead to the war of 1812, the burning of Washington DC, and a curious American alliance with the pirate Jean Lafitte. It ended in a draw. After this situation calmed down, the Brits bought cotton from the Americans down south and we all know how that worked out between 1861 and 1865. What is less well known is that England was actually on the side of the Confederate South.

The American public was pretty well committed to neutrality as the English and Germany were fighting WW I. The war started in 1914 but it took until 1917 for America to get involved. Another little-known fact: Franklin D. Roosevelt was the Secretary of the Navy and Winston Churchill was the Lord of the Admiralty when the Lusitania was sunk by a German submarine. It seems clear that this ship was carrying arms and therefore in violation of America's neutrality. Furthermore, it seems equally clear that the Germans knew it did. This incident is what finally got America into the war. It is less clear, but arguable, that both Roosevelt and Churchill may have had something to do with the whole incident. Clearly, it didn't hurt either of their careers.

After WWI, America and England began what FDR would call a 'special relationship' and this was a big thing during WW II. The Yanks and Brits would be allies in the Korean War, Cold War, Gulf War, and the War on Terror. The Yanks had to sort out Viet Nam on their own, but the Brits had to sort out the Falkland Island without America's help, and they got it done a lot better than America did in Viet Nam.

Much aside from war and history, one way to understand the Brit's thinking about the Yanks, is to get terribly subjective and consider some anecdotes and snarky quotes.

"American food means taking everything you learned about moderation and healthiness growing up, and completely ignoring it."

"I mean, isn't American baseball basically *rounders*?" (Yes. Rounders and baseball are very much alike.)

"America football... that's just rugby with pads and lots of commercials."

"The USA has a constant obsession with women with big_____, or big _____, or both. "

"Why are all Americans obsessed with high school? It looks like the most awful experience of all time where if you have anything in the least bit unusual about you, you get your head flushed down the toilet and all learning occurs though pop tests." (And this from the place where all the rich kids used to be packed off to boarding schools -apparently to be sodomized.)
"Nobody needs a gun. Not even for sport. Americans are paranoid they need a gun to protect their house, they don't."

"I have a problem with their spelling."

In summation, what the English think and say about Americans is not much different from what Americans think and say about themselves. Or what southerners say about northerners who say things about the people on the west coast who have opinions about people in the mid-west who are amused by people in the south. And so it goes.

American Plan   -a hotel room with meals included. American Hotels no longer follow the American Plan, but it lives on in England.

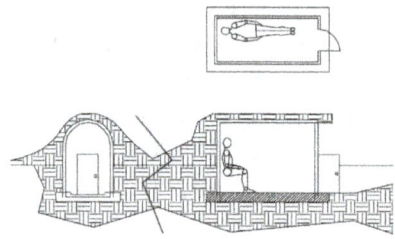

Anderson Shelter   -a prefabricated bomb shelter, buried in the back yard and used to good effect during WW II.

Anglo Catholic   -a high church somewhere left of Catholicism, but a little to the right of Church of England.

angel delight   -a powdered desert which, when mixed with milk makes a mousse-like desert. (Yanks would call it pudding.) It is iconic of all that is horrible about nutrition and instant food.

angels on horseback   -an old fashioned appetizer of grilled oysters wrapped in bacon. *Devils on horseback* are prunes or dates wrapped in bacon and are served at Christmas.

Anglo-Indian   -an English person either born in India or one who has spent a lot of time there. It is not an Indian who has immigrated to England.

Anglo-Saxon   -a catch phrase for supposed new and improved ethnic crowd that would replace the original Celts and finally become the British white-people.

The Angles, the Saxons, and the Jutes were a rather warlike crowd; tall, blond, and coming from Germany, Denmark, and the Netherlands -or what would eventually become Germany, Denmark, and the Netherlands. (Add Norway to this list, and you would have also have a pretty good description of where the Vikings would be coming from about 500 years later.) The Angles and Saxons first invaded England in the 4th century, but the Romans kicked them back across the channel. The Romans then left about 450 and the Angles and Saxons came back and stayed. They were joined by the Jutes who settled in Kent -and called themselves the 'Kentings.' The Angles settled in East Anglia, and the Saxons settled in Essex, Sussex, Middlesex, and Wessex.

There is a controversy among historians as to why the Angles, Saxons, and Jutes all came to England. One bunch holds that the Anglo-Saxons were invited to invade or settle in England in order to protect the locals from the Welsh and Scots. Another says that farmland was better than in the Low Countries. Both sides agree that when the Romans left, the Angel-Saxons stayed and melted in with the local Celts.

While the American use of the term *Anglo* to refer to pale white English people, (WASP -White Anglo Saxon Protestant), the English use it to refer to people who lived in Wessex & Anglia and were thought to be even less civilized than the (Franks / French) Normans.

In the 1800's, the therm Anglo-Saxon became shorthand for racial superiority, particularly as compared to the locals being colonized whether they wanted to be colonized or not. It brings to mind the term *Aryan* that was popular in the middle of the 20th century in Germany. We all know how that view got sorted out.

Anne Boleyn (1500-1536)   *Henry VIII's* second wife and mother of the future **Queen Elizabeth.** She was born around 1500. (There is some doubt as to exactly when.) She was the daughter of a high-level diplomat and by all accounts a bright, educated, popular girl who served in the various courts in Netherlands, France, and England. Things started going down-hill for her in 1522 when she and her dowry were negotiated off to an Irishman who was her cousin no less. This was to sort out a confusing political difficulty, but **Cardinal Wolsey** decided it wouldn't be quite proper. She was engaged again a year later for similar reasons and to another almost-relative. The good cardinal once again said 'No'.

Her big sister, Henry VIII's mistress at the time, got her a job in Henry's court and he tried to replace the big sister with little sister Anne. She resisted till he split with the Pope and had his marriage with **Catherine of Aragon** annulled. Anne and Henry were married in 1533, they had a daughter that same year, but by 1536 she had failed to produce a son and heir for Henry so he had her investigated for treason and beheaded about a month later. There is some controversy as to her treason, but it seems she was largely, if not entirely, innocent. The important take-away here is that Catherine's banishment and Anne's execution pretty much put an end to the relation between the English Monarchy and the Catholic Church and the earliest hints of the coming of the **Protestant Reformation.**

anorak   -a rain coat that is usually made from what the English call *American Cloth* and the Americans call *oil-cloth*. No one kows why.

apartment   -originally, the living quarters attached to some other functional building, i.e. the judge's apartment in a law-court building. In the 19th century, it meant a single room rented in a house. What Yanks think of an apartment is a *flat* in England. see also **homes**, and **bed-setter**.

apothecaries -druggists and/or pharmacists.

apprentices and apprenticeships   It's hard to say if the guild system with apprentices was more about keeping the supply down and the cost up, or about professional quality control with a mild form of slavery tacked on. Apprenticeships were common throughout Europe, a good bit of the world, and America too for that matter. Even to this day, many trades and their attached trade unions require some number of years learning the craft and *paying ones* dues' as an apprentice.

Craft guilds existed in medieval England and apprenticeships came along shortly thereafter. In 1563 England passed the ***Statute of Artificers*** which set some minimum ground rules for the master. He could have no more than three apprentices at any given time, and had to feed, clothe, and board them. The apprentice was indentured for seven years. It was common for parents to send their 12 to 14-year-old sons off to be apprentices, and then often taking in someone else's child.

approved school   -what Americans would call a reform school for juvenile delinquents.

Archbishop   -the head of the Church of England. There are actually two of them, the Archbishops of Canterbury and York, but the one in Canterbury is the real deal. They rank at about three and a half steps up the peerage toward the King and are right up there between dukes and marques.

architecture, English   A discussion of English architecture must begin with a mention of Stonehenge, some 1500 years older than the oldest pyramids in Egypt. A good bit later, the Romans came and went. They left behind fewer baths and fortifications than there are in Italy, but England certainly has its share of Roman ruins.

When the Romans left, Norman architecture might be considered the first recognizable 'style' in England, but it was really a knock-off of the Roman, (Romanesque), and furthermore, more French than English. Big buildings in England follow the arc of European architecture in general, but residential architecture took on a distinctly English style only in the 1700's.

The vernacular architecture unique to England and typical of where the common man lived was half-timber framed, ***wattle and daub***, with a thatched roof. Very picturesque for people like Snow White and her friends, but not built to last.   In big buildings, Gothic architecture with its pointed windows replaced Norman  influences during ***Henry VIII***'s reign, particularly for churches, but building churches in England became a dicey proposition as the Protestants and

Catholics were sorting things out. Still and all, Gothic architecture was typical of all of Northern Europe and therefore hardly 'English'.
England joined the rest of Europe in its fascination with all things Greek and Roman about 1700. We now begin to see assorted revivals, and the first

uniquely English style -particularly in residential architecture. It fits loosely under the label 'Georgian.' The English were a little more willing to set aside the gratuitous ornamentation of the Rococo and built houses with rigorous symmetry, emphasis on windows, and classic proportion.

Georgian refers a series of four King Georges that ran from 1714 to 1820. (**George III** was the same George who so annoyed the American Founding Fathers, but we will return to the Yanks shortly.) George III was either barking mad or severely depressed, (to use modern terminology), and his oldest son took over as his *regent* from 1810 to 1820. This gives us a sub-set of Georgian, the Regency Period with architecture that was even more restrained than Georgian, but still symmetrical, classic, and big on windows.

In the meantime, the Americans were not getting along with England (the revolution of 1776 and the War of 1812 and all) so they rejected the idea of copying England's architecture in favor of the French and their fascination with roofs. But they didn't go very far down this road. Federal architecture is more ornate than the Regency, but still symmetrical, carefully proportioned, and–you guessed it–still big on windows.

armourers / armorers   Not what you might think, the Armourors and Braisers Company made things out of copper and tin like pots and pans.

Army   Begin with the idea that in the past, England has no army as such; it has a bunch of *regiments*, and these regiments have not always been the king's regiments. Going way back, a rich nobleman would appoint himself a *colonel*, gather up his vassals, knights, and what ever naive peasant he could persuade to come along, and go off to take some other rich guy's stuff, typically his land and the appurtenant peasantry, but maybe his wife, or his horse, or whatever-damn-thing he pleased. Occasionally, an even richer guy like the king would have need of some fighting men and hire the whole lot at a price sure to make the rich guy even richer.

After the Civil War, Parliament was very leery of having a lot of organized, belligerent, and possibly Catholic men hanging about with weapons so they told everyone to go home and go back to farming. They only authorized and paid for a few of these regiment as the king's personnel Guard. (Note the capitol G in Guard who were the coolest and meanest most loyal mamma-jammas to be found. Even to this day, being in a Guard regiment means you were better than anyone else. They also had the prettiest uniforms.)

This worked well enough up until the Napoleonic Wars when England found she needed some serious military people to round out the Navy. (Remember, the fractious English citizenry in the American Colonies were a bothersome footnote to the bigger European theater.) So they organized 109 regiments of infantry, and 31 of cavalry. But they kept them off-shore as much as possible and paid them as little as possible.

Even this didn't work during the ***Crimean War***, which was a dismal failure for the English, so in 1871, Parliament bought up all the ***commissions*** of the colonels and officers that *owned* the regiments. Today THE *army* organizes pay, ranks, duties etc., but it still thigks if itslef as a collection of ***regiments***. Enlistment was for life until 1841, but reduced to 21 years for enlisted men, and 22 years for officers, but some of this time could be served in a reserve battalion. There was *conscription*, (Yank's *draft*), during both WWI and WWII, but today the army is all-volunteer, all-professional, and among the best in the world. Indeed, it must be said the they are every bit as good as America's Army today.

America has organized its Army much like the English have (with some help from the Prussians) but with some subtle differences in vocabulary. These differences are best left to the military / history freaks to hash out. For the casual reader, the following will help understand what's what, or at least what's the bigger and more important plop of soldiers.

	Highest / Largest		Smallest	
Infantry	Regiment (2 or more Battalions)	Battalion	Company	Platoon
Cavalry	These three are administered by a general (external) staff.	Regiment	Squadron	Troop
Artillery			Battery	
Engineers			Squadron	

Commands:
   Regional: North, South, East, West, and Scotland Commands as well as two Overseas Commands. These are lead—administered actually—by a general staff and some Generals.
Corps:
   2 or more Divisions of 50,000 people
Division:
   Commanded by a Major General with about 10,000 soldiers. Consists of 3 to 4 Brigades
Brigade:
   Commanded by a Brigadier with 5,000 soldiers in 3 or 4 Battle Groups or Battalions / Regiments.
Battle Group
   Lieutenant Colonel with 700-1000 people. Consists of various ad-hoc units for a specific purpose.
Battalion / Regiment:
   Lieutenant Colonel, 720 men. Consists of 4 to 6 Companies.
Company / Squadron:
   Major, 120 men made up of 3 or 4 Platoons
Platoon / Troop:
   Captain, Lieutenant or 2nd Lieutenant, 30 men in 3 Sections.
Section:
   Commanded by Sergeant or Corporal, may have 2 Fire Teams

ARMY

Fire Team:

    Commanded by a Lance Corporal and having 4 men.
    see *regiment, commissions, navy, ranks, dragoons, lancers,*
    grenadiers etc.

Army and Navy   -a popular department store in London that originally specialized in selling to military families. It is iconic for conservative tastes and completely unlike America's Army Surplus store which sell camping equipment.

arse   -a very crude word for ass in England. The word *ass* is either a donkey or a stupid annoying person and not at all crude or not as crude as *arse*.

Arts Council   -much like the American National Endowment for the Arts, (NEA). It is publicly funded and like the Yank's version, it seems to always fund the wrong & controversial stuff, at least to the minds of the more conservative taxpayers.

Ascot   -an important horse race where the swells dress up all fancy because the Royals will be there and men wear an ascot, the silly necktie / scarf worn under the shirt.

ashes, the   The trophy for the cricket test between England and Australia is an ugly little terra-cotta urn reputed to contain the ashes of a burnt wooden cricket ball. Or if not a cricket ball, then a bail, no one is quite sure. Australia won for the first time in 1882. The Sporting Times in England reported this sad event by saying that English cricket died and "...the body will be cremated and the ashes taken to Australia." Think of The Ashes as yachting's America's Cup, but with considerably more fans. see *cricket*

at home   -from 1800 to about 1940, being *at home* meant the lady of the house was at home and receiving callers. The butler's job was to carefully admit those guests who were of the proper pedigree per their calling cards.

aubergine   -eggplant. Both are ridiculous words.

Australia   -discovered by the Dutch in 1606, claimed by the Brits in 1770, and used as a penal colony from 1788. Prisoners or otherwise, things went well and the population grew. In 1901, they federated and became a self-governing *commonwealth*. Today the Brits feel pretty good about the Aussies, who play cricket, soccer, and rugby all three. It's all like how the English feel about the Canadians, (or that end of Canada that speaks

English), despite the fact that the Canadians do not play much cricket and furthermore, are fans of American football.

BTW, the Brits feel pretty good about the Aussies (Australians) at 79% approval, but they think just slightly better about he Canadians & new Zeelanders (the *Kiwis*) at 80% approval for each.

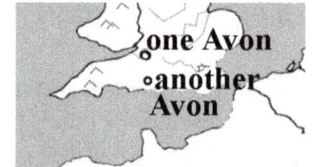
1949 Ford Prefect

Automobiles   A discussion of English cars would be only slightly shorter than one about American cars. While the sexy expensive ones like the MG, Lotus, Jaguar, Rolls Royce, and James Bond's Aston Martin etc. are well known in America, the less glamorous ones show up in literature and deserve a few words. Some popular ones include...

| Morris Oxford | 1920 - 1930 | Morris Minor | -post WW II |
| Ford Prefect | 1938 - 1961 | Morris Mini | 1959 - 2000 |

A single picture is sufficient because they all look silly, small, and boxy to the American eye, but in their defense, they are efficient in a place where gasoline (petrol) is expensive, parking is limited, and roads are narrow.

avenue   -the driveway to a house or the long tree lined drive up to the manor. In England *avenues* are rarely streets.

Avon   -a smallish river that would have had no great importance if Shakespeare had not been named the Bard of Avon because he was born in Stratford-upon-Avon. There are actually three or four Rivers Avon and the largest and only navigable one has nothing to do with Shakespeare. Just to confuse things a little more, there is also a Stratford, London.

away with the fairies -crazy, in la-la land. It comes from Irish mythology with the little people and fairies and all.

From the Egyptian picture-letter for foot. (?) It shows up in English words like *debt*, and *subtitle* where it is not pronounced because that's the way the Roman spelled it and there was a time when Latin was THE language of the well educated. The pronunciation freaks call *b* a *voiced bilabial stop*.

B   -the designation for paved country roads. See *A* & *M*

back-bench / back bencher   -Parliamentary member of the **Loyal Opposition** party who has little to say about how things go in Her Majesty's Government. They sit on benches behind the **Cabinet** Members, who are located on the *front bench*. They are a little like America's congressional minority but even less influential.

back stairs   -the stairs at the back of the house to be used by the servants. Anything *back stairs*, like gossip, was to be ignored by the family who generally ignored the servants anyway and used the exclusive front stairs. see **below the stairs**

bagman   -a traveling salesman

bags   -pants. Debagging in England is like the American *pantsing* a kid. It also means lots and lots of something, i.e. *bags of nerve*.

Bailiff   -a sheriff-like officer. They were mostly used in matters of debt, bankruptcy, evictions and other such unpleasant matters. When you encounter a bailiff in your reading, someone probably ends up being homeless or in debtor's prison but depends on the era.

baker's dozen   From the 13th to the 19th century there were various and serious penalties in London if a vendor cheated a customer on the weight of a purchase. In order to protect themselves from this, bakers would toss in a thirteenth bun, loaf, or whatever.

ball   Prior to the 19th century, balls were for courtly rich people and at least as much about political intrigue as fun and dancing. They didn't get much better during the Victorian era. Balls for fun, dancing, and seduction or mild flirtation were American. The Victorian ball was a deadly serious and ritualized ordeal to sort out who married whom. A ball had more in common with a stock exchange wherein things like young men and women were appraised, valued, bought and sold in a matrimonial market. Night-clubs and the like where young people could finally meet without adult supervision put an end to it all in the 1920's.

bangers and mash   -sausage & mashed potatoes, classic pub food. During WWII food—and especially meat—was rationed. Sausages were made with cheap filling and more water than usual; they fizzled and banged around in the pan more than proper sausage should.

Bank Holiday   England has lots of them and they are not just for banks, everyone gets the day off, or non-emergency people anyway. But it's not quite so simple; England, Wales, Scotland and Northern Ireland have slightly different holidays. Works out as follows:

Holiday	England & Wales	Scot-land	North Ireland	Rep. of Ireland	Isle of Mann
New Years Day January 1	√	√	√	√	√
January 2		√			
St. Patrick's Day March 17			√	√	
Good Friday	√	√	√		√
Easter Monday	√		√	√	√
May Day May 1	√	√	√	√	√
Last Monday in May	√	√	√		√
1st Monday in June				√	
1st Friday in June					√
Tynwald Day July 5					√
Battle of the Boyne, ('The Twelfth') July 12			√		
1st Monday in August		√		√	
Last Monday in August	√		√		√
Last Monday in October				√	
St. Andrew's Day Nov. 11		√			

Holiday	England & Wales	Scot- land	North Ireland	Rep. of Ireland	Isle of Mann
Christmas December 25	√	√	√	√	√
Boxing Day December 26	√	√	√	√	√

There Is one important exception to the non-emergency part; in 1968 an Emergency Bank Holiday was declared when the ***Prime Minister*** and his P*rivy Council* closed the London gold market to stem the losses to the British pound.

Bank of England   -a private bank founded in 1694 and nationalized 1946. It's role in England is closer to various roles of the Department of the Treasuries and Central Bank in America, but it is less political and arguably does a better (or at least a more conservative) job of managing things.

banking   In England, banking is a far more conservative and time honored business than in America with all its marketing, credit cards, and free toasters. Banking in England is also less regulated and arguably needs less regulation, it also has more history. *Charles I* seized all the gold rich people and been storing in the Royal Mint (this was one of the reasons they chopped off his head). But the rich people also decided it was better to store their gold with reputable goldsmiths who would then issue negotiable receipts. In 1650, a cloth merchant opened what was almost a commercial bank, with the ancestors of modern-day checks / cheques / bank-notes etc. In 1694 the Bank of England got its start, but its job was solely to lend money to the crown. Two years later, the Bank of Scotland opened to lend money to Scottish businesses.

In the 1700's the industrial revolution combined with England's growing foreign colonies (and the beginnings of *mercantilism*) to prompt the development of merchant banks. By the end of the century two banks dominated this industry, both were started by Jewish German immigrant families -the Rothschilds and Barings.

Early in the 1800's the first joint stock company was formed, various bank collapses and legislation led to a generally improved banking system that by the end of the century would be the best in the world. Barclay became the biggest stock company. It was also formed by investors from religious families, this time Quakers.

The 20th century was cluttered up with two World Wars bracketing a world-wide depression, so it wasn't until about 1950 that English banking got interesting and then it largely paralleled American banking with computers, credit cards, deregulation and aggregation of smaller banks. Sadly, they have also followed the example of America's banks in risky instruments and investments, though not quite to the same extent.

Today England's commercial banks are like what Americans would think of as a bank; with deposits, checking accounts and small loans. Mortgages, on the other hand, come from building societies. Nonetheless, the English *post office* and its *Giro* serve many of the common man's banking needs.

banns   -a Medieval Catholic requirement that the intention to marry had to be announced on three consecutive Sunday services in the home parish of both parties. It was all part of the "If there be anyone knows any reason why these two shall not be joined..." thing.

Baptist   -a Protestant sect founded in 1611. It split in two in 1638 and went downhill. Then the Methodists made evangelism popular in the 1800's, reunified the Baptists in 1891, and today the Methodist flavor of the Baptist sect is mostly a working-class crowd.

   Their doctrine holds that baptism must be as a matter of mature choice, rather than the Catholic practice of baptizing infants. Like the Protestants, they do not recognize the strict authority and hierarchy of the Catholic Church and Pope, but rather rely on reading scripture and following a pastor who was essentially hired by the church members rather than someone assigned by or sent from the church. The largest population of Baptists are in America,

barmaid   -a useful character in a lot of 19th and a little early 20th century literature. She tended bar and was therefore around men and alcohol all the time but was never to be thought of as a prostitute; rather she was more of a pretty and out-going little sister to her customers.

Barmy -not quite crazy, but eccentric and daft.

barkers   -made tannin from tree bark to tan leather. A carnival *barker* is American.

Baron / Baroness   -the lowest order of British nobility. In England, Barons are addressed as 'My Lord / My Lady Puff'en-Stuff'. 'Barron Rothenbottom' for example, would be someone from the continent. The word derives from Latin *per baroniam,* meaning tenant in chief (tenant being different from owner). Nonetheless, the barons were the ones who forced King John to sign the **Magna Carta** in 1215. Barons are hereditary positions, their children (or the oldest son anyway) inherit the title. They were an invention of **William the Conqueror** and a means to raise money. Today there are about 50 or 60 hereditary Barons in the UK. A *baronet* may inherit the title and sit in the **House of Lords**. A Baron is above a **knight**, but is not actually noble.
see *peerage*

barrel   -lots of stuff gets put into barrels in English literature of a certain age. It is worth knowing that a pin holds 4 1/2 gallons, a firkin holds 9 gallons, a kilderkin holds 18, a barrel holds 36 gallons, a hogshead -54, a puncheon is 72 gallons, butt-108, and a tun is good for 252 gallons.

BTW *Pork butt* comes from the pig's shoulder. It's called a butt because the Royal Navy used to buy salt pork by the 108 gallon *butt*. Furthermore, the 252 imperial gallons in a *tun* would weight 2525 pounds which is neither a long, short, imperial, nor an American ton. I do not know why this is so.

barrister　　-high level lawyer specializing in courtroom advocacy. He or she has been 'called to the bar.' They are often hired by, or consult to *solicitors*, who deal more directly with the public. They are also the chaps who wear the silly white *wigs*. Barrister or Barristers-at-law or Bar-at-law may draft legal proceedings (as opposed to contracts), argue in superior courts, and are considered legal scholars. 'Barrister' may also be an honorific title.

Barristers	Solicitors
Advocate (in the courtroom)	Legal advice
Hired and instructed by solicitors	The client's point-man
Wear the silly wig and gown, and work in the higher levels of courts.	Business law, children / family law, divorce, criminal, wills & probate, and general ambulance chasers. In general -the same specialties we see in America
EDUCATION: After undergraduate work, both do a year of Common Professional Exam or Post Graduate Diploma, then...	
1 year Bar Professional Training course	1 year Legal Practice Course
101 year 'pupillage'	2 year training contract

bath　　-take a bath, often in cold water to build character. To *bathe* is to go swimming.

bathroom　　-the room with the tub but not the toilet. The biffy, loo, W.C. etc., was in a separate room or in the back yard back in the day.

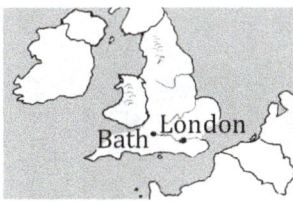

Bath, City of　　-Home to about 89,000 people in the ceremonial county of Somerset, named and famous for the ruins of Roman baths, hot springs, the River Avon, and Georgian *architecture,* all of which all led to its becoming a World Heritage Site.

batman / batsman　　-An officer's personnel servant was his **batman** in the 19th century. In cricket a **batsman** was the chap with the flattened bat standing in front of the *wicket* and returning the *bowls*. In American baseball, the batter stands at *home plate* and returns the *pitches*.

Battersea Park / Fields　　-a 200-acre park across the Thames River from Chelsea. In the past, it had what would be called an amusement park in America with roller coasters etc. but today is more like Golden Gate Park or Central Park with museums and art galleries and all, but with a convention center also thrown in.

Battle of Agincourt   -In 1415 Henry V won a decisive battle in France. The French had a much larger army but the English using better technology (long bows!). This battle was so decisive that it failed utterly to end the Hundred Years War which went on for another sixteen years, but it DID occur 100 years after the war started. The French king was back home chewing on the furniture—literally, he was insane. The French forces were lead by a committee of self-serving noble-twits who didn't actually talk to one another.

Battle of Britain / Battle of England (July 1940-June 1941)
Early in WWII Germany bombed England and England defended herself with a small force of young fighter pilots. In all of the history of warfare, this was the first major campaign ever to be fought entirely in the air. The Germans planned to force the English to negotiate a peace. Initially, they bombed ports and shipping in order to blockade food and war materials, later, they bombed factories, and still later, they bombed civilian centers as part of a 'terror bombing' strategy. The Germans lost 1887 of 2550 aircraft (largely bombers) and the English lost 1547 of 1963 working aircraft (entirely fighters). The English won, but it was a very close thing. *Winston Churchill* said of the Battle of Britain that "never have so few done so much for so many." see also the *Blitz*

Battle of the Atlantic (1939-1945)   -unlimited submarine warfare during WWII where-in the Germans tried to prevent England from importing food and war materials. Another WWII record holder, this time for duration, it ran from 1939 to the end of the war in 1945. It was actually two opposing blockades, Germany attempting to starve the English with submarine warfare and to choke off supplies of war material and soldiers, while the Allies (mostly America, Canada, & England) attempted to blockade Germany from importing much of the same. see *food*

It was a close thing. 72,000 sailors and Merchant Marines died on the Allies side, while the German lost 30.000 sailors. The Germans sank 3500 merchant ships and 175 war ships against their loss of 783 submarines. None the less, 90% of shipping from America to England made it through.

Battle of Trafalgar (1805)   This pretty much put-paid to any plans Napoleon might have had about invading England. This naval battle was fought in 1805 between England's numerically smaller fleet against the larger combined French and Spanish fleet off the southwest corner of Spain. This is one of the many battles the defines England's military pride and their deserved sense of invincibility -or at least their utter security on the island fortress.

The battle was fought between ships-of-the-line, the largest of the floating cannon platforms of the day. These ships tended to be slow and unwieldy -particularly when compared to the lighter *frigates*, that carried fewer cannons, but were faster and more nimble. Trafalger is also where **Admiral Horatio Nelson,** one of England's greatest heroes, was killed.

Bayeux Tapestry   -a long, (230 feet x 20 inches), embroidered tapestry depicting the **Norman Invasion**. Lots of curious pictures of guys on horses and some in boats. It was made in sometime in the 1070's in England, not Bayeux France. It is astonishingly old, at least for fabric, and thought to be an excellent example of Anglo Saxon art.

BBC   -the British Broadcasting Company. It goes back to 1922 and has been a public monopoly since 1925. Yanks think of the BBC as being better than America's vast commercial television wasteland, but they only ever see the best the Brits have to offer. The Brits, on the other hand, think of the BBC as being too conservative and a little stodgy. It started with radio and began fiddling with TV in 1936 and got serious about it after the war. Each household pays a little under £150 a year for a TV License. This is about $160 year and collected by an unpopular door-to-door functionary. They have the choice of 10 different TV channels, but BBC 1 and BBC 2 does the job about 80% of the time. There are also 15 radio stations each catering to a specific taste and with even more demographic variety among viewers than among the various TV options.

beadles   -elected officials in smallish towns who were also the bell-ringer and town-crier with minor and various duties like keeping order, whipping vagrants and looking after the poor. see **police**

Becket, Thomas (1120 – 1170)   -variously *Saint Thomas of Canterbury* or *Thomas of London*. Becket was the *Archbishop of Canterbury* and a Catholic back when it was possible to be both. He got cross-threaded with Henry II over issues that would seem to presage both **Henry VIII**'s and **Oliver Cromwell**'s difficulties with the church. Becket felt that people in the church like himself were privileged in various ways and should get to keep the taxes extracted from the citizenry. Henry thought differently. It is not historically clear, but in the excellent 1966 movie <u>Becket</u>, Henry he was overheard to say, "Who will rid me of this troublesome priest?" and four knights rode off to assassinate Becket, who the Pope promptly canonized.

bedsitter   -the most basic urban living quarters. Today a bedsitter is much like an American studio apartment, but in the past, they may have been only a private bedroom with a common bathroom down the hall. There may have been a lounge for sitting about and socializing with the other tenants. The landlord provided one or two meals, somewhat like the American rooming house but a little less disreputable.

beef   For a nation with Beefeaters, (the nickname for her Majesty's **Yeoman Wardens**), the Brits don't eat a lot of the stuff. Per capita, the Brits eat about three fifths of what Americans eat and it's trending down sharply. The Danes are the winners when to comes to eating cow, about 12% more per capita than even the Yanks. When the English do eat beef, they don't cook it right. What Yanks enjoy as steaks, the Brits call a chop and fry it. Otherwise, they roast *joints*, or simply boil it. Enough said. see **food**

beefeater -see **Yeoman**

beer   -the mildly alcoholic beverage not much different from what Americans drink. Before tea came to England and the need to boil water to make it safe to drink was figured out, brewing beer was a common way to kill the wee bugs responsible for things like dysentery. English beer is a little stronger that American beer both in terms of flavor and alcohol content, but this is changing as Yanks are discovering all the different types of beer that micro-breweries are producing. While it is true that Brits drink their beer at room temperature, it must be remembered that room temperature in England is lower than in America. Furthermore, as the German style lager is growing in popularity, the Brits occasionally even permit a little refrigeration -if only on particularly warmish summer days.

　　　As far as per capita beer drinking goes, the countries in central Europe win with between two to three quarts a week for every man, woman, and child. The Irish drink just under two quarts per week, Americans at about one and half and England about one and one quarter quarts.

Belfast   -the largest city and capitol of Northern Ireland. Originally it was an unimportant part of the gentle countryside of Ireland. Then in the late 1650's there came Protestants to practice a religion different from Catholicism, weave linen, and start all manner of troubles. Tobacco processing, rope making and finally ship building made Belfast a prosperous city. For example, this is where the Titanic was built.

　　　In 1888 Victoria granted Belfast city status -the only such city in Ireland. Northern Ireland was made a part of the United Kingdom in 1920 and things really started going downhill between the Irish Catholics and Protestant English. The Troubles came to a head in 1969 and for the next 25 years the city's economy was all but ruined. Today Belfast is coming back as a center of shipping, film making, aerospace, and education. It's now home to 330,000 citizens.

below the stairs   -much like **back stairs**, it refers to matters involving the servants who often did their work and ate their meals in the basement where they were out of sight.

Beowulf -written sometime between 700 – 1010. It is the oldest English literature. It is a long epic poem about Scandinavians battling the evil monster Grendel.

bespoke -made to order rather than off the rack. *By Appointment to…* refers to products the crown has used for at least three years running.

Bethlehem -a hospital for lunatics in London from the late middle ages. The corruption of the word -*bedlam*- gives us the term for chaos going back to Shakespeare. As a particularly vivid example of the Victorian 'rectitude,' a visit to Bethlehem was thought to be cracking good fun just to laugh at the poor souls imprisoned there.

bib and tucker -fanciest dress, tux & tails, or dressed to the nines etc. In the 1700's, a bib was the front of a man's shirt and a tucker was for a woman –because it was tucked in. (A *pinner* was pinned.) see **_Piccadilly Circus_**

Big Ben -it's actually just the bell, but it has come to mean the tower and the clock. It's all a part of Westminster and Parliament. The clock is thought to be the final arbiter of the correct time. If the science weenies with their atomic clocks come up with a time that differs by milliseconds from that of Big Ben, then science is wrong.

bill -much like legislative bills in America, but with some differences. In America, a bill is introduced by an individual (or a couple of legislators) from either the majority or minority. In England, a bill is introduced only by the **_government,_** which **_is_** the majority party that makes up both the executive cabinet and legislature.

billion There is much linguistic confusion here; it works out as follows. These numbers are not much used except for describing the distance to stars or the American national debt.

Number	British	American
1,000,000	million	million
1,000,000,000	thousand million -milliard	billion
1,000,000,000,000	billion	trillion
1,000,000,000,000,000,000	trillion	thousand billion

binky -a babies' pacifier

Birmingham -England's second largest city. The City (and metropolitan borough) of Birmingham has a population of 1.1 million. Its history is as a market town in the medieval period and an important industrial center as the industrial revolution unfolded in the 18th century. It was a little like America's Detroit, Pittsburgh, and Milwaukee all stirred together. The steam engine, soccer league and lawn tennis were all invented there. Today Birmingham makes its living with finance, service, retail, transport and conferences. The people call themselves *Brumies* and have a distinctive accent. The city's nick-name is Brum. Note the <u>U</u>, but the city is spelled B*I*rmingham.

By 1791, Birmingham was the world's leading manufacturing city and it
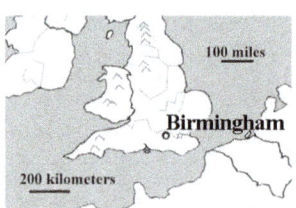
was from all this designing and building that Birmingham's people, economy, and perhaps most importantly, its atypical social diversity a hotbed for democracy and enlightenment with a little *e*. Birmingham, Edinburgh, and Glasgow, were the origins of England and the world's ***Enlightenment*** with a capital ***E.***

biscuits -cookies. Yank's cookies are *sweet biscuits* or a *tea biscuit* in England. Dipping your biscuits in tea was quite common -provided you were quite common yourself.

biscuit tin -cookie jar in America, but in England they are actual tins and used to hold odds and ends (odds & sods) when the biscuits are gone.

water biscuit -cracker.

ship's biscuit -hard tack. It was vile stuff and hard as a rock, but it lasted forever.

take the biscuit -Americans might say *take the cake*.

bishop To understand the importance of bishops in English history and literature, Americans need to consider medieval feudalism wherein the two biggest things on the horizon were the lord's castle and the bishop's cathedral. If you look closely at feudalism, it becomes clear that religion and the whole nobility system were both effective ways to keep the peasantry in its place. Arguably the religion may have been more humane, but it was probably the more efficient, involving threats of excommunication and eternity in the fires of hell and all. While kings were off fighting wars, the church tended not only to matters of the soul, but also what we might think of local government and education. Indeed, up thru ***Henry VIII***'s time, the monarch's best and most educated advisers were from the church. After he fired the pope and started the Church of England, the bishops were even better able to tend to things without the pope's meddling from off in Rome.

Another reality a that is little hard for Americans to get a hold of is that bishops were already rich when they were appointed by the king for political reasons, their religious devotion had nothing to do with it. Up until the industrial revolution in the late 1700's, bishops show up in literature as fat bloated gitts with venereal diseases at least as often as the king and his dukes.

The general increase in literacy after the Reformation and the more specific need for educated workers with the industrial revolution diminished the advantage the bishops had enjoyed by virtue of their monopoly on literacy and education.

Even so, they remained politically important. A bishop was automatically a member of the **House of Lords**-at least until the **Reform Bill** of 1832 which redistricted the various boroughs to represent actual people. It was not until 1872 that the number of bishops who were given an automatic admission to the House of Lords was limited to 25.

By the 20th century, bishops were mostly still wealthy, but expected to act with some pious restraint and look after the members of his (or her, but only quite recently) diocese. Today there are two Arch-Bishops (the big one for Canterbury and a back-up one for York). There are also another three for London, Durham, and Winchester. The third-string runs at about 60 more bishops of here and there, and some have additional duties like health, education, prisons, urban life, etc.

Despite huge wealth and power, a bishopric was not a hereditary position. Whatever of the diocese's wealth the bishop was not able to squirrel away as liquid assets went back to the crown till the next bishop was appointed.

bitters   In the 18th and 19th centuries, *bitters* was patent medicine for bad tummies, i.e., *digestifs*. The stuff is made from herbs and spices steeped in a strong alcohol solution and like any good medicine it tasted awful. It was bitter, sour, or bitter-sweet. Eventually bitters evolved into something to add zing to cocktails.

black death (1346-1353)   In 1347 rats and their fleas brought a fatal pestilential fever to Turkey and by 1349 to Europe, and finally to southern England by 1353. It killed as many as half the people in certain places. There are historians who say that fewer people sharing resources, horrible as it must have been, was one of the things that kicked off the **Renaissance**. BTW the nursery rhyme *Ring Around the Rosie* does NOT actually come from a morbid description of the plague in London contrary to trivia you occasionally see bouncing around the internet.

blackguard   -rhymes with *placard* -an utter louse. It goes back to Shakespeare when a *black guard* was the lowest form of laborer and often black with filth.

black pudding   -breakfast sausage. It's not pudding, but sausage with the usual meat ingredients, but with oatmeal and sometimes grits or barley. Its color comes from blood and it might be thought of as a toned-down version of **haggis**.

Black Watch   -the 42nd Royal Highland Regiment. They are sometimes called the *Black Jocks* (Jock being a common Scots nickname), or the *Ladies from hell* because of the kilts. The Watch first saw action in Egypt in 1882, and every war England has been in right up to 2009 in Afghanistan.

blimey   -a cockney expletive for *Gorblimey* pronounced *Gor, blimey.* which in turn is from the medieval oath *God blind me*.

Blitz, the   The German bombing offensive that led to the **Battle of Britain.** It's a less an academic term but a more historic one and more along the lines of what the people who lived thru it call it. The bombing of London and other industrialized cities was so intense that they boxed up all the children and shipped them off to foster homes in the country out of range of the Germans. The *Blitz Sprit* has been mentioned with some pride in response to terror attacks even today.

Bloodless Revolution   see the *Glorious Revolution*

bloody   -simply means *very* or even *very very*, but it has an interesting history of varying vulgarity. From Shakespeare to the middle of the 1700's it was respectable, but vulgar during the Victorian era (but what wasn't?). After WWI it starts showing up again, but often written as "b____". After WWII, it was sometimes replaced with *bleeding* or *blooming*. It is increasingly acceptable today, particularly in Australia.

Bloody Mary (1516-1568)   -*Henry VIII's* daughter Mary I, by his first wife **Catherine of Aragon**. She was a devout Catholic like her Spanish mother. During her reign from 1553 to 1558 things went very badly for Protestants. About 300 of them were burned at the stake.

Blue Cross   -a charitable organization helping the poor with vet bills for their pets.

board school   -not to be confused with **boarding schools** but rather a primary school administered by the local board like an American Board of Education in a given town. They go back to the late 1800's. see **education**

boarding houses   Renting out a room was a very common way to bolster the family income, but if it was more than one or two rooms, and if anything more potent that small beer was served, a whole lot of licenses, guilds, and trades entered the picture. see **inns & taverns**

boarding schools   These show up in a lot of English writing and by all accounts, were & are as bizarre and horrible as described. The Harry Potter stories got some things right; many boarding schools are very old, (as far back as 12th century medieval monastic schools), bullying etc. has not been exaggerated, (it was thought to be character building), and boarding schools were expensive and admission often depended on who your daddy was, and finally, blazers and school ties were de rigueur. Like Hogwarts, there are co-ed schools, but the oldest and most conservative are still strictly for young men. Like Hogwarts, which specializes in which-craft and magic, today there are boarding schools specializing in preparing students for further education and careers in the military, performing arts, and religion, as well as schools for students with what is politely referred to as having b*ehavior challenges* and/or other learning difficulties. Today about 1% of English kids attend boarding schools.

In defense of the whole thing, in the 1700 and 1800's, England was spreading itself all over the globe and people were sent off to look after England's interests, be they diplomatic, mercantile, or military. They understandably wanted their kids to get a proper English education so they packed their kids off to boarding school before they left England's shore. On the other hand, sometimes they brought the kids along and schools were set up in the bigger colonies. This had the additional advantage of permitting some of the local (native) rich kids to be thoroughly indoctrinated in the English way. Other than a curious insistence that people be able to speak and read Latin, these schools arguably did a good job of teaching children what society thought was important, at least until well into the 20th century when the need for scientists and engineers became more important than the need for rhetoricians and linguists. see *schools* & *mercantilism*

bob -slang for one shilling. It depends on the era, but think if it as about $5.00 see *money*

Bodecia, Queen (circa 25 – 60 AD)   -a Celtic queen and right pain to the Romans. Bodecia's husband was a king (a tribal chief actually) and more or less a Roman ally. However, after his death they flogged the widow Bodecia, raped his daughters, ignored his will, and took all his land. Big mistake. Bodecia lead a revolt against the Romans, killed a bunch of them, and very nearly beat them. She did succeed in burning down London (Londiniun -a Roman fortress and market-town at the time) before she either was captured and killed, or almost captured and killed herself first–no one is quite sure. She was supposed to have flaming red hair, been a beautiful woman, and an utter hell-cat. As such, she makes for great legends for the Brits.

bobbins -rotten or rubbish

Bob's your uncle   -something that is dead easy. For example, "Two right turns and the first left, and *Bob's your uncle,* you're there". It also has a hint of sarcasm implying it's not what you know, it's who you know.

bog   -a wet muddy area common in Ireland and north-east England. Or the bathroom.

Boers   -Dutch farmers who resented England's rule in South Africa. They fought two guerrilla wars against them in 1880 and 1899-1902. It's also sometimes spelled *boor;* but it's not a *bore* is which is a tedious person.

boff -variously to masturbate, f___ , or fart.

bollix / bollicks / bollox etc.
-to confuse something (verb), or a confused mess (noun), or an annoying difficult person (insult). *Bollocks* are testicles.

Bond, James Bond   Before he was a mainstay of the movies, Bond, James Bond was a character in a series of 12 novels and short stories by Ian Fleming published between 1953 and 1964. Bond was a Commander in the Royal Navy working for MI-6, the Foreign Office's Secrete Intelligence Service. Ian Fleming, on the other hand, was an officer in the Royal Navy's Intelligence Office.

Bond Street   -a shopping district in London for tailors and handmade suits for the very rich and the very conservative. see **Carnaby Street**

Bonnie Prince Charles (1720-1788)   -one of England's colorful pretenders to the throne. Born in 1720, he was the grandson of James VII and leader of an unsuccessful Catholic insurrection in 1745. He then philandered his way around Europe till his death in 1788. He was kind of a nebbish.

Book of Common Prayer   -more than a prayer book, this is the liturgy the **Church of England** used to stave off Catholicism. It was first published in 1549, revised in 1552, 1762, 1927, and adopted by Parliament in 1965. Its importance to the English language is second only to **Shakespeare** and the **King James Bible**.

boot -a car's trunk. The *bonnet* is the hood.

borough   -originally a town with the right to make its own laws, but through history the meaning has changed. As Parliament unfolded as a real legislative force, a borough was a town that had its own **MP**. By **Henry VIII**'s time a borough probably had a cathedral, and a cathedral had to have a bishop. The industrial revolution made some boroughs the largest towns in the land and they were granted city status by the crown. (This had no special benefit other than status.) Some other quite large towns were neither boroughs nor cities, but were technically mere **parishes** with no MP. Throughout all of this, boroughs were Parliamentary divisions, but divisions based on old Reformation demographics and there were some large industrial areas that had no representation at all, and some -the **rotten boroughs**- may have had a rich MP representing just himself, his family, and his servants.

In 1832 they sorted it all out with the **Reform Bill** and in 1835, they standardized the municipal laws and procedures across the land. In 1965 London did away with all its boroughs, and in 1972 all boroughs in England were changed to either metropolitan counties or districts. Except some were allowed to remain ceremonial insofar as the Brits have always been big on ceremony and some of the ceremonial boroughs have some pretty colorful history.

An *open borough* is one wherein neither party has a majority and therefore is what Yanks would think of as a swing district. A *pocket borough* is the opposite -the landlord had all the votes in his pocket. see **divisions**

bosun   -a sailor in charge of a ship's sails and rigging. He is the highest enlisted man and equivalent to the army's sergeant. The bosun's whistle was a call to work.

bound over   -a little like probation in America. It is not so much a sentence as a promise that arrest and sentencing will quickly follow any further bad acts.

bounder

 -not merely a cad, but a cad who has bounded above his proper state.

bowler   -a derby hat. Originally a bowler was worn to protect a rider's head from low branches. Take away the horse, add a rolled umbrella and you have the iconic conservative English gentleman. The verb to *bowler-hat* meant to retire from the military and put on such a hat. In cricket, the *bowler* is the pitcher and has nothing to do with hats.

Boxing Day   -the day after Christmas. It has nothing to do with pugilism. Boxing Day is when servants and trades-people are given their *Christmas Box* by their masters or employers. Think of it as an American Christmas bonus, but going way back. Today, Boxing day is also a huge shopping opportunity when stores mark down everything that wasn't sold during the Christmas rush.

braces   -suspenders for the trousers. English suspenders hold up a man's socks or a woman's stockings. Braces are for trousers. A garter was the belt to carry a sword -as in the **Knights of the Garter**.

brass-slang for money. To *brass-up* is to pay off a debt. *Brassy* is impudent, but in America is takes on more of the sense of loud and vulgar. A *brass hat* is a high ranking military officer with lots of brass fiddly-bits on his hat or simply the boss.

breach-of-promise   -getting cold feet after the proposal but before the wedding is a big deal to the English, particularly after the middle of the 1700's. For an American to understand this, two things must be born in mind. First, for the **middle class**, marriage was hugely important not only to the bride and groom, but the whole family. Huge amounts of effort and cost went into **balls**, negotiations, and intrigues. When a proposal was accepted, it was game-over and if a better or richer suitor happened along, well, that's just too bad. Second, it was common for sex to start before the actual ceremony and pregnancies occasionally came about. The money awarded in these cases was considered a form of alimony awarded to a woman of now doubtful virtue for what presumably would be a life of spinsterhood. There were some few men who sued for breach of promise, but presumably they were not preggers.

The whole thing got out of hand at the end of the 1800's when there were a number of sensational cases wherein chorus girls brought such suits for huge amounts of money. It all wound down with changing attitudes about women owning property in their own names.

bread   -much the same as American bread, except white bread made from wheat was for the wealthy up until about 1800. Before that the common folk ate rye or barley bread and the Scots ate oat bread. The English do bread pretty much the same way Americans do, with one or two exceptions. At the beginning of the 20th century, they fried thick slices in lard and ate it with a fork. More Brits like to slice their own bread than do the Yanks.

breakfast   Back in the day, breakfast was bread and butter or cheese and beer. The iconic English breakfast at the manor was served as a buffet for the convenience of family and guests who arose at various times. The continental breakfast of tea and bread was a pitiful thing compared to the rich people's spread of fried egg, kippers, sausage, bacon, fish with rice, tomatoes, toast, and fried bread. The poor ate porridge or gruel. Coffee was not a large part of it all. The sugary stuff Americans eat cold out of a box with milk has only recently began to make some appearances on the English breakfast table. see *food*

breeches   -what Americans think of as knickers and worn by men. In England, *knickers* are women's underwear. see *pus-fours*

brevit   Up until the middle of the 1800's an officer would occasionally be assigned, or *seconded* to work outside of his own **regiment** and do so at a rank higher (with higher pay) than within his own regiment. This temporary rank was called a *brevit rank*. see **commissions** and **army**

brigade   *-a military unit temporarily made of two regiments and* commanded by a brigadier -not a *brigadier general* like in America -just a *brigadier*.

Brighton -an unimportant fishing village until George IV (1762 – 1830), got in the habit of going there for various pleasures. It then followed a common trajectory; first the royals made it a play-ground then the ***middle class*** came for a season or two, then, because it was a pleasant 50-mile train ride from London, the working class came and Brighton came to be seen as tasteless and tawdry, at least by those with real taste. It's still a popular weekend get-away for the younger set who enjoy the quirky glitz. Think a little bit tacky or 'schlocky', but today it is very LGBT friendly, considered the hippest place in all of England, and THE place to live if you are young and can write computer code and want to get paid a lot to do so.

100 miles

Bristol

Brighton

Bristol -an important port city from the middle ages that exported wool and imported fish, wine, grain, and dairy. It lies at the confluence of the Rivers Avon and Frome and was among the most important cities in England up until the Industrial Revolution when cities like Manchester and Liverpool surpassed it. Today its population is around 440,000 people. It is a little like San Francisco which was an important port until its land, particularly water-front land, became too valuable to waste on cranes and docks, so shipping moved across the bay. Bristol's waterfront is now a Center of Heritage and Culture and this business of loading and unloading ships has moved to Avon Mouth in the distant suburbs.

British Invasion In the early 1960's, American R & B music crossed the Atlantic, became rock music, and crossed back to America where it became hugely popular. Bands include: the Beatles, the Dave Clark Five, the Kinks, the Rolling Stones, Herman's Hermits, the Animals, and The Who.

In addition to music, other counter-cultural elements crossed the pond to and from America; things like like fashion, literature, pop-art and assorted protests.

Britain/ British -a slippery word with lots of curious and often or contradictory meanings. It goes back to the Romans who called it *Britannia*. This was news to the Celts who lived there and thought it was part of Gaul, or what the Romans called Normandy, which would eventually become France. By comparison, *England* is simple. It's Old English for the Germanic for the *Angul-land* -land of the Angles of Anglo Saxon fame.

The words *Brit* and *Brits* are mildly vulgar. Better to say someone is a Briton, but no one does. The *British Council* promotes British culture all over the world, and the *British disease* refers to a long economic slump in the 70's and 80's. It is possibly due to greedy unions or greedy rich people. Take your pick.

British justice - isn't just and often violates common sense.

British luck -is an ironic comment on good luck that goes to no good end.

British Museum   -a huge museum containing artifacts more or less politely looted from Greece, Rome, and Egypt by English archeologists before anyone else knew what archeology was. It also has a library that has every book or magazine ever published and the central reading room under a dome bigger than that of *St. Paul's Cathedral* about a mile down the street.

British Telecom / BT   -was originally part of the post office, then independent but still nationalized and finally privatized in 1984. see **BBC British Rail** was also a national asset until it too was privatized between 1994 and 1997. By all accounts it was well run, certainly better than America's Amtrak.

broderers / broiderers   - men, and most were men, who did embroidery. Women made lace. Rich women sitting about in drawing rooms doing fancy things with needle and thread would wait till late in the 1800's.

brogue   -a thick Irish shoe originally worn by Irish laborers who spoke with a thick Irish brogue.

broom   -an interesting example of word meanings being a moving target, broom is a wild bush whose twigs could be gathered and tied around the end of a stick to make a *besom* for either sweeping or for witches to ride. The coarse broom twigs were more suited to sweeping a barn than a drawing room, so about the same time *besoms* became *brooms*, the material in choice became broom-corn -which is not corn at all, but grass.

BTU -British Thermal Unit   -the amount of heat necessary to raise one pound of water one degree Fahrenheit. BTU's measure the same thing as calories do. A BTU is just over one quarter kilo-calorie, or 252 of the sort of calories that a slice of pie might contain, but commenting that a piece of pumpkin pie has about one and a half BTUs would make you look like a sodding wank.

bubble and squeak -left-over vegetables and potatoes fried up till they bubbled and squeaked.

Buckingham Palace   -the official London residence and administrative center of the Monarch. They hold lots of receptions and official doings, but parts of it are open to the public from time to time. 775 rooms, 19 state rooms, 52 royal guest bedrooms, 188 staff bedrooms, 92 offices, and 78 bathrooms. (This works out to slightly more than three guests sharing a bathroom and this does not include the people working in the offices. They presumably have to go to the gas station across the street?) see

buffer / old buffer -an old foggy or an old duffer in America.

bugger -sodomy (vulgar). The non-vulgar use is a friendly reference to a silly person with no implication as to sexual practice. ***I'm buggered*** means I'm confounded. ***Bugger-up*** is to screw up. ***Bugger off*** means to go away and stay away. ***Bugger about*** is to fiddle about, ***Bugger-all*** is none at all, and ***play silly buggers*** is act stupidly. Finally, ***bugger's grips*** are sideburns or mutton chops.

bum -the bottom. From before Shakespeare it was standard word for buttocks. It was considered vulgar during the early Victorian era and replaced by bottom. Then bottom also went to the lower class and bum came back to polite conversation or polite conversations that needed such a reference. Bumfodder is toilet paper and now shortened to bumf. Bum fluff is peach-fuzz in America.

Burberry -raincoat, but unlike a Mackintosh which is made from rubberized cotton, a Burberry is made of more expensive waterproof wool. It used to be upper-class, but is now associated with football hooligans.
burgess -originally, a full citizen of a borough, later a mid-level swell, and in the 20th century, a middle-class businessman similar to and derived from the same root as *bourgeois*. ***Burgesses*** are either a ***MP*** for a smallish area, or a freeman of a borough It's not to be confused *The House of Burgess*, the legislative body in the Virginia Colony from 1619 to 1776.

Burke's Peerage and ***Burke's Landed Gentry*** The definitive lists of who's who and how important they are. First published in 1826. The 2003 version is 4700 pages long and will run you £399.00 (a little under $500 US), but now it includes Baronetages and Knightages.

Burns, Robert / Robby / Rabbie (1759 - 1796) Robby Burns is the national poet of Scotland and did much of his work in the Scottish language but he also wrote in English and what we might call Scottish-Lite. He sold more of it in England that way. Among the fans of historic poetry, he is considered important to the romantic movement, liberalism, and socialism. But perhaps his greatest work was in the area of Scottish folk tales and folk songs. For it all, he wrote some beautiful poetry. For example, he wrote *Auld Lang Syne* which is sung every new year's eve by drunken party goers all over the UK, the US, Canada, Australian and a bunch of England's colonies and possessions. BTW, *Auld Lang Syne* means–roughly–*in the old long since* which is a profoundly nostalgic sentiment. The poem Red,

Red Rose is worthy of inclusion here:

Red Red Rose:

My love is like a red, red rose
That's newly sprung in June
My love is like the melody
That's sweetly sung in tune.

As fair thou are, my bonnie lass,
So deep in love am I:
And I wil+-l love thee still, my dear,
Till a' the seas gang dry.

Till a' the seas gang dry, my dear
And the rocks melt wi' the sun:
I will love thee still, my dear,
While the sands o' life shall run.

And fare thee weel, my only Luve,
And fare the weel a while!
And I will come again, my Luve,
Tho' it were ten thousand mile.

burser   -either the treasure or a *bursary* which is a student on a scholarship.

bus, double decker   -from the days of the horse drawn stage-coaches these were the economy-means of getting around. So much so that passengers were sometimes stuck up on the roof. This gave way to London's iconic double-decked buses, with the top deck only enclosed about 1940. see *coach*

butler   Originally, this was the chap in charge of the master's wine cellar. By about 1850 the butler came to be the supervisor of all the servants, but only in the very largest households. In most literature, the butler was more apt to fulfill the role of valet and /or steward. see *servants*

by-election   The equivalent of the American special election when a MP dies or otherwise leaves office before his term is up and a new one is elected.

The letters *c* & *g* started out as the same letter, but by the time the Irish got a hold of Latin and taught the English how to read and write, the Old English, *c* got tangled up with *k*, and so it remains today. Words with a hard *k*-like *broken,* were originally spelled *brocan.* The soft *c* in words like *spice* are probably from the French speaking Normans. To make it even more complicated, words with a *qu* in English today were spelled with a *c* in Old French.

cabinet   It's like the American cabinet, but made out of English *Members of Parliament.* In America, the cabinet is made from—we hope— non-partisan experts in the various subjects whose advice the president needs from time to time. The English Cabinet is more political because the cabinet *ministers* are selected from the current party in *government*. The English get their professional expertise from non-partisan *Permanent Undersecretaries*. There may also be a small number appointed by the *Prime Minister* from the *House of Lords*. They are all variously referred to as *Ministers* of This or *Secretaries* of That.

cake   -nothing at all like the American two or three layer things covered with frosting. English cakes are smaller and they are often closer to what Yanks might think of as sweet-roll, with some varieties are made with fruit like raisins or currants. The expression for the good life, *'cakes and ale'* goes back to Shakespeare who stole it from the ancient Greek story teller Aesop who pointed out *"Better beans and bacon in peace, than cakes and ale in fear."*

cake hole   -mouth, as in "Shut your cake hole."

call   -to visit, not to make a phone call as it is in America, but an English phone-booth is called a call box.

Cambria -the Latin word for Wales. 'Cambria 'is important to the fossil guys because Wales was where a bored English rich guy (Edward Lhuyd) who was interested in geology discovered all manner of fossils that

would give raise to the expression 'Cambrian Explosion' which in turn would give raise to what is called the 'Pre-Cambrian' Eon followed by the Phanerozoic Eon. (The pre-Cambrian was NOT followed by the Cambrian, because the Cambrian was an <u>era</u>—a subset—of the larger Phanerozoic <u>Eon</u>.) It's all terribly important to the lab-coated dinosaur crowd. BTW *Phanerozoic* means 'visible life' or the little animals that could be seen *without* a microscope.

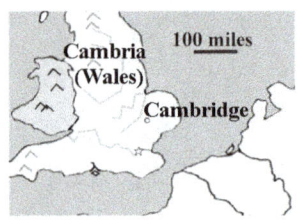

Cambridge A city of 123,000 people about 50 miles north of London named after a bridge over the minor River Cam. Cambridge University goes back to around 1200 and today about one-fifth of its population are students. Cambridge is nick-named Silicon Fen and is a high-tech center for software and the world's largest bio-science research center. Over 40% of its workforce has a college degree or about twice the rate in the rest of England. Cambridge actually got its start when some scholarly types got cross threaded with the townspeople of Oxford and decamped about 80 miles to the southwest to do their own thing. See *education*

Camelot -no such place, but the center of King Author's legendary kingdom.

can -a large metal container to carry liquids. Gasoline is carried in a *jerrycan*, and hot water goes into a *billycan*. What Yanks call a tin can for food, the Brits simply call a *tin*.

candy floss -cotton candy.

cane -the stick or switch used in corporal punishment of students as well as the verb for applying the cane. The English do not carry canes, but rather *walking sticks*.

canon -a clergyman involved with a cathedral or large church. Usually one of a staff of similar clergy and similar to the priest(s) of a Catholic *parish*. Canon law(s) are the rules of behavior. (A *canNon* is a piece of artillery.)

CANOE Committee to Ascribe Nautical Origins to Everything. In fair disclosure, your author is an enthusiastic member. If you find here-in too many references to ships and the sea, remember that for most of mankind's history the highest technology of any civilization floated. Furthermore, England, being an island, got very good at making things that floated. They would also get very good at making things that shot cannonballs. The combination of these skills lead in a more or less straight line from *Henry VIII's* navy to the *English Empire.* Go read some of C. S. Forrester's *Hornblower* or Patrick O'Brian's *Aubry-Maturin* novels about the British Navy during the Napoleonic Wars. Great stories!

cap   -the proper headgear for a tradesman etc. Going *cap-in-hand* was for a working stiff to go ask something of a swell.

capital punishment   -hanging, or slow strangulation actually, was for commoners; the nobility got to be decapitated. Crimes and dates work out as follows; in 1783, it was taken from the town square and brought inside of the prison. This spoiled the fun for the townspeople who before then would take the day off to go enjoy a nice hanging. Up until 1838 any felony was good cause for a hanging, but thereafter capital punishment was limited to murder, treason, arson or piracy, and after 1965, murder was also taken off the list. Now capital punishment is still available for treason or piracy, but it hasn't been used since 1964 when two men who murdered a robbery victim were hanged. see *hangmen*

capon   -a castrated cock. It was supposed to taste better that way.

caravan
-a camping trailer, usually towed by the family car on *holiday*, (on vacation).

card
-what American's might call a *calling card*, but much more complicated. Back when servants were all the norm among the middle class, the card with just the caller's name engraved was carried by the butler to the master or the mistress of the house who would than decide it the caller were to be admitted or sent away. The complexity dealt with folding down one corner or the other to indicate the caller would come back, would not come back, was shopping for any available unmarried daughter, or was in actuality, a monkey. There are not enough servants these days to play this game.
        Business cards now are used in England much as they are in America. Playing cards were for gambling until early in the 20th century when the Brits and Yanks went crazy for bridge and proper women were finally allowed to play cards.

Cardiff   The capitol and largest city in Wales and a popular tourist destination. It's chalk full of castles and music. Its history is like that of most of the British Isles with various foreigners tromping thru, but unique in it's importance for iron and especially coal from the late 1700's. There was some impressive—for the day—engineering done to the harbor and canals to move that coal. Today it has a population of about 350,000 *Cardiffians.*

Cardinal Wolsey, Thomas (sometimes **Woolsey** 1473 ? - 1530)

The Archbishop of Canterbury was a hugely powerful politician and friend of **Henry VIII**. He was sometimes referred to as 'alter rex,' or the *other king*, at least until he failed to get the Pope in Rome to let Henry set aside **Catherine of Aragon** and marry **Anne Boleyn**. He fell out of favor and in 1529 went home to York to tend to ecclesiastical matters he had been neglecting while in London. The next year he was summoned back to London to face charges of treason, and in all likelihood, be beheaded, but he died along the way.

carmen, carters, carriers:

Delivery men, but their license strictly prescribed what they might carry. At varying times and in varying places, one could carry only agricultural products, another only passengers, and still another, only cargo.

Carnaby Street
-a small street off Soho synonymous with 1960's fashion.

carriage   -almost any type of horse-drawn rolling thing, but all of them needed a horse, and place to store both the horse and carriage, and a servant to take care of the whole mess. It was all very expensive, so the *carriage trade* refers to a wealthy clientele.

cartwrights   Ben, Little Joe, and Hoss clearly had an ancestor who made carts.

cassock -the long black garment worn by clergy. Until comparatively recently it might be thought of as business wear for such people. Only when it was worn with a white linen surplice, was it for services or sacred ceremonies.

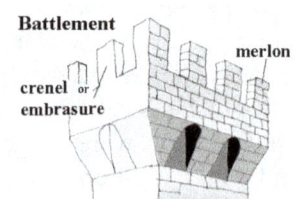

castle   -a fortified administrative center, home, and sometimes granary. Rich people lived in medieval castles and in theory allowed the common folks to hang around if the area was under attack. They were designed for defensive warfare, which is to say withstanding siege. This gives castles their most iconic architectural features, the battlements or crenels from which arrows or crossbow bolts could be fired or even rocks and boiling oil could be heaved. (Moats and drawbridges were not universal.) From the 12th to the 16th century, rich people needed a *License to Crenellate* from the king to fortify their homes. In-so-far as doing so could make it harder for the king and his knights to come along and take over again, such a license was a pretty cool thing for a noblemen to get; it meant the king trusted him. An ordinary manor house became a castle when it crenelated. Palaces came along later and while they had battlements etc, these were an architectural feature just to impress the neighbors. Palaces were built for comfort and luxury -not defense. see *royal residences*

cathedral -the seat of a bishop. From the Latin *cathedra* meaning *seat*. A cathedral is probably a huge imposing church, but not necessarily so. It can, in theory at least, be a small unimpressive church, but it must have a bishop, (and his diocese), attached to it. If the bishop and / or the surrounding countryside was poor, the cathedral might be small. For example, *Westminster Abbey* is not a cathedral. It is big and impressive, but it is the seat of an abbot, not a bishop, therefore not a cathedral. These ecclesiastical distinctions and all tended to

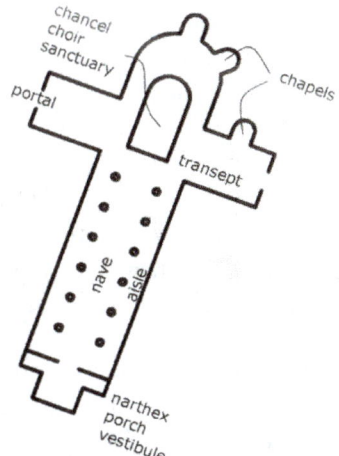

go out the window after the *Protestant Reformation* when life got difficult for bishops and Catholics in general.

Catherine of Aragon (1485–1536)   *Henry VIII's* first wife and mother of *Queen Mary.* She was one of his wives who was *not* executed. Her parents were Queen Isabella and King Ferdinand of Spain, (the same Isabella who financed Christopher Columbus), and in 1501 she married England's Prince Arthur who died five months later. She was the ambassador for Spain to the England and the first woman to serve as ambassador in all of European history. She married Arthur's younger brother *Henry VIII* in 1509. In 1513 she served as Henry's *regent* for six months until his eighteenth birthday. At about this time, she was instrumental in one of England's victory over Scotland. In 1516 she gave birth to her only child *Mary I,* (later known as *"Bloody Mary'*), but no sons. By 1525 Henry was infatuated with *Anne Boleyn* so he used the lack of a son and heir as an excuse to try to get their marriage annulled. *Pope Clement VII* refused and Henry assumed the supreme power over the church. (This was not quite the start of English Protestantism, but it was an important first step toward the coming *English Civil War.*) Henry then was able to annul his own marriage and send her off to live out her life in the country. She died in 1536.

One tends to think of Catherine of Aragon as one of histories' most hapless victims if not quite to the extent as some of Henry's other wives, friends, and advisers who lost their heads, but she was an impressive and accomplished woman by her own rights. Her banishment was widely resented and her death was mourned by the English public. She was a proponent of educating women, spokesman for the poor, and an important intellectual part of Renaissance Humanism. If nothing else, she lived in the center of very interesting times for England and for Europe.

Notice the poor woman's chin. The Spanish Hapsburg Dynasty was so inbred that the recessive genetic deformity–the Hapsburg Jaw–ran thru generations of this family. Catherine didn't have to too badly, but one of her younger cousins was so deformed he couldn't chew, could barley talk, drooled constantly, and died at age 30 looking like a very old man. Over a period of about 200 years, there were nine marriages between Hapsburg cousins and even two between uncles and nieces.

Catholics   It is a dicey thing to be a Catholic in England, but it wasn't always so. For the time between Christ and the Romans leaving about 450, it was OK to be a Christian. When the Romans left, they took Jupiter, Neptune, Venus and all the other planets / Gods with them. Things went back to the old Celtic pagan gods. In 597 the pope sent what we might think of as a *Catholic* missionary effort to England. (Catholicism being the new and improved flavor of mere Christianity.) The old-fashioned pagan gods, (Roman and Celtic Gods stirred together), and the trending Catholics got along fine, at least until **Henry VIII** wanted a divorce. It was about then that things started going downhill for the Catholics. There was some back and forth between the Protestants and the Catholics, but under **Queen Elizabeth I**, (1558–1603) and again under **Oliver Cromwell**'s **Commonwealth,** (1649–1660), it was a decidedly bad time to be a Catholic. It didn't improve. Catholic priests were regularly executed if caught, and only after the restoration in about 1700 could you even be a Catholic, but you were not allowed to hold office until 1791. In 1829, Catholics could be in Parliament, and 1853, they could even go to Oxford.

Today England is comparatively non-religious, and no one much cares about the whole thing, but even so, Catholics were viewed a little like Americans would view communists today. Things are changing, but to the English mind, being Catholic implies being Irish, poor, and uneducated if only a little bit.

caution   -the warming given to someone being arrested along the lines of *Anything you say may be taken as evidence*. As a verb *-to be cautioned*, it is like being *Mirandized* in America.

cavalry   This is a generic term for soldiers mounted on expensive horses, or later, driving various machines. From the times of the mounted and armored **knights**, they were distinct from infantry, but some cavalry got there quickly and then climbed down to do a little actual fighting. The Calvary was for gentlemen who could afford **commissions** and horses. Living, fighting, and getting killed in the mud was strictly for the infantry which was largely made from commoners.*

The cavalrymen were THE coolest soldiers up until WW I when it was discovered riding a horse did not keep you alive against machine guns. Even so, England keeps a few of them and their horses around in the *Household Cavalry* for parades and whatnot. see **dragoons, hussars, lancers, regiments,** and the **army.**

BTW. Do not confuse the word *cavalry* with Mount *Calvary* where Jesus was crucified.

*An interesting bit of American History attains. During the American Revolution, the colonists had very accurate hunting rifles that could not be reloaded quickly and furthermore, needed to be taken apart and cleaned every few shots. So they used what we might think of today as guerrilla tactics. They would shoot from a long ways off and do so from behind a rock or tree. They would then have to run off and reload etc. They also liked to shoot the guy on a horse -an officer. The English thought this was deucedly uncivilized. The foot soldiers were supposed to line up a short distance from the enemy, who was also lined up all neat and proper, Then they would each bang away at one another with short range muskets that could be reloaded quickly. Whichever side ran out of common soldiers first lost, and the officers on both sides were able to be back in camp in time for dinner.

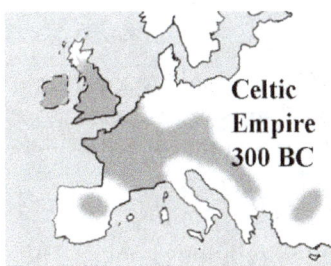

Celts   Bronze age people from central Europe that flourished and spread all over the continent and British Isles between 500 and 100 BC. Then the Romans came along. In Britannia, the Romans didn't bother with Wales, Scotland, or Ireland so versions of the ancient language are still spoken in these places at least by some of the old folks.

Celtic Empire 300 BC

CH   Order of the Companions of Honor. Started in 1917 for civilians who contributed to art, literature, music, science, politics, industry and religion. The rules are that there will never be more that 65 of them plus the monarch.

Chad   -England's equivalent to America's *Kilroy.* Both military and both WW II era. While Kilroy was satisfied to simply state he was here, (there?), Chad was a little more inclined to complain "Wot, no beer / sugar / internet etc.?"

chair / sedan chair   All the rage form about1600 to the early 1800's when streets and roads got good enough for horses and carriages. King **Henry VIII** was a big fan, but by the end of his life, it took four big guys to do the job.

chalk & cheese As similar as chalk and cheese -not at all alike.

Chancellor   -originally the king's secretary and therefore the primary administrator. Now there are various chancellors including the Chancellor of the Exchequer, (treasury) and Lord Chancellor overseeing judicial matters. see ***government, cabinet, Prime Minister***

Chancellor of the Exchequer
This office is the equivalent of America's Secretary of the Treasury and the second most powerful office in ***Her Majesty's Government***. (Numbers three and four are the ***Foreign Secretary*** and the ***Home Secretary***.) He or she is appointed by the Queen on advice of the ***Prime Minister***. This is a very old office and until 1923 was filled by the same chap who was also the Prime Minister.

Channel Tunnel / the Chunnel

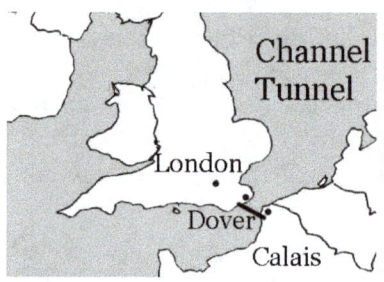

Channel Tunnel

-31 miles of high-speed rail-road tunnel from England to France running under the English Channel for people, freight, and autos. It's is not the longest tunnel in the world, but it is the longest under the ocean. It goes as deep as 250 feet and runs at 99 miles per hour.   Started work in 1988 and finished in 1994. It is said to go from Dover to Calais, but it doesn't; it really goes to the suburbs -Folkstone in England to Pas-de-Calais in France. It carries north of 50,000 car passengers per day, 85% of whom are English, presumably on holiday.

chapmen   Chaps or chapbooks were small often religious books. The door to door peddlers who sold them from the back of a donkey or horse were called *chapmen*. They also sold cloth, looking glasses, toys, combs, knives, and all manner of knick-knacks. There were so many of them that in 1696 they needed to be licensed.

char /char woman / charlady   -a cleaning lady or a servant who does not live in and is sometimes called a *daily.*

charcoal burners   -nothing to do with BBQ, but rather the peopple who made smokeless hot-burning charcoal from trees and used in steel making, black-smithing and making gun-powder. They were also called *wood colliers*.

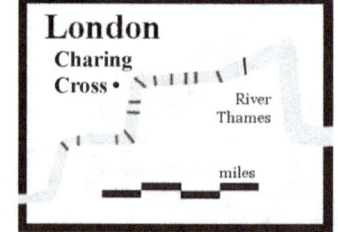

Charing Cross   An intersection in London by Trafalgar Square. It is considered the very center of this city and the location of a main rail-road station. Its name is a combination of the Old English word for a bend in a river, 'cierring,' and Elanor's Cross erected by Edward I in 1291 as a memorial to his wife.

chartered accountant -like an American CPA.

Chaucer (1343 – 1400) Geoffrey Chaucer, was an author, (fiction, nonfiction, and a little pornography), poet, philosopher, bureaucrat, and diplomat. The most popular of his many works is <u>The Canterbury Tales</u>. This was the first book written in Middle English vernacular rather than the usual Latin used by the intellectual swells of the day. (This is not to say it's easy reading to those who speak American. It's not even easy for the people who speak British.)

chav / chavs -a 21st century juvenile delinquent snot. These are from the lower class and wear what they think of as designer clothes to go about being "brash and loutish". The origin of the word is unclear, but it apparently does not derive from "Council Housed And Violent," but this is thought to be as good an explanation as any. (*Council houses* are like America's *housing projects*.)

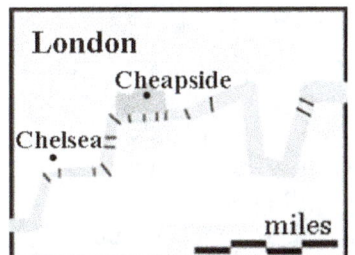

Cheapside -a street in London and the financial center of the realm. Think of it as England's equivalent to America's Wall Street. It comes from the Old English *ceapan* to *buy* or *shop*. Many other towns have Cheapside Streets or market streets. It has nothing to do with the inexpensive meaning of *cheap*.

cheddar cheese The most popular cheese in England and second most popular in America (behind mozzarella) and the most popular in the world. It goes back to at least AD 100 and it is possible the Romans brought the recipe to England. During WW II and for many years after, *government cheddar* was pretty much all there was to eat cheese-wise. Mack and cheese was a popular meal on both sides of the Atlantic during WWII because it could be gotten with fewer ration stamps than other foods, particularly meat and dairy. see *food*

Chelsea -an extremely expensive and largely residential neighborhood in London. Chelsea is bordered by Sloane Street. This gives rise to a number of deprecating terms for what American might call spoiled yuppies and hipsters. For example, 'Sloan Rangers' are women who ride horses. Chelsea also has more Americans living there than anywhere else in England. No one knows why this is.

chemists Pharmacists made drugs in apothecaries, but chemists made industrial chemicals, often nasty ones. Druggists etc. became *chemists* only in the 20th century.

cheque -a check from a bank. Working Brits received a pay packet with cash because few of them had bank accounts as late as the 1990's.

chimney sweeps Yes -like the guy in the movie who was as lucky as lucky could be. But if you were a young orphan, the smaller the better, you were hired / adopted / bought to crawl up and down a chimney scraping off tar and soot. It was a tossup to see if you died of lung problems before you got to be too big for the job. It got worse when England went from burning wood to burning coal. The round brush on the end of a long flexible handle was only invented in the early 1800's.

chin wag -chat, as in "Have a nice cup of tea and a bit of a *chin wag*."

chips -French fries ("Freedom fries"?). *Crisps* which are potato chips.

Christmas England's idea of Christmas is increasingly as commercialized as it is in America, it has not always been so. The Celts did a mid-winters festival of lights with yule logs, naughty frolics, and lots of wassail. The Catholics kept much of the fun of it all, but stirred just a little solemnity surrounding the birth of Christ. During Shakespeare's time, ***Twelfth Night*** was the big thing. Then the Protestants decided it was entirely too much fun and sinful so they went back to work right after church service on Christmas morning and that was about it for Christmas until Charles Dickens came along. He got a little help from Queen Victoria's husband Prince Albert who was from Germany where they still liked a little fun. Prince Al insisted on a proper Prussian Christmas tree and such became popular among the swells. Even so, it was a gradual thing that had involved little more than Christmas cards and the ***Christmas goose***. December 25 was far less important than ***Hogmanay***, January 1, in Scotland and ***Boxing Day,*** December 26, when gifts were given to the ***servants.*** Even now, the Brits only go shopping crazy for about two weeks before the holiday, rather than beginning right after Halloween like the Yanks do.

Christmas Goose -the traditional Christmas dinner. English Christmas Dinner is very much like America's Christmas dinner, apart from England's insistence on a pudding for desert rather than pie. The history of the main course shuttles back and forth between turkey, (***Henry VIII***'s favorite), and goose, with a little boar tossed in and even swan and peacock among the very posh. But goose was the thing for dinner during the Victorian Era; *Goose Clubs* which were sort of a poultry lay-away plan that allowed the common folk to save up all year for a nice fat goose. BTW -the famous Christmas dinner from Dickens's <u>A Christmas Carol</u> was turkey.

Chunnel -see ***Channel Tunnel***

Church of England As far as doctrine is concerned, the church straddles Catholicism and Protestantism. It is the *official* church of England and therefore it had be a compromise. From its earliest history, the Church of England was as much a political thing as a religious thing. The **Restoration** (1660) gave some of the Catholic bishops back their property and made them rich and powerful once again. It was only during the 1700's that the Church began to take on what we think of today as charitable Christian functions with things like parish **schools**, poor relief, and concern for widows & orphans.

This straddling things and not being Protestant enough, lead to war both among **Thomas Cromwell**'s Protestant crowd, as well as more strife between Protestants and Catholics. The real fanatically intense Protestants like the Puritans, Pilgrims, and Calvinists went off to the colonies for more religious freedom & tolerance. Once there, they could be intolerant of anyone with whom they disagreed.

Today, much of Brits self-identify themselves as Church of England, but the number who actually attend church is small and getting smaller. This is, however, the case with most Christian religions in most of the world.

Churchill, Winston (1872 – 1965)

Ask ten Brits who the most important Englishmen (or women), were thru history and you will get eleven answers, but Winston Churchill would be near the top on every list. He was the middle son of a politician from an illustrious old English family, but not a terribly rich one. His mother was an American socialite and a famous beauty. Without the prospects of his eldest brother (and even these were limited) he went off to fight in, and write about the Cuban War in 1895, India in 1896, the Greco-Turkish War

in 1897, the Sudan in 1898. He was recognized both as a great writer and heroic soldier throughout. In 1899, he returned to England, ran for Parliament, but lost, so he went off to South Africa to fight in the Second Boer War where he was taken prisoner, escaped, saved a bunch of other people, and was just all around heroic once again. He was considered for the Victorian Cross, until someone noticed he did all this as a civilian and was therefore not eligible.

Between 1900 and 1915 he took a something of a breather and went into politics. In the summer of 1914 a royal inbred nitwit got himself assassinated in Serbia and it was off to the races with WW I. Churchill resigned from government and went into the Army -first as a Major and then as a Lieutenant Colonel. Along the way, he was the Lord of the Admiralty at the same time Franklin Delano Roosevelt was the Secretary of the Navy in America. (The two politicians knew and respected one another and some few historians have suggested that this friendship was no small part of what got America into WW I, but this is a subject for other pages.)

Between the world wars, Churchill was out of politics or *in the wilderness* because he was in favor of India's Independence, warned against Nazi

Germany, and finally, was vehemently opposed to the fashionable intellectual's dalliance with socialism. All of these views were contrary to popular notions of the times, and all would later come to be proven to be spot on. In 1940 he was once again the First Lord of the Admiralty, and when Neville Chamberlain got done trying to appease Hitler and resigned, Churchill then became the Prime Minister.

Churchill probably did more to win WWII than anyone else in the world, but the English were astonishingly ungrateful so he was out on his ear again between 1945 and 1951 when he was back in until 1955. He died in 1965 at 91 years of age.

There are a few stories about Churchill that need telling. One supposedly happened at a party when a woman marched up to him and said. "Sir, you are drunk, very drunk." He replied, "Madam, you are right. Furthermore, you are ugly and tomorrow morning you will still be ugly." At another party, another woman told him that if he were her husband, she would put poison in his tea. His reply: "If I were your husband, madam, I'd drink it." But my favorite story about him involves a nanny and her young charge visiting her friend one morning. The second woman was one of Churchill's varied servants. The two women were having a nice cup of tea and a chin-wag, while the wee lad grew bored and wandered off until he came to the great man's bedroom. Churchill was well known for staying in bed doing paperwork well into the day and the boy was entirely in awe of the man, and asked, "Sir, is it true you are the greatest man in the world? Churchill looked up and answered, "Yes, now beat it."

There is much to be said about and learned from Churchill and his life. An extraordinary man by all accounts. Perhaps the biggest take-away for the American reader is that he was half American, 1/64 American Indian, and loved Americans. One writer suggested he was more comfortable among Yanks than any other Englishman has been before or since.

There are some excellent movies and a couple of TX mini-series about Churchill. Perhaps among the best is THE DARKEST HOUR. It's all about the very beginning of WWII and Churchill's struggle to convince Parliament and all of England that it was vital that England enter the war.

Circus   from the Latin for 'circle' and a roundabout or traffic-circle; there are no elephants nor clowns. see ***Piccadilly Circus***

civil parish   -the smallest or lowest political division involving local administration. While it is an oversimplification, Yanks might think of a civil parish simply as a town that is concerned with elementary education, local roads, fire protection, libraries, and some planning. It is below—smaller than—*civil* districts and counties, but some of then are as large as 80,000 citizens, but some are villages with as few and a hundred inhabitants. They are not to be confused with an *ecclesiastical* parish which divides up parishioners from one church to another. All is probably less important to an American reader -other than being terribly confusing anyway.

Civil Service   Her Majesty's Civil Service is the permanent professional bureaucracy or secretariat of the Crown. They are employees of the crown rather than elected members of *Her Majesty's Government. Cabinet Ministers* are chosen from *MP*'s, of the majority party and liable to be replaced every 5 years, but the Civil Service in perpetual. In America, the civil servants may be a local, but in England, they are considered Crown employees (England's "the Crown*"* equals America's *Federal.*) Set aside an hour or so, and type "BBC Yes Minister Youtube." You will learn about the English and Geo-politics as well enjoying dry British humor at its best.

Civil War, English   Three wars actually, between 1642 and 1651 between various factions of Protestants vs. Catholics and Parliamentarians vs. Royalists. Worked out roughly as follows: Catholics were generally loyal to King Charles but the Protestants were in favor of the Parliament being in charge. Charles was beheaded in 1649 and things went badly for the Catholics under *Oliver Cromwell*. Cromwell was something of an ass and things weren't all that great for the Protestants either particularly if one of them annoyed Cromwell. The final brief war between 1649 and 1651 saw *Charles II* return to the throne with Parliament giving its consent, but Parliament kept hold of the purse strings, not unlike what congress is supposed to do today in America. see *Oliver Cromwell, Commonwealth, the Protestant Revolution, the Protestant Restoration, Charles I*

claret   A somewhat slippery term for a dark red wine from France that came to be cliché for snooty wine in England from the 12th to the 15th century. The French do not use the word 'claret,' but instead drank Bordeaux.

clergy   Members of the clergy have long shown up in English literature. They are either pious and poor, or rich and rapacious. There seems to be no middle ground and there are a lot of them.

As is often the case, a historic perspective is the best way to sort it all out for the American reader. When the Romans left, things were increasingly owned by a king or by the Catholic church. A little later it was owned by the Normans and the church and later still, rich English guys and the church. The church was the constant and the church also had a monopoly on literacy. This brings us to one of the church's first responsibilities; they kept track of births, marriages, and deaths in a given parish until at least till the middle 1800's. (Looking after people's souls was only incidental.) From the earliest days of the organized church, it also served an educational role, but originally it was just to educate more clergy. English priests were not expected to have a degree, but were expected to have at least a little college. (It was only after WW II that the Catholic church required a theological degree.) Indeed, history, science, archeology, literature all benefited from work done by the clergy. (Later science and exploration would be done by otherwise bored rich *gentleman*.) The following roles may be Catholic, Protestant, or both in one form or another.

Archbishop	The top bishop in the Church of England. There have usually been only two of them, the Archbishops of Canterbury and of York.
Bishop	Supervised a large area and had their own cathedrals. Bishops and Archbishops are the highest level of cleric administration and automatically became members of the **House of Lords**.
Priest	A mid level clergy. Priests usually had their own church and Church of England priests were usually married.
Deacon	The lowest level of the church's hierarchy. Deacons in England were priests-in-training, not *church elders* like in America.
Archdeacon	Not so much a supervisor for deacons as an assistant to the bishop.
Dean	Supervises a cathedral's canons.
Canon	A member of a cathedral's staff of priests and one who conducts service
Rural Dean	Supervises several churches in a *see.*
Curate	An assistant to a rector.
Rector	The head priest out in a parish and entitled to that parish's tithe.
Vicar	If the rector didn't want to be bothered looking after his parish, he could hire a vicar for some minor portion of the income he derived from that parish. Vicars in literature were usually devout, if poor.
Chaplain	A priest without a church. He might serve at a nobleman's private chapel or serve a military function.
Warden	Supervised the church's charitable undertakings.
Beadle	When the church oversaw local law enforcement, beadles were the village policeman. In the more modern Church of England, their role was to keep order during service.
Sacristan	Looked after the church or cathedral's holy vessels etc.
Precentor	The church's choirmaster.
Sexton	Maintains the church grounds.
Verger	Maintains the church building.

There is one final role in the clergy that shows up in literature, that being the wife. (Catholic priests etc., did not marry, but Protestant and Church of England clergy could.) The Vicar's wife was usually the center of all matters involving the women of the parish, notably charities & appurtenant fund raising, local morality and culture, and she often did a little common sense matchmaking.

clerk -pronounced *clark* -an office worker or an agent for a *barrister.* American sales clerks are referred to as *shop assistants* in England.

climate   England's is a *temperate maritime* climate. England is cooler than the rest of Europe in the summer, but warmer in winter, rarely below freezing or above 90° F. Rainfall averages about 30 inches per year, but with great variation from west, (wet, windy and mild), to east, (dryer and cooler). There is no rainy season –it rains all year round, with January and October being the wettest. It does snow in England, but rarely and it melts quickly. None the less, the Scottish Highlands have five or six ski areas and there are even a couple in northern England, but none are as large, high, popular, or having seasons as long as those in the Alps or Rocky Mountains.

The sun shines thru clouds etc, for about one third of the time and June is the sunniest month. Fog is also a year-round phenomenon, but is heaviest in the winter.

Incidentally, should climate change bring about a raise in sea levels, England will suffer greatly because much of the River Thames is essentially a long tidal basin.

clogs   Not just the Dutch, but people living in rainy wet Wales and Northern England wore clogs. They are made by two separate licensed guilds; the *clogger* who made the wooden sole, and the *clogmaker* who made the leather upper.

clothing   To understand clothing in England, it is important to remember two things, First, England is wet and chilly -never seriously cold, but never toasty warm. Second, until the industrial revolution, fabric was hugely labor intensive to make and therefor very expensive. The old portraits and historic moves show people wearing astonishing amounts of fabric back in the day. This is because it was only rich people who could afford lots of clothes and had their portraits painted. The common man probably wore a knee-length wool tunic and his wife wore one a little longer.

Consider scratchy wool as underwear. Two solutions attain back in the day. You would simply go without, or wear linen if you were a little richer, or you did so until about 1666 when the English discovered cotton from India. Oh Happy Day! At least until 1721 when Parliament passed the Calico Act because English hand weavers were facing too much competition. The solution came from the Industrial Revolution and vast improvements in spinning and weaving that allowed England to import raw cotton. India became both a source of the raw product and a market for the much more valuable finished fabric etc. The Calico Act was repealed in 1774. Note the date; the Crown was of the opinion that the American Colonists were also supposed to buy finished products–for example tea–from England. But England would also import cotton from the American South and was, in fact, on the side of the Confederates during the Civil War a little later.

The reader will encounter confusing bits of clothing throughout English literature and history that are *almost* familiar, as well as costumes and formal-wear that have no equivalence across the pond. There are also items with contradictory meanings as follows:

Article	England	US
knitted long-sleeve top, closed in front.	pullover, jumper, jersey	sweater or a knit dress
woman's sleeveless dress.	pinafore	jumper
knitted sleeveless top	slip-over, tank-top	sweater vest
sleeveless undershirt	vest, singlet	tank-top, 'wife-beater'
sleeveless formal garment	waistcoat	vest
a woman's sleeveless dress w/ a blouse worn under	frock	jumper
man's undershirt	vest (This is changing,)	T-shirt or simply a T
simple skirt wrapped about the waist and tied	wrap over	wrap around

clotted cream   -somewhere between butter and cream cheese. It's spread on scones or crumpets and a necessary part of a proper *cream tea*. In America, it would be classified as butter because of the fat content.

club   Before the days of hotels in London, the rich guys who came to town on business or to do their parliamentary duty needed a respectable place to stay that was more comfortable than a rooming-house or an inn. Furthermore, it needed to be a place that was respectable if only from the outside. Some clubs were a refuge for the gentry to indulge in things that were frowned upon—but enjoyed by—the gentry, gambling being but one of the more innocuous possibilities.

After WWII, the relaxing of the idea of respectability, as well as the increase in restaurants, hotels, as well as the ability to drive in from the country in your own car, changed London clubs back to exclusive refuges for snooty old-guys. Today, what Yanks think of night-clubs were never quite as popular in England as they were in America, particularly during prohibition. Only after the mod era of the *British Invasion*, and later, *disco*, gave a new éclat to England' night-clubs.

coach   Back when, it was an enclosed house drawn vehicle and bigger than a carriage. Later it was not unlike an American stage coach that traveled, literally, in stages and on a schedule. In the 19th century, it came to mean the passenger part of a train. Now a carriage is a bus traveling between cities.

Coalition Government   When the largest party political party in Parliament does not have a majority, a coalition may be formed. The alternative is a *vote of no confidence* and that is disruptive for everyone, especially the politicians. Such a coalition is sometimes called a *national unity government* or a *grand coalition*. There were coalitions during both World Wars and they are now more the rule than the exception. This is probably more civilized than, for example, one party or other in the American congress shutting down the entire government altogether.

cockle   -a small shellfish sold from push carts in times past. (Sweet Molly Malone sold cockles and mussels, calling 'Alive, alive-o.') A cockle is also a small purple flower. A cockleshell is a small rowboat. It is not clear why, but feeling something from *the cockles of one's heart* is a very warm or sincere feeling.

Cockney   An insult going back to Chaucer when it referred to a pampered city dweller. It has variously meant a swell or (ironically) the opposite, a working class individual. It has always meant a Londoner and probably one from the *East End*. Finally, tradition holds it is someone born within earshot of the bells of St. Mary-de-Bowls or the *Bow Bells*.

Cockney rhyming slang

This was all the rage in 1840 when the speaker takes a common phrase of two or three words wherein the last word rhymes with the word the speakers really wants to use. Then he or she says only the first word. For example, to express *wife,* it becomes *trouble* because *wife* and 'trouble and strife' rhyme, but the '…and strife' part is dropped. Phone becomes *dog and bone*. Mate (buddy) becomes *China* by way of Chine plate.
Very confusing and that is the point; to confuse the uninitiated.

Cocktail   An interesting and confusing word. The cock-tail made from spirits and mixer is probably American idiom that traveled back eastward to England some time after 1800. Before then, an English cocktail was a working horse whose tail had been docked or cocked. It later morphed into an insulting term for a working man putting on the airs of a swell. Punch was the preferred way for the Brits to suck down strong alcohol throughout the 18th century and well into the 19th. (Not to dismiss wine and beer.)
Here are a few typically English cocktails:

Gin and Tonic
   For so simple a drink, much needs to be said about gin and tonic. Gin is perhaps England's most iconic liquor and it is so in a lot of places the Brits hung out. It was originally a Dutch medicine during the 17th century. Now there are four ways to make gin with London Gin being the fanciest and most difficult to make.
   Tonic came about a little later and also as a medicine, but a medicine that actually worked. It was made from the bark of a tree with an unpronounceable name from the tropics that contains quinine. It also tasted filthy, but quinine was an effective treatment for fevers brought on by malaria. The British who lived in South Asia and Africa would often get malaria, but it was the Brits in India that first came up with the idea of mixing the bitter quinine powder with sugar, soda water, and gin to make a very nice cocktail. (If you

happen to like drinking Christmas trees. Americans and other enlightened people prefer rum and tonic or vodka tonic.)

- o   1 or 2 ounces gin
- o   3 or 4 ounces tonic water
- o   lime wedge

Partially fill a tall glass with ice, pour in a shot or two of gin, squeeze in a lime wedge, top up with tonic, and stir. For an interesting change of pace, skip the lime and instead use a slice of cucumber and / or sprig of thyme. Drink while watching something on **BBC**.

Sloe Gin Fizz

A *sloe* is a small blackthorn berry related to plums and sloe gin is gin that has been steeped with sloes and sugar. Turns it red.

- o   2 ounces sloe gin
- o   1 ounce lemon juice
- o   4 ounces club soda
- o   1 teaspoon simple syrup
- o   lemon slice

Chill a highball glass. Put ice, gin, lemon juice, and syrup in a cocktail shaker and shake till chilled. Pour into the glass and top it up with soda. Garnish with the lemon slice.

Pimms Cup / Pimms #1 Cup / Pimm's Cooler.

Pimms is only about 25% alcohol rather than the roughly 50% of liquor. It is sweet with a vaguely spicy citrus flavor. It might be considered more liqueur than liquor and is the classic drink for cricket matches and perhaps more of a cooling refreshment than a means of getting even mildly drunk. There is much controversy as to what to name this cocktail, let alone how to make it.

The simplest possible recipe and one that can be made easily in America follows, with a list of options to customize the drink.

- o   Pimm's #1, 2 ounces
- o   7-Up, 4 ounces
- o   cucumber, sliced about ¼ inch thick
- o   mint leaves, 3 or 4

Put a few ice cubes into a cocktail shaker and a couple of slices of cucumber and a few mint leaves. Shake it gently to muddle the greens. Pour in the Pimms and shake it some more. Pour it all into a tall glass, and gradually top it up with 7-Up.

Substitutions:

Replace Pimms #1 with Pimms #'s 2 thru 5 -if you can find any of them.

Replace the 7-Up with lemonade, beer, ginger beer, ginger ale, sparkling wine, or tonic.

Replace the mint with thyme.
Replace the cucumber with a dash of bitters.
Skip the greenery altogether and add whatever fruit is on hand.

Sidecar

It's not clear who or where this cocktail was invented, but mixological historians agree it has to do with WW I and motorcycles.

- sugar
- lemon wedge
- 1 oz Cointreau, Triple Sec, or orange liqueur
- 1 oz lemon juice
- 2 ounces cognac
- ice

Rub the rim of a chilled martini glass with the lemon wedge and sugar the rim. Shake everything in a cocktail shaker and strain it into the glass.

Pimm's Iced Tea

Another summertime favorite. (For warming wintry drinks, see rum and whiskey)

- 6 ounces tea, chilled, (orange pekoe, mint, or whatever you like)
- ¼ oz lemon juice
- 3 oz Pimm's #1
- ¼ oz agave nectar (or sugar)
- orange wedges, mint sprigs, or cucumber slices as garnish

Mix everything together, pour over ice, and garnish.

Rum Punch

There is some question as to who said it, but it is clearly and often repeated that the proper way to make punch is "1-part sour, 2 parts sweet, 3 parts strong and 4 parts weak." This being so, a half gallon or so of a respectable punch can be made by picking something from each of the following:

SOUR 1 cup	lime juice or lemon juice
SWEET 2 cups	grenadine syrup, agave nectar, simple syrup, mango nectar, (You might back off on the SWEET if you are also using a particularly sugary WEAK)
STRONG 3 cups	rum -light, dark, or amber, vodka (Once again, if you are using a wine for the WEAK, back off a little on the STRONG.)
WEAK 4 cups	orange juice, pineapple juice, ginger ale, 7 UP, club soda, watermelon juice, apple juice, sparkling wine

MISC. / GARNISH	grated nutmeg, orange slices, pineapple chunks, ginger sugar, 2-4 dashes bitters

Serve with a block of ice in an appropriate punch bowl. Be ever mindful of the fact that when drinking punch out of fancy wee cups, it's much harder to monitor one's progress toward salubrious attitude adjustment, than it is when drinking familiar cocktails out of regular glasses.

Mother's Ruin Punch

Setting aside rum and turning back to gin, we find this comparatively modern party favorite.

- ½ cup sugar
- 1 cup club soda, chilled
- 1 ½ cups gin
- 2 cups grapefruit juice
- ¾ cup lemon juice
- ¾ cup sweet vermouth
- 2 ½ cups champagne or sparkling wine, chilled
- grapefruit slices as a garnish

Mix everything but the champagne & garnish with ice in a large punch bowl. Gently pour in the bubbly and garnish with the grapefruit.

Hot Gin Punch

Now we also set aside summertime refreshment and finally take up a warming winter punch.

- 2 cups gin
- 2 cups Madera or sweet red wine
- 1 lemon , juiced & pealed
- 1 orange, juiced and pealed
- ½ pineapple, diced
- 2 tablespoons brown sugar
- 2-3 cinnamon sticks
- 1/8 teaspoon ground cloves
- 1/8 teaspoon ground nutmeg

Put everything into a medium pot and warm gently for 10 - 15 minutes with the lid on. Serve in a teapot.

Some Historic Perspective: At about the same time the Brits were perfecting punch, Americans were drinking punch made with whiskey that was so bad that its flavor was improved by steeping a plug of chewing tobacco in it. Some recipes went so far as to suggest including gunpowder. **BTW** James Bond's *"Shaken, not stirred"* notwithstanding, the martini was an American invention.

coddiwomple   -to travel to an unknown destination with dispatch -old English slang. *Cattywompus* means the same thing in Ireland, but in parts of America it means uneven, crooked, or even *skew-humple*.

codswallop -nonsense

coiners   Copper coins go back to about 100 BC in England, and 1500 first saw machinery being used to make coins. Coinage, silver & gold bullion, money, banking, National Treasuries, indebted kings, and various forms of fraud complicate the issue, but the Royal Mint has overseen English coinage since 886.

cold dish / cold plate   -a cold meal usually consisting of cold cooked meat and bread, but with history. Single ***middle class*** people were not expected to even know where the kitchen was, so a servant would leave a cold meal out for them following an evening's carousal.

Cold Stream Guards   -England's oldest standing regiment. It got started in 1661 from odds and ends of Cromwell's army to guard ***Charles II*** and still does so for the monarch. These are the guys in the fluffy tall bear skin and old fashioned uniforms standing unmoving outside ***Buckingham Palace***. And the rifles and bayonets they carry? They are real bayonets, and real rifles, with real bullets.

college   As in America, colleges are the bits and pieces that make up a university, but as is always the case in England, colleges have lots more history. Originally and theoretically, colleges had more to do with research than teaching. Lectures, reading, and exams were pretty relaxed. Schools with regular classes, schedules, grades and all the to-do that Yanks might think of as college were called *academies* up to the middle of the 19th century and even then, they might were more like what Americans would think of as a high-school. Note the spelling of the word *colleagues* and *colleges*. Going way back, a college was a company of colleagues, perhaps even more or less a ***guild***. see ***education, schools*** etc.

collier   May have been a coal miner, a cargo ship which carried coal, or a ***charcoal maker***. Dirty jobs all.

collywobbles -a somewhat old fashioned slang for a bad tummy. Usually preceded with *the*

colonel   -the commander of a ***regiment*** or the owner of a regiment until about 1871 when the crown bought out their ***commissions***. This lead to a lot of surplus colonels who were loath to give up the status of their rank so they insisted on being address as Colonel Whoop-De-Do, even though they were retired. They show up in literature of the late 19th and early 20the century as well as on the side of buckets of fried chicken in both America and England to this very day. The word *colonel* comes from the Latin *columna* who was the leader of a column of soldiers.

Colonial   -someone from the colonies, but of European descent. They are from places like Australia, Canada, or New Zealand, but never Hong-Kong, Africa, or Jamaica. Caucasians born in India or America may or may not be considered Colonials.

colonies, the   In no particular order and at various times, the colonies were Ireland, America, Canada, India, Australia, Hong Kong, Bermuda, parts of the West Indies, lots of Africa, and parts of the Middle East.

Americans tend to think of the thirteen original colonies, but English possessions were far more extensive. The first one was Ireland and called an 'over-seas settlement' or a *colony*. This is to say real live Englishmen went there to live, like America, but with an important difference; the people who came to America did so to farm and work, whereas the people who left England to go to Ireland were right gits who did so to exploit the Irish and return to England for parties and fox hunts, or so the Americans and Irish remember it. Bermuda and the West Indies were also over-seas settlements.

The English also established trading posts, or *factories*, in the East Indies and coastal India, and picked up Bombay and Tangier in West Africa as the dowry of a Portuguese princess whom Charles II married in 1661. To round out the list of possessions / colonies / settlements etc. consider Gibraltar, Hong Kong, Nova Scotia, and the Falkland Islands.

Hong Kong is an interesting example. After the First Opium War (1839–1842) it became a colonial cession, but England transferred sovereignty to a special administrative region of China in 1897.

To understand English history, one must understand the English Empire at least as much as one understands the monarchy. Both are huge complicated subjects, but for the reader, it is perhaps sufficient to understand that a LOT of their best stories, particularly those set from about the beginning of the 18th century and extending to WW II, take place in exotic places. America has the Wild West, and the Brits have the Colonies. But here again, there is an important difference between the Brits and the Americans; America has held on to its legendary wild west and it is where they keep many of their mines, ski-areas, casinos, and Californians. England has lost most of its exotic possessions.

Today the English are ambivalent about the loss of their possessions. Arguably self-government is a better thing than economic exploitation for the people involved, and the English are nothing if not civilized, but England is still nostalgic for her colonies; at least the older folks are. Perhaps like an American old-timer might feel about the old west and the good old days, real or imagined. The younger generation of Brits view the colonies as interesting settings for books and movies and don't give it much thought otherwise.

As one reads English stories, one is struck at what wonderful travelers the English are. They seem to be able to effortlessly appear at dinner in full *bib and tucker* after having spent all day traveling on the back of an elephant.

A final word on the subject; as some of her possessions were breaking away from the crown, some others sent delegations off to *Whitehall* to say – in effect- "Thank you very much, but we would much rather keep things just the way they are." and they drink a toast to the queen at every cricket match to this very day. see *Commonwealth*

combinations   -warm long underwear for men, or a warm top and bottom combination for women.

come out   Originally, it was when a young woman was presented at court. Later, from about 1700 to 1900, it referred to a young woman coming out of her house for parties and balls for the *season* in order find a suitable husband. The American meaning of *coming out of the closet* to acknowledge one's homosexuality, is a comparatively modern expression.

comforter   -either a baby's pacifier or a nice wooly neck scarf.

Commissions, purchasing Army

To get a grip on this confounding bizarre practice, it's helpful to compare the English Army to the Royal Navy. The navy needed some few people who could do clever things -things like doing math and trigonometry in order to navigate, or people who understood enough physics to shoot cannons and later, to tend to steam engines. Therefore, the navy adopted what was at that time the wildly radical policy of promoting people based on their ability rather than who their daddy was. The army, on the other hand, needed people who looked good riding around on horses while wearing uniforms.* Lest this seem too strong a statement, consider the English view of the barbaric American colonists who persisted in shooting and killing officers rather than foot-soldiers. Foot soldiers couldn't afford houses after all, and so killing them was only the civilized way to fight a war.

There is some small logic to the practice. The commission served as sort of a deposit. If the officer deserted, or was a coward, or was found to be incompetent (and the bar was set pretty low) be was cashiered or kicked out of the army and the crown kept his commission. On the other hand, if he lasted, and most of them did, he could sell his commission to a young hopeful and retire to go raise roses as sort of an 18th & 19th century retirement plan.

Over and above this apparent logic, there were some more compelling, if less obvious, reasons for buying and selling commissions among rich people. Mostly, it kept power where it belonged, among the rich, who would preserve the status quo. There was to be none of this pesky revolutionary notion that all men were created more or less equally. If the officers were already rich it kept looting down to a minimum and there was less of a tendency to cheat the real soldiers. Mostly however, it gave rich daddies a convenient way to keep their younger sons out of the casinos.

The Napoleonic Wars killed more than a few officers and so sometimes someone would get promoted based on need and presumably, ability, but such people were looked down upon by those officers who bought their commissions all proper like. Clearly, this lead to some incompetent leadership. This sad incompetence reached its highest (lowest ?) level during the Crimean War between 1853 and 1856. One chap -Lord Cardigan of sweater fame paid a record $5,200,000.00 (in 2016 dollars) for a Colonelcy. He led and was one of the few survivors of the reality that inspired Alfred, Lord Tennyson's famous *Charge of the Light Brigade*. There is some debate if Cardigan was more incompetent than his boss, Lord Raglan, who invented the raglan sleeve. (You can't make this stuff up.)

To attach some fiscal perspective to the whole thing, in 1837 Queen Victoria was just beginning her reign, the telegraph was patented, and Lee and Perrin began making Worcestershire sauce. There were no wars to speak of. Nonetheless, prices of commissions in the army ran roughly as follows:

Rank	Branch	Cost then	Cost now -US
Cornet / Ensign	Infantry	£450	$58,500
Lieutenant	Life Guards	£1785	$232,050
Captain	Cavalry	£3225	$ 419,250
Major	Life Guards	£5350	$695,500
Lt. Colonel	Foot Guards	£9000	$1,170,000

As to why the Foot Guards were the most expensive club to join, understand that the foot officers rode horses, and had the prettiest uniforms. As silly as this sounds, the prices of commissions varied with rank but also with whatever branch was most fashionable at the time. It all started unraveling in 1855 when Parliament tried to figure out why the Crimean War was such a dismal failure. They did the *Commission on Purchase,* (of Commissions!?), and found unfavorably. It ended completely in 1871 when the crown bought its army back from the officers for some £40,000,000

*There were two exceptions to this practice and once again, education, particularly math, was the issue. The Royal Engineers and the Royal Artillery needed people who could build things or shoot things. These officers had to graduate from a military school, and were promoted based on seniority. They didn't go quite as far as the Navy who promoted on ability, but at least it was a start.

common -pejorative for ordinary or lower class.

commons, the -from the old legal term of common land meaning resources in the environment owned, or at least used, by everyone. In medieval times, the commons were part of the manor and therefore owned by some rich guy, but everyone could at least walk on the commons. Today *commons* refers to air, water, and public land.

Commonwealth At the end of the Second ***English Civil War*** in 1649, England considered itself a republic. Technically, it became a Commonwealth rather than a Monarchy, but the Commonwealth also refers to the period between the execution of ***Charles I*** and the restoration of the monarchy in 1660.

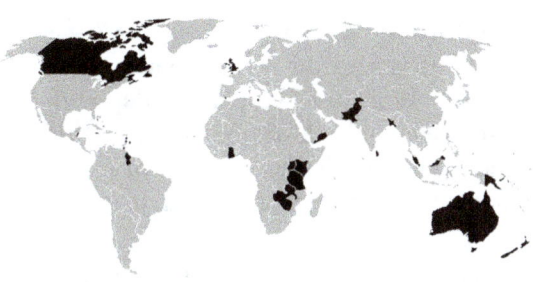

In contemporary use, the word refers to former British Colonies with various ties to England, either political or ceremonial. Typically, these are places where they either play cricket or call soccer 'football'. America does neither and is therefore not considered part of the Commonwealth.

Etymologically, a *commonwealth* is a voluntary association of political entities for the common good. Virginia, for example, is not technically a state; it's a commonwealth.

comprehensives England reorganized what Americans would think of as its public school system between 1965 and 1972. These secondary schools are tax-supported and any student between the ages of eleven and eighteen could attend, much like America's middle and high-schools. This is to say there are no admission requirements. And much like American schools, they struggle with various problems, some of their own making, problem. Race is not the issue, but rather class.

confectioners Once the English were able to get their hands on cheap sugar from the Caribbean about 1750, candy making got to be big business.

conscription -the draft, not that the Brits did much of it, despite a long history of pretty successful wars. They did so for a short time during WWI, but only two years after it started. Again in 1939 but then only 20 and 21-year-old men. Between 1940 and 1942, conscription was expanded to men from age 19 to 40, and single women. From 1947 to 1962 all fit men had to do two years of national service.

There is one notable but extra-legal exception practiced by the Royal Navy; they pressed / kidnapped / Shanghaied, anyone the could find on the waterfront and a lot American sailors they happened across on the high seas. This was one of the reasons for the War of 1812.

consenting adults   In England, the term refers to involved homosexual men.

Conservative Party   -similar to America's conservative party but with lots more history. They derived from the older *Tory* party in 1832. The Tories supported the monarchy and rich folks. The later Conservatives pretty much stuck to this script. Think Winston Churchill, Margaret Thatcher, free enterprise, monetarism, and privatization. see *political parties. Tories, Whigs, liberal* and *labor*

continentals   Historically, these were the pesky and disloyal people that lived off across the Atlantic late in the 18th century. To the English mind, the continentals were rather ungrateful for all the mother country had done for them and not without some justification. These days, it means anyone who lives on the continent of Europe and is therefore someone of somewhat suspect manner and up-bringing.

coopers   -a barrel maker but not quite that simple. There were white coopers who made household barrels, bowls, buckets, etc. Dry coppers made barrels for apples, butter, fish, gunpowder, and soap. Wet coopers made barrels for jam, sauce, and most importantly, wine and liquor. see *barrels*

Cornwall   -a vacation spot in the far southwest corner of England. It calls itself England's Rivera, but not the only place making this claim. During the middle ages, the Cornish mined tin & copper to make bronze, but mining there goes back as far as the actual Bronze Age. Metal mining petered out and they started mining china clay for porcelain. At the very western end of Cornwall is Land's End, which shows up in literature as the first site of England for east-bound ships. Cornwall was remote from London and wealthy in the past, but now it might be thought of as England's Montana. It is relatively poor, but with annoying rich people moving there to buy land so they can enjoy nice views of the ocean.

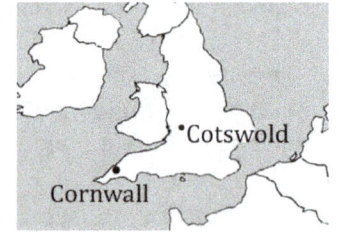

correspondent -the third corner in a divorce triangle.

corn   America's wheat or any grain like oats. America's *corn* is *maize* in England. Corned beef clearly has no corn. It carried the old-fashioned name of the method it was used to cure it in large *corns* of salt.

Corn Laws   Between 1816 and 1848 steep tariffs were imposed on imported grain to protect the price of corn, (wheat), and thereby, the wealth of the rich land-owners. It was repealed only when it sort of bumped into the Irish *potato famine* of 1846 to 1852. About a million people in Ireland starved before they did so.

costermongers   A street vendor with a permanent stall -think farmer's market, flea marker, and craft fair all together, but every day of the week except Sunday.

Cotswold   -very pretty rolling hills west of London. *Cotswold* means *sheep enclosure* in the Saxon language. There are lots of sheep to this day and lots of fossils as well as Cotswold stone which are used to build lovely yellow colored stone houses. Agatha Christie liked to send Hercule Poirot there to solve crimes.

count   -not English at all; there are no English counts. They lived on the continent, often from Germany and all, but they partied in England from time to time where they variously got drunk, seduced governesses, and got themselves involved in intrigues and English stories.

county   There are three varieties of counties in England. Some are not counties but districts, and sometimes a given piece of land may be in two overlapping counties of two different varieties at one time.   It's terribly confusing. Nonetheless, it works out as follows:
   -39 traditional counties (shires) going way back to the Anglo-Saxon times.
   -33 non-metropolitan counties. Six have set aside their district functions
      and are now unitary authorities. They are supervised by councils that are
      called *county councils*, but they are really *district councils*.
   -48 Ceremonial counties that may take on several unitary authorities.
This is one more of those things that American probably don't need to understand all that well

County Council
To simplify, it's the local government, but *county* is not a single entity in England. Think of them as smallish states by American standards. Nonetheless, they fulfill equivalent functions taken on by America's states, counties, and cities. These include education, social services, fire & rescue, libraries, planning and some local roads & highways.

Covent Garden   -a suburb just west of the City of London. It used to be the place to go to buy fruit and vegetables, but now is a touristy shopping area including the world's largest Apple Store. Covent Garden Square and Covent Garden Market and The Royal Opera House all go by the name of Covent Garden. It confuses the English too.

cream tea   a light afternoon meal of *tea, crumpets, clotted cream*, and jam.

cricket   Take a baseball diamond and throw out all the bases, add more outfielders, and put an extra home plate behind the pitcher's mound and you would almost be ready for an exciting game of cricket. A mention of something like cricket showed up in court records as far back as 1597. By 1660 at least a few people got paid to play cricket, and by the mid 1700's, it was a huge spectator sport. Cricket's 'golden age' was the 20 or so years before WWI, which was about the same time football, (soccer), was becoming more popular.

International matches (tests) are played between England, India, Australia, Pakistan, Sri Lanka, the West Indies, Zimbabwe, Bermuda, and Bangladesh; in short, pretty much everywhere England colonized except America, where the game morphed into baseball. One of the most popular tests is between England and Australia and the trophy is referred to as "*The Ashes.*

A complete explanation of cricket would need an entire book. If you are that interested, ask a British fan, but settle in for a long spell. To compare it to American baseball…

Issue	Baseball	Cricket
The field of play	The infield is very carefully measured and laid out. The outfield fence may vary slightly from one field to the next.	Only the pitch, the flat path between the blower and batsman, is defined as 66 feet. The pitch sits in the middle of a big field of whatever size it happens to be.
Hits	The ball must land within the foul lines –toward the bases and outfield.	The batter may hit the ball which ever direction he wants to –even backward if he is that good.
Runs	The maximum number of runs per batter is four –if the bases are loaded and the batter hits a home-run.	The batsman keeps running back and forth between the wickets as many times as he can while the other team chases down the ball, and then he gets another chance to bat. 20 to 40 runs is the about average for test level at-bats. One guy averaged just under 100 runs. If his hit clears the boundary, he automatically gets six runs without even needing to run.
Outs	Three strikes at bat, his hit is caught on the fly, or he is tagged out running the bases.	The wicket is broken, (the bail gets knocked off the wickets), his hit is caught on the fly, he puts his leg in front of the wicket to protect it (he cheats), or is run out -the wicket is broken when an outfielder throws the ball at the wicket when the hitter is off running between the wickets.

Crisps -potato chips -not to be confused with *chips* which are what Yanks call French (or Freedom) fries

Cromwell, Oliver

Cromwell, Oliver (1599–1658) Yes, he was related to **Thomas Cromwell**. Oliver's great-something grandmother was Thomas Cromwell's sister and she kept her name for confusing reasons having to do with title and inheritance. Ollie was born in 1599 and didn't show up much in history till he became a Member of Parliament in 1628-9, but was still a comparative nobody. He was, however, a devout Puritan, and a tolerant Puritan, at least initially. He did another stint in Parliament starting in 1646 and was one of the signers of Charles's death warrant in 1649.

He surfaced as a military leader during the English **Civil War,** and killed a lot of Catholics, particularly the Irish and Scottish ones. He appointed himself the **Lord Protectorate** of the Republican **Commonwealth** from 1653 to 1658 when he died. Historians disagree, but no one less that **Winston Churchill** thought he was a genocidal dictator.

It might be valid to think him as inventing a model followed by a lot of little tin-pot dictators in much of the world's troubled places; you find a parade, get out in front of it, take credit for everything while quietly killing any potential rival.

The movie CROMWELL (1970) is an excellent movie on both the man and the **English Civil War**. Make lots of popcorn and buckle-up, it's just under two and a loaf hours long.

With two Cromwells, Henry executing people all willy-nilly, and the Catholics & Protestants burning one another at the stake, it's all a little confusing. There's nothing like a time line - even a crude one- to clarify things.

1480	1490	1500	1510	1520	1530	1540	1550	1560	1570	1580	1590	1600	1610	1620	1630	1640	1650	1660
Columbus (born 1451)																		
Sir Thomas More																		
	Sir Thomas Cromwell																	
		King Henry VIII																
				Queen Elizabeth 1														
					William Shakespeare													
						Oliver Cromwell												
															Civil War			

Cromwell, Thomas

Cromwell, Thomas (1485–1540)   He was an ancestor of **Oliver Cromwell**. Tom was a lawyer and chief minister to **Henry VIII**. You may take your pick, he was either a political hack who betrayed all and sundry (including his one-time friend **Anne Boleyn)**, or the chief architect of England's Reformation and Parliament's ascension over the monarchy. The monarch in question, **Henry VIII**, was one monarch badly in need of some Parliamentary supervision.

Cromwell was the 1st Earl of Essex and the king's right-hand-man from 1532 to his execution eight years later. He engineered Henry's annulment to **Catherine of Aragon** but failed to get the pope's blessing, so Henry said to hell with the pope and made himself the head of the **Church of England**.

Cromwell set up the rules of how the church would work and Henry made him the vicar general as well as the vice regent. This was new; one guy who was second only to the king in both matters political as well as religious, but politics and religion were much more intertwined then.

Things bumped along well for Cromwell as he saw Henry thru three more wives (one died in childbirth, one was divorced, and one was executed) until Cromwell engineered Henry's sixth marriage to a German princess. He had hoped to stir some German rectitude into the English Reformation, but it turned out Katherine Parr was not attractive enough to suit Henry so he had Cromwell tried for treason and promptly executed. Years later, Henry would admit he felt badly about how things turned out for his old friend and adviser.

cross sweeps   -not so much a craft, as the last way to earn a few pennies. A cross sweep would take his broom and sweep the horse manure from a path across a street so a rich person would not dirty their shoes.

crown   -five shillings or one forth of as pound. Today it would be about a nickle, but in the Jane Austen's time, for example, a shilling would buy you a modest meal. see ***money***

crumpets   -a biscuit-like thing, but cooked in a frying pan. It's not split nor subsequently toasted like the English muffin which is actually American. Both are very good at soaking up butter etc. A cook might find it interesting in the fact that they use both yeast and baking soda for leavening.

Crumpets
Find four crumpet rings. These are little sheet metal things about 3 inches in diameter and an inch high. (Or cut up a couple of tin cans of about that size.)
>   2 cups flour
>   ½ teaspoon salt
>   1 teaspoon sugar-
>   2 cups milk
>   2 teaspoons fast rising yeast
>   ½ teaspoon baking soda
>   a little vegetable oil

1. Mix everything EXCEPT the baking soda thoroughly. You should end up with a thickish batter but not as thick as bread dough.
2. Cover and let it do its yeasty foamy thing in a warm place for about an hour.
3. Stir in the baking soda and knock down the fluffiness. Let it ferment for another 30 minutes.
4. Preheat the pan, (ideally a heavy cast-iron job), and rings over low heat. Add enough oil to your pan to get to a non-stick state.
5. Pour the batter into the rings till they are about half filled.

> Cook about 8 to 10 minutes for the first side. The first side is done when the top is full of little holes and looks dry.
>
> 6. Remove the rings and flip them over to cook for another minute or two. Serve with jam or jelly and entirely too much butter.

Crusades, the   There were seven wars off and on from 1095 to 1456 -or eight; it depends on whom you ask. The Crusades were in the Mid-east and England was far enough away not to get too wrapped up in this mess. The Normans (French) were in charge during the crusades and the Norman kings viewed England as a possible source for only passable soldiers, but these kings rarely

ORLANDO BLOOM   EVA GREEN   JEREMY IRONS   ...LIAM NEESON

KINGDOM OF HEAVEN

actually cleared their own calendars enough to schlep off to that hot, dusty, dry, poor, miserable corner of the world to kill and be killed. One important exception involves the legend of *Robin Hood* and the evil Sheriff of Nottingham filling in for King Richard who might–or might not–have been off in the Holy Lands. There are any number of movies about the Crusades. KINGDOM OF HEAVEN is a comparatively recent movie (2005) on the crusades. There are a couple of niggling details; the hero, Balian of Ibelin)1143 - 1193), was more French than English and was actually born in Jerusalem.

Cunard White Star Line a luxury passenger ocean liner company They sailed (mostly) between Liverpool and New Your. Cunard was started in 1846, merged with White Star lines in 1934, and went out of business in 1949. Before the merger, White Star owned the Titanic which sank in 1912. If you come across either company, the writer is talking about very rich people.

curate   -a clergyman, (or now a clergy woman), who assisted a *rector* or *vicar*.

currants -either raisins or a little dried berry like the gooseberry.

curriers   -one of the many processes to cure leather. The currier would take hides from the tanner, (or the *shedman* who flattened the tanned hides) and shave them to the desired thickness.

curry   Chicken *tikka masala* has been called England's 'true national dish' with good reason. This version of curry comes on potatoes, rice, chips, pizza, and is served everywhere.

To understand the English love of curry, you need to begin with the notion that while it comes from India, Indian curries and English curries are not necessarily the same thing. For starters, Indian curry has a lot of hot chilies. More confusion comes from England's first cook book The Forme of Cury published circa 1390. The word 'cury' (one R), is from the French 'cuire' *to cook*. It appears to have no connection to the Tamil (Indian) word for sauce, *kari*. And for that matter, 'curry' in India means sauce or gravy rather than a whole dish. "You want a nice dish of curry?" in India would be a little like asking "Do you want a nice bowl of gravy?" in America.

In England, curry–the English version of curry–goes back to 1747 and used only black pepper and coriander for spice. Later it would also include turmeric and ginger, and later still, the hot spices. "Curry powder" is entirely an English invention with a long list of spices. Any good cook in India would have his or her own recipe to make a curry sauce.

Between 1858 and 1947, the English were big in India with civil servants and soldiers running back and forth between the sub-continent and home, all the while fetching home a fondness for curry. After WWII, there were also a lot of immigrants from India and curry became even more popular. Today in England, curry means meat, (any meat or fish, but most often chicken or lamb), with a thick mild curry sauce often served over rice.

Chicken Tikka Masala: (A fast and easy version)
    2 pounds of chicken -leg and thigh meat are very good
    Marinade:
        1   quart plain yogurt
        4   teaspoons salt
        2   teaspoons cumin
        2   teaspoons cinnamon
        2   teaspoons cayenne
        2   teaspoons black pepper
        2   teaspoons fresh minced ginger or 1 teaspoon ginger
        powder
        OR, instead of all the above, just go with...
        3-4   tablespoons of curry powder
    Sauce (curry):
        1   tablespoon butter
        1   clove garlic
        1   jalapeno pepper diced fine
        2   teaspoons cumin
        2   teaspoons paprika
        1   teaspoon garam masala
        1   tablespoon salt
        1   8oz can tomato sauce

    1 cup heavy cream
¼ cup chopped parsley
Anything else you like of a vegetable nature, i.e.,
   chopped tomatoes, bell peppers, diced onion, as well
    as left-over asparagus, peas, green beans etc.

1. Mix all the marinade ingredients in a large bowl and coat
   the chicken thoroughly. Refrigerate for an hour or more.
2. Pre-heat the oven to 350°F
3. While chicken is marinating, measure & prep the garlic,
   jalapeno (remove the seeds and white pith for a milder
   heat), cumin, paprika, and garham masala. Melt the butter
   over medium heat in a large non-stick frying pan and toss
   in the powdery spices to bloom -till they sizzle and smell
   nice. Then sauté garlic & jalapeno. If you are adding
   other vegetables like onion that need cooking, now would
   be the time. Add oil or butter as needed. (Some
   vegetables will probably best be added to the sauce when
   it's done, it all depends on what you are adding and how
   much cooking the veggies need.)
3. Reduce the heat to simmer, add tomatoes sauce, cream, and
   any extra (cooked) vegetables. Cover and simmer for 15 -
   20 minutes till it thickens.
4. Skewer the chicken on long skewers. It is supposed to be
   grilled, and grilling is very good, but the yogurt makes an
   astonishing effective glue to stick things to a grill as it
   cooks. Much easier and almost as good to skewer the meat
   and place the skewers over a rectangular baking dish.
   Roast the chicken at 350° for 20 minutes or so till the juices
   run clear.
5. Carefully pull the chicken bits off the skewers and gently
   stir them into the sauce. Serve over rice, noodles, potatoes,
   or plain.

custard   -not to be confused with pudding in England. Pudding is
(almost) any desert. What Americas think of *pudding* is called custard in
England. English custard is thick, sweet, with cooked milk or cream, eggs,
sugar, vanilla, and sometimes things like chocolate, butterscotch, or
raspberry, or lemon, but a proper custard is only vanilla and often with little
black vanilla been seeds floating about.

Vanilla 'Custard'

This is an Americanized version. A proper English custard involves multiple mixing bowls & pots, and a double boiler. Wonderful stuff, but his version makes a respectable homemade custard / pudding. If you are feeling like you are cheating to much, pour in into a graham-cracker crust before refrigerating it and call it a vanilla custard pie. Hit with some whipped cream.

   1/3 C Sugar
   1/3 C Flour
   ¼ t Salt
      4 Egg Yolks -or just use 3 whole eggs
      2 C Half and half -or whole milk and whole cream   mixed 50/50
   1 T Butter optional
   1 ½ t Vanilla Extract

1. Mix flour, sugar, and salt in a heavy sauce pan.
2. In a separate bowl, beat egg and half-and-half together till smooth
3. Gradually whisk the wet into dry over medium low heat.
4. Keep stirring until it thickens.
5. Remove from heat, melt in the optional butter.
6. Let it cool a little and stir in the vanilla extract
7. Chill

cutaway   -a man's coat going back to about 1840. By 1900 it was only worn for very formal occasions.

cutlers   -made cutlery as well as scissors, skates, razors, swords etc. -basically anything with a sharp edge.

Dee comes from Semitic picture-letter for door or fish. Later it came to be Delta -Δ- in Greek and a handy letter for algebra and such. In Old Scottish and Gaelic, D is pronounced as an unvoiced aspirated apical alveolar stop. This is to say it's pronounced like a T.

dawn chorus, the -birds singing in the morning.

deal -pine or fir wood. A *deal table* probably refers to a rustic planked kitchen work-table. Hardwoods like oak or mahogany were for more serious furniture.

degree   English students matriculate in colleges, but only universities hand out degrees after exams. Degrees are far less common in England than in America, and by far the greatest part of higher education is done in their polytechnics, which are what Yanks would think of a cross between junior colleges and vocational technical schools. see *schools*

Department of State see *Secretary of State*

devolution   After all the bother of gathering Scotland, Northern Ireland, and Wales under English control, Parliament has been very carefully giving some of the authority back to the local folks. They have been at it for about 200 years now and it bumps along in fits and starts.

Devon   -a ceremonial county to the south west. DevonSHIRE is the old name. Exeter is the county's *administrative center.* (American's

Devon County

might say it was the 'county seat', but 'state capitol' would be more accurate.)

A mild climate makes growing things profitable. This and the coast make for lots of tourism. It's sometimes called the *English Riviera,* but the ocean is way too cold for swimming.

Devonshire cream see *clotted cream*

different from / to / than   Grammar teachers in England insist that it is *different to,* but American teacher say it's properly *different from.* Neither crowd approves of *different than.*

digestive -a small bland cracker like a soda cracker.

dinner   -the largest meal of the day. The timing has shifted around thru history and among the classes. Among the wealthy, dinner would be eaten late in the evening. Among the common folks, dinner might be eaten mid-day, but this is possible only if work and home were very close together. The Elizabethans all had dinner at noon, and 18th century swells had it around 3:PM as did all the classes for Sunday dinner. With the coming of railroads and autos, work and home moved further apart and going home for a midday meal became the exception. Dinner was pushed to later in the evening. If the kids were fed before the grown-ups, they were fed what was called tea -with or without a pot of tea. see *supper*

dinner jacket   -a tuxedo suitable for a formal dinner, but not the one with tails. James Bond often shows up in a diner jacket.

diocese   To Catholics, a diocese is a division of England under the supervision of a Bishop. There are 22 of them in England and they are gathered into Ecclesiastic Provinces supervised by one of two Archbishops.
     Dioceses in the Church of England are called bishoprics. There are 41 dioceses but only two provinces, These are supervised by boards and councils that are more democratic than ecclesiastical.

disco   -much less sexually fraught than American the disco nightclub. English discos might even be sponsored by the church or *council.*

divisions, political, of England   For starters, *England* is probably not what Yanks think it is. It is just part of *Great Britain* along with Wales and Scotland. Add Northern Ireland and you have the *United Kingdom* -the UK. Yanks might be forgiven for being a little fuzzy on the vocabulary, with one important exception. The **Republic of Ireland** is NOT a part of it all -not since 1922 when the Irish War of Independence undid a previous war in 1801 when the English more or less invaded and occupied the entire island. (They politely called it the "Act of Union.") Northern Ireland is still part of the UK. The Republic of Ireland to the south is an independent sovereign nation that was actually neutral during WWII.

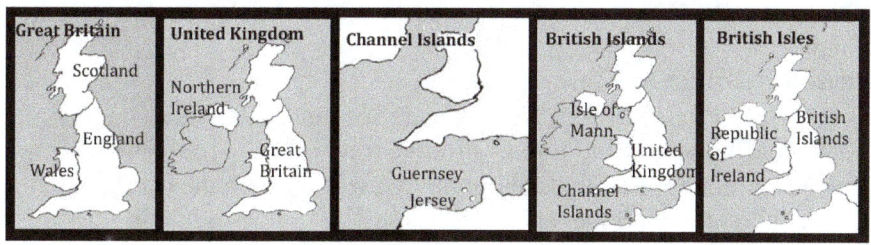

Should a Yank find himself chatting with an Irishman, he or she would be wise to tread softly until it was clear which end of the island he came from. There are also a few other much smaller islands, Mann, Guernsey, and Jersey that add to the confusion, but the last two are much closer to France than to England. There is lots of interesting history as to why they are part of British Isles, but it's probably not important to American readers.

What is important, however, is that England is divided up into somewhere between 8 or 9 regions. It depends on what you do with London. These regions are useful in tourist publications and for statistical number crunching more than any political purpose. They go way WAY back to the Anguls, Saxons, and Jutes. London is an important exception and a very confusing overlapping mess of authorities.

Smaller than the regions are the unitary authorities, and the counties. Counties are further subdivided into metropolitan and non-metropolitan counties. Think of counties as smaller that American states, but bigger than American counties. For the American reader, they are somewhat like big American cities wherein the political duties of both the city and county are combined, but in England, they are more like a combination of state and county. Some are large and rural, and others are a collection of almost big cities. Finally, there are traditional counties which are different from the ceremonial counties. In both, there is the opportunity for old timers to dress up in funny old-fashioned costumes and march in parades. (The English do love their tradition and ceremony.)

History attains throughout. Originally, counties were the possessions of dukes -the top of the peerage heap. Sometimes mere earls could run things, but dukes and earls both appointed a **Lord Lieutenant** to make sure the income kept coming in. Change happened and populations moved around so eventually they had to reshuffle and re-sort just to keep Parliament more or less Parliamentary with the **Reform Bill of 1832.** Even before this, however, government was getting increasingly complicated and so the crown and Parliament in London needed local help to keep things running smoothly.

Below counties etc., are districts that may also be called cities, boroughs, royal boroughs, or metro-boroughs or metro-districts. These were sometimes further divided into civil parishes. These last are rare, small, and when they exist, they are important historically because they are what remains of the Catholic church's local authority from before the Protestant Reformation.

If an American reader were to spend the time to understand the modern-day layout of it all, and it would be a thankless effort, then he or she would have to start all over again to figure it out for Scotland, Wales, and Northern Ireland.

Takeaways for the Reader:
- All of England -the UK -England, Scotland, and Wales- would fit comfortably into California.
- The modern Brit feels about *the council* in much the same way a Yank would feel about *city-hall.*
- The local church ran things in town until the Protestant Reformation.
- The Lord of the Manor ran things on his manor but occasionally the reader will find a rapacious Lord who also ran things in town to greater or lesser degree. Conflict arose.
- The English tried to sort it all out legislatively in 1956, 1972, and once again in 1995. Progress has been made, but there is still some ways to go.
- One possible reason for the UK withdrawing from the European Union was the appalling possibility that the whole mess would have to be adjusted some more to comply with the Union's thoughts on how it was to be done.

The following table might be of some use if the reader really wants to understand it all -if only a little.

Regions	County	District	Parish
1.North East 2.North West 3.Yorkshire & Humber	6 Metropolitan Counties	36 Metropolitan Districts	(many) Civil Parishes
4.East Midlands 5.West Midlands 6.East of England	27 Non-Metropolitan Counties	201 Non-Metropolitan Districts	
7.South East 8.South West 9.North East 10. North West	56 Unitary Authorities		
11. Yorkshire & Humber 12. East Midlands 13. West Midlands	Greater London	32 London Boroughs	
14. East of England 15. South East 16. South West		"City" of London	
Scotland, Wales, & Northern Ireland all use a completely different set of rules and organization.			

divorce   Divorce thru English history marriage and the roles of ***women,*** and it's not a pretty picture in some ways. For starters, it was difficult to get divorce thru most of England's history, especially for the rich. This is because marriages were negotiated deals combining two estates and lots of wealth, divorce would have been an impossibly complicated mess to unravel. It simply wasn't worth the effort. Much easier to keep the spouse and simply take a lover.

On the other hand, marriage was expensive and difficult for the common couple, so they often didn't bother. Divorce might have been marginally easier for the common man, but death at a young age and especially during childbirth made divorce a little redundant. Barrenness and adultery -**flagrant** adultery- were grounds for divorce,* but only if the wife was the adulterer. (Their understanding of biology was such that a childless marriage was also thought to be the woman's fault.) Up until about the time of Shakespeare, a divorce could only be granted by *Parliament.*

Henry VIII's invented the *Church of England* so he could set aside *Catherin of Aragon*, but this did not make divorce easier for anyone but Henry. In 1875 they set aside the 'flagrant' part of the definition of adultery and replaced it with a more normal work-a-day adultery but it was not until 1923 that adultery on the part of the husband also came to be ground for divorce. WWII had an interesting effect on the whole thing. There was some 'allowance for wartime indiscretion' that made a divorce a little harder to get. Since then, England has not quite caught up to America in their divorce statistics, but it is coming right along.

* Desertion was tentative and only problematic grounds for divorce. Little Known Fact: Benjamin Franklin never married Debora Read, the mother of his two children and whom he loved and with whom he lived happily for 44 years till her death in 1774. She had been married before, but her husband disappeared. It was rumored he had run off to be a pirate, but it could not be proved, so there could be no legal marriage.

DL's   -Deputy Lieutenant -appointed by the Lord Lieutenant. It's not clear what they do other than go to ceremonies, but "DL" is a cool thing to put behind one's name. It could also stand for Drivers License

dock -where the accused sits during his or her trial.

dog collar -slang for the cleric's collar.

dole   -originally money paid out from the parish to various people and for various ends. It applied to unemployment benefits only after 1919 and was a derisive term. *On the dole* is not charity, but more like America's unemployment insurance. The length of the *dole que* where people went to collect their money, is considered an indicator of the economy.

don   Originally a senior member of a college, but later it came to be a derisive term for an arrogant academician and was thought to be reminiscent a Spanish Don, (capitalized), at a time when the English were fighting with the Spanish.
donkey's years -a very long time -think of it as America's *a coon's age.*

doolally / go doolally   -gone crazy or insane. It probably refers to a soldier and is considered a consequence of battle fatigue.

dormitory   -what American's might think of a bunk house or barracks with many beds in a large room, particularly in a *public school*. A *dormitory* *suburb* or *dorm town* is like what Americans think of a *bedroom community*.

Doomsday Book   William the Conqueror sent out what we would think of today as county assessors to determine every man's holdings and what they were worth for purposes of taxation. Because the decision by these assessors was absolute and could not be appealed, it came to be called The *Book of Judgment* and later, the Doomsday Book.

Dorset   -both a county and a region on England's south coast. Dorset is a *ceremonial county*, a *non-metropolitan county*, and has its own **County Council**. Despite all the confusion as to its political and governmental status, it is a nice place to vacation because of the scenery. see *divisions*

double cream -whipping cream.

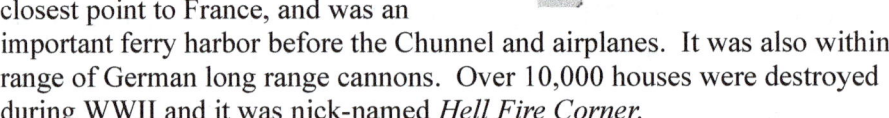

Dover   A town of 33,000 people on the south-east corner of England. It is the closest point to France, and was an important ferry harbor before the Chunnel and airplanes. It was also within range of German long range cannons. Over 10,000 houses were destroyed during WWII and it was nick-named *Hell Fire Corner*.

Dover, White cliffs of   -a geological formation of chalk, (calcium carbonate which is squished together skeletons of wee algae), that sticks up out of the ocean as much as 350 feet

They are hugely popular to the Brits as a natural wonder and even more so as a symbol of protection against the rest of Europe, i.e. Napoleon and Hitler. If you read about WWII pilots, you will surely come across the relief they felt when the nursed a damaged plane over the English Channel and at long last spotted the White Cliffs of Dover.

dowager   -initially a widow who got to keep her husband's title and / or property after his death. This was often because she was the mother of the inheriting peer. Now it likely means any woman of wealth, a certain age, and with whom one ought not trifle.

dower and curtsey   Dower was the property a woman could retain when her husband died -hence the word *dowager*. Curtsey is what a surviving husband got to keep. You would have to be an 18th century lawyer to entirely understand it. A *dower house* was a small house on the far corner of the estate where the inheriting son would store his mother in order to keep her away from his new wife's household. Kind of a nasty practice to the modern American mind.

dowry   This is the seemingly archaic system of buying and selling daughters, but for two things: It lasted well into the 20th century, and it had more to do with making sure that daughters could continue to live in the manner to which she had grown accustomed while living with her parents. Back in the day, the money was given to the father of the husband who guaranteed things for the daughter if the son and husband ran off or died. None the less, a rich young woman's dowry made some cracking good stories of contemptible young men, often in pretty uniforms, and sad brides who often took ingenious revenge on the swine. While the aristocratic practice of dowry diminished, it really took a hit in 1882 when women were permitted to own property in their own names. Prenuptial agreements have now made the whole thing passé. see *dower and curtsey*

Downs, the   A sheltered area at the south-east corner of England off the coast of Kent County. It wasn't quite a harbor, but more of a staging area for fleets during the age of sail. It has shallow water with good anchorage.

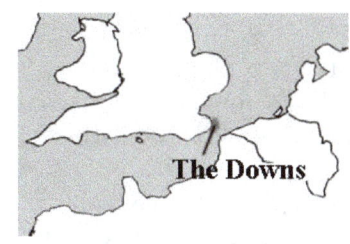

Do you hear there?   In the Royal Navy "Do you hear there?" proceeds a ship-wide announcement. It's like America's "Now hear this."

dragoon   -a mounted soldier who got off his horse to fight with a musket and saber when he got there. Their dragoon muskets got their name because the 16th century versions belched fire like a dragon. see *Army, English*

dram   -not very much at all and certainly not enough to be useful. A dram used to be one 16th of an ounce, (1/256th of a pound) under the avoirdupois system, which no one uses any more. In very old cookbooks, it is more or less a teaspoon. If a reader runs into the word in another context, it probably means some small but non-specific measure of liquor.

drapers / linen drapers   These were the only people licensed to buy cloth from manufacturers or to import it from the continent. The modern system of going into a store and buying something off the rack that was ready-to-wear simply didn't happen until early in the 20th century. A customer would buy his fabric from a draper and take it to a tailor who would then make the garment.

drovers   English cowboys that drove cattle from Scotland to the rich grassy midlands to be fattened and then drove them on to market. Drovers were, however, much more civilized than America's cowpokes, and probably rich, at least until the railroads took over. Drovers had to be licensed as early as 1552, had to be landowners, and had to be married. Forget the American cowboy and his house. An English drover would be a rich guy brokering deals involving lots of cows that he perhaps never saw. Finally, drovers are not to be confused with teamsters, carters, porters etc. who used animals to haul things, people, and materials from place to place.

drawers   -underwear or a swimming suit. In the old days, they were men's stockings and later, long underwear. see **combinations**

drawing room   -the room where women withdrew after dinner or in a public household, where the family could withdraw to enjoy some privacy. see **houses, English**.

duel   The English were sensible in this matter, or at least after the days of mounted knights bashing the stuffing out of one another in medieval jousts. Dueling never gained the faddish popularity in England that it did on the Continent, particularly among the French. It is estimated that 10,000 French twits got themselves killed during a dueling fad late in the 16th century and about 4,000 more during a similar fad about a hundred years later. Even so, one historian suggests the only about 20% of these *single combatants themselves* got killed. Americans were no slouches in this direction either. Andrew Jackson who claimed he fought 14 duels. Exceedingly rare movie western cowboy gunfights were uniquely American *affairs of honor* but with considerably less ceremony than was thought to be proper form involving rules, seconds, and witnesses as it was in Europe.

Duke / Duchess   Just under the Monarch, dukes are the highest of the English peers. The oldest son of the king is always the Duke of Cornwall, and others are always the Duke of Somewhere. There are only about a dozen of them these days.

dustman   -a garbage collector in the old days, but to use a more current and accurate word, a *recycler.* There was value in rags, metal bits, bones, wood scraps, etc. in an economy where everything was made by hand. Today the English dustman, like the American garbage man, simply tosses it all in a truck and hauls it away to the *tip.*

dyers   Here is an example of a seemingly simple thing by today's standards that was complicated back in the day. *Elizabeth I* was concerned about the amount of money being sent overseas for dyes, so tariffs were erected as a matter of course. To her government's credit however, they did some 16th century R & D and came up with local sources of blue, black, purple, orange, red, maroon, brown and yellow dyes. Cochineal (beetles) for bright red, and indigo, (a flower), for blue-purple still had to come from somewhere else.

E is THE single most popular letter in English and a lot of other languages as well. It descended pretty much unchanged from Greek (epsilon) to modern usage. It is important to math people who insist that 2.7182 is the natural logarithm. It has to do with exponents, but this is only important to math geeks. On the other hand, ***e*** sits smack in the middle of the ***Great Vowel Shift***, but this is only important to language history geeks.

Earl / Countess　　　-the third level of the peerage, below the Marquess, but above Viscounts. There are no official titles for Earl's wives because there are no female earls -only men may inherit earldoms. *Countess* is the best we can do for the wife of an earl, but there are no English Counts. There are not a lot of female peers who are not married and none at all before about the 17th century. There are now about 25 to 30 earls and some of them are also Marques. This is another area wherein you would have to be English to even begin to understand this. It has to do with one guy owning stuff over here where he is an Earl and owning some other stuff over there where he is a Marques.

East Anglia　　-the eastern most part of central England. It is named for the Angles and is very flat and marshy -at least until the Romans built sea barriers. More land was turned to farmland in the 17th century with drains and diversions. At about this time it's also where England kept its Puritans until they went off to America. During WWII it was where the Brits and Americans kept their bombers. Now it's where they keep the counties of Norfolk (*northern folks*) and Suffolk, (*southern folks*).

East End　　-the poor part of London to the east of the city. Back when London was a small walled village, there was a separate area of docks, warehouses, and what we would call slums today. Crime, prostitution, dive-bars etc. were all part of it. In the 19th century it became a center of small manufacture and sweatshops. Throughout and to this day, it is where new poor immigrants first make their way in England. It is also the center / origin of *cockney*.

East India Company   In 1600, a private stock company was set up to do profitable things in India. First, they set up trading posts, then they had to oust the French which they did with a private army. Next, they had to corrupt the local leaders and nobility. They did this with admirable British efficiency by making the locals richer than they were before. Things started going downhill in 1857 with the Sepoy / Indian Mutiny. A lot of people died and the crown dissolved the company and took over things in India in 1873. see *colonies, commonwealth,* and the *English Empire*

Edinburgh   -the capitol of Scotland and its second largest city. Edinburgh is on the Firth of Forth and was the trading center for eastern

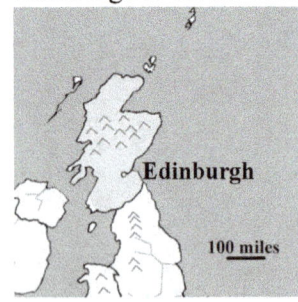

Scotland and a center for brewing and medicine. During the 18th century, it was also an intellectual and cultural center -often called the *Athens of the North,* (Edinburgh was more philosophical but Glasgow leaned more toward science and engineering). Today its population is just under half a million and is second only to London in financial machinations. BTW -it's pronounced *Edin burro.*

Edward the Confessor   The Anglo-Saxon king born in 1003 crowned in 1042 and died in1066 Edward the Confessor was thought to be very pious and so his nickname. He was probably a pretty good king but had the misfortune of having being king when the Normans invaded.

Edward VIII: Born in 1894, died in 1972, Edward was the king in 1936 for about ten months when he abdicated the throne to marry Wallis Simpson. He was a fan of the Nazis, didn't like court fussiness, and perhaps worst of all in the eyes of the powers that were, the object of his affection Walla Simpson was an American and had two previous husbands. He had to go. Edward was given the governorship of the Bahamas as much for the allowance it paid as to get him out of the public eye. The couple spent the rest of their lives in France. Edward was a rather sad character.

egg   It is strange that something as ordinary as a hen's egg can be telling in England, but it is so. Rich people boiled eggs and served them in silly little porcelain egg cups or had the cook gently poach them. Working people on the other hand liked their eggs fried and often put them in sandwiches. English *egg mayonnaise* is what Americans could call egg salad. English *eggnog* is powerfully alcoholic and while it may have an egg, it does not have cream.

Egypt -an English possession / colony / protectorate from about 1800 when they took it away from the Ottomans and the French. They kept it till 1936. What is interesting about this is that this explains why they write books and make movies about Victorian Herpetologists being pestered by re-animated mummies. It's also why some of the best collections of ancient Egyptian artifacts are in England's museums. see ***Suez***

elections National elections in England are for Members of ***Parliament***. The members of the majority party then select the executive part of the ***government*** made from the ***Prime Minister*** and his ***Ministers / Secretaries.*** The elections are scheduled every five years, but if the ***majority party*** is not major enough, they have to either form a ***coalition government***, or start all over with more elections. Local elections might be held more often, but usually every two years.

eleven: -a cricket or football team
first eleven -to be on the varsity cricket or football team at school
eleven plus -an exam given to children at about age 11. It was discontinued as schools converted to the ***comprehensives.*** see ***schools***
elevenses -morning snack at 11:AM

Elizabeth I: (16th century) Born 1533, crowned 1558 at age 25, died 1603 at age 70. Elizabeth was the daughter of Henry VIII and ***Anne Boleyn*** -his second wife. She was born a year after Anne and Henry were married, but there is some confusion as to when they were married publicly rather than secretly. When Elizabeth was three years old, her mom was executed.

She was crowned eleven years after her father's death and a confusing royal family squabble. Edward the Sixth was the next king. He was the son of Henry and Jane Seymour, his third wife, and the only one to give him a male heir. The boy was about ten years old when he was crowned and died at sixteen. Next up was ***Mary 1*** -the daughter of Henry and his first wife, ***Catherine of Aragon.*** Catherine and Mary were both devout Catholics and Mary won the title of "Bloody Mary" for her habit of executing Protestants. She died five years later and finally Elizabeth got to be queen at age 25.

She was a pretty good queen and never married, hence the nickname the 'Virgin Queen', but her status
in this direction is more than a little apocryphal. She was Protestant, but not rabidly so. She also followed the advice of some reasonably honest councilors. She fought some inconclusive wars against the French, Dutch, and Irish. The most important war was with the Spanish, but she got some help from the weather which sunk the Spanish Armada in 1588.

During her 46 year reign the English did some pretty important things. William Shakespeare and Christopher Marlowe were writing. Francis Drake sailed around the world, and the Catholics and Protestants more or less got along. All of this was not so much her doing, as it was the consequence of her being a long-term survivor, skillful in foreign policy, and predictable in her policies.

Elizabeth II: (20th century) (1926 to 2022) -crowned in 1952 at age 26 when her father George VI died. (Who became king when **Edward VIII** hung it up and ran off with an American divorcee.)

She was thirteen years old when England entered WWII and this became her entree to public duties. Other than some discussion among the Brits of Republicanism and the abolition of the monarchy, she is a popular

queen, who has traveled all over the world to visit England's **possessions** in ceremonial or PR roles. There are, however, twelve fewer now than there were when she was crowned because some of them have gained independence.

England has gone thru some significant changes during her long reign, and like Elizabeth 1, the changes were not so much her doing as her having lived thru a lot of history. She reigned longer that her great-great-grandmother Queen Victoria, (64 years), and is the longest lived British monarch ever, (96 years when she died in 2022). Elizabeth has four children, her oldest son Charles was married to Dianne, and fathered her grandchildren William and Henry. In his turn, William has given her two further great-grandchildren, George, (born 2013) and Charlotte, (born 2015).

Elizabethan Era   When you come across this expression, think of William Shakespeare. Or if you read about the Shakespearean Era, think of Elizabeth. She was born in 1558 and Bill was born 6 years later. She died in 1603 and he shuffled off in 1616. They knew each other. She was a patron and he wrote some beautiful poetry about her in <u>A Midsummer-Night's Dream</u>.

While art and literature flowered in Tudor England, there was more to it than that. She saw the beginnings of colonial expansion, (Virginia and Canada), significant economic growth, and even the little guy was doing better, or at least eating better.

Empire   -almost, but not quite, the colonies. Go back far enough in history and northern France might have been a part of the English Empire, but they gave it back to the French about 1550. Then there were the American Colonies, but that also proved to be temporary. The real English Empire upon which the sun never set, involved parts of the Caribbean, Africa, & China, and the jewel in the crown of empire, all of **India**. see **colonies**

Enclosure Acts (old spelling *Inclosure Acts)*   Farming way back in the day was so primitive and inefficient that land was not a limiting factor -labor was more important.* In modern economics, we would say that agriculture was more labor intensive than land intensive. This being the case, there was plenty of land–the common land or simply the *commons*–to go around. If one plot of land was depleted and no longer good for growing oats, the farmer would simply plow up the next patch of land. Starting around 1500 farming and land husbandry was beginning to be understood and practiced and so farmers began to take care of the land. They used fertilizer etc., but this effort only made sense if the farmer owned the land or had a very long lease. One popular proverb of the time ran...

> *Lime and dung for yourself. Marl for your son and grandson*

...and another one ran...

> *Manure for yourself, sand for your son, marl for your grandson*

Sanding is just that, hauling sand into the field to break up heavy soil and marling is to treat the acidic soil with lime or calcium carbonate. Both are expensive and difficult, but over the long term, these practices made for more profitable farms.

The Inclosure / Enclosure Acts then were all about taking land from the commons, and putting it under the care of long-term investor-farmers. Presumably this was a good thing as far as feeding people was concerned. Not so much if you were one of the guys who had been farming in the commons. Between 1604 and 1914[†], some 5,200 individual acts took 6.8 million acres of the commons and enclosed it so rich people would recover their investments in soil improvement and conservation.

   * An added challenge was that if a farmer planted a pound of seeds back in the medieval, he might harvest three or four pounds of grain. (Today, the ratio is closer to one to twenty depending on the grain.) This meant that if your family was starving because of a poor harvest and you ate your seed stock, you might make it thru to spring planting, but there would be nothing to plant.

   [†] The greatest majority of the Enclosures came during the last half of the 1800's. Arguably, the science that contributed to the industrial revolution also helped farming.

engineers   This occupation has evolved alongside science and technology. The first mention of engineering functions in England goes back to the early 1600's and dealt with draining fens or swamps. They built bridges and roads a bit later and were surveyors in the 18th century. They only started doing things with actual engines after James Watt invented– perfected actually–the steam engine about 1781. But the guys who built these engines and railroad locomotives, as well as power looms and such, were called *machinists*.

English Civil War   Several wars actually, two big ones, one from 1642 to 1646, another from 1648 to 1649, and several smaller ones in Scotland and

Ireland. There were some distinctions between these wars, but it all came down to the Catholics against the Protestants.

Catholics	Protestants
Loyal to the king	Supported the *Parliament*
"Cavaliers" because they were big on the flamboyant fashions of the day.	"Roundheads" because they didn't go in for fashion and cut their hair short.
Didn't actually execute anyone, but killed a lot of Protestants anyway.	Executed *Charles I* and exiled his son Charles II.
Loyal to the pope.	Called Catholics "papists."
Felt the king's authority was absolute.	Were pretty sure the king could govern only with Parliament's consent.
Would eventually crown *Charles II* and see some of the church's property be restored.	Lead by *Oliver Cromwell.* Allowed *Charles II* to be crowned, but kept him well under Parliament's control.

Record-keeping being what it was back then, it's hard to say, but about 100,000 people died from disease and famine brought on by war, but only 90,000 died from actual fighting. (This ratio was pretty much the norm for wars until the 20th century.) One big important exception was in Ireland where some 100,000 Protestants died against 500,000 Catholic dead. Combined, this was not quite half the population of Ireland at the time.

The importance of these wars comes down to two things; the *Protestant Reformation* that split off from the Catholic church, and the ascendancy or *Parliament.* This was not yet our modern notion of democracy by any means, but getting closer.

English Commonwealth see *commonwealth*

English Muffins   -not EVEN English. They are an American invention. Not quite like a *crumpet* and even less like a *scone*, but all are equally good at soaking up butter at breakfast or tea-time.

English Peerage   -basically, rich people. The Peerage of England was replaced by the Peerage of Great Britain in 1707 with the Act of Union with Scotland. (Ireland and Wales were still out in the cold.) Up until the House of Lords Act of 1999, all peers could sit in the House of Lords. (Women peers were admitted to this club only in 1963.) In order of snootiness, it works out as follows:
1. Duke / Duchess
2. Marquess / Marquesses
3. Earl
4. Viscount
5. Baron / Baroness

These positions are hereditary; the oldest kid gets the title. Baronets are hereditary, but not peers. *Knights*, Dames, and *Ladies* etc. don't rate at all. All of these peerages come from long ago and have confusing histories that are made all the more so by between England and Scotland.

Enlightenment   After the Renaissance, (roughly 1400 – 1600), spread from Italy to the north, the Enlightenment* spread south from France, Germany, and in no small measure, from Scotland. The French philosopher Descartes, Englishmen John Locke, Francis Bacon, & Isaac Newton, and the Dutch Baruch Spinoza, are all responsible for the notion that *reason* might be more useful in sorting out things that Catholic dogma. The Scottish Enlightenment stars the proto-economist Adam Smith and the skeptical empiricist David Hume among others.

   To oversimplify to a huge degree, French Enlightenment concerned itself with the proper role of government, the Germans pondered the proper role of every-man, and the English, the Scots actually, either ignored it or found a way to make a buck out of it.   Benjamin Franklin visited Europe and fetched a pile of Enlightenment back to his buddy, Thomas Jefferson, who used it to good effect in some of his writing.

   * There is some argument as to when the Enlightenment started. Some historians place the start of the Enlightenment in 1620 with the beginnings of the scientific revolution and others put it in 1715 when Lois XIV died. Either way, a reader would be justified in thinking the Renaissance led to the Enlightenment in pretty short order.

enquiries -what American call (called?) information on the phone.

enquirie agent -an American private detective. Inquiries is the plural.

ensign   -either a military unit's flag, or the young officer-in-training who carried it. Ensigns were replaced by sub-lieutenants in 1880. The US Navy still has ensigns as its lowest ranking officer.

entail   Entail still exists in American law, but only as a historic footnote in ponderous legal texts. In England, entail is an entire chapter in similar books. Basically, it means that property may be entailed to several people successively. Consider knights and their non-hereditary estates that could not be given to their heirs. This basically meant that someone could live off the income of the property, but when he died, it went back to whomever, probably the king. Entail could also be used to assure that the property went to the oldest son. It made for convoluted plot twists of Reformation literature involving second sons, and furthermore, explains why finding the correct husband for many of Jane Austin's characters was such an important issue.

Esquire   "Esq." is an abbreviation for *squire,* but lots of men tacked it onto the tail end of their names up until about the middle of the 20th century. Thereafter, *Mr.* was good enough for all but the most pretentious **gentlemen**.

Essex   -the county just north-east of

London on the North Sea. There is industry to the south, very high unemployment to the west, and wealthy bedroom communities to the east. in the 1990's *Essex Man* was the stereotype for people a bit like Americans would label as rednecks. see *Essex Girls*

Essex Girls   Think of Essex girls in England as America's dumb blondes, promiscuous and dim. The expression got started in the 1980's and now applies to such women all over the country.

estate agent -an American real-estate agent.

Eton
-a small town known for an old (1440) and prestigious *public school*. The *Eton crop* is a woman's short hairstyle a little like what American flappers wore at about the same time (the 1920's), and an *Eton jacket* is a short jacket for children, but occasionally coming into and going out of style for women.

euphemism & understatement   Until readers get a handle on the ideas that the English are unfailingly polite (and this is not a bad generalization), and recognize their fondness for understatement, and finally, appreciate their dry sense of humor, a simple translation of the polite things the English may be useful.

What the Brit says:	What they really mean:	What a Yanks thinks:
"I'll bear that in mind"	I will have forgotten this whole chat by teatime"	They will come thru.
"This is an interesting / original point of view"	You are barking mad or at the very least, very silly.	They like my idea.
"This is rather a bother."	Something is a right-royal pain the ass and someone must die for it.	This chap is patient / tolerant / unflappable beyond all understanding.
"This is in no sense a rebuke."	I'm furious and you will be fired tomorrow.	Don't worry about it.
"This is not bad."	This is very good indeed.	This is -at best- mediocre.
"Correct me if I'm wrong."	I'm right. Now shut-up.	Let's keep talking about it.
"QUITE good"	A bit disappointing	Pretty good.
"quite GOOD"	Pretty good.	Pretty good.
"Would you be so good as to..." "Perhaps you would...	This is an order! Do it now, or be ready to justify yourself.	Do what you can, when you can.

Eurasian   -not people from China & Japan etc., like Americans might think of them, the English *Eurasian* is European and Indian. see *wog*

European Economic Community   -founded in 1957, it is an organization to simplify certain matters regarding the movement of goods and money between its members including Belgium, France, Italy, Luxemburg, Netherlands and West Germany. may be called *European Common Market* of just the *Common Market*. Initially it concerned itself with customs & tariffs, coal & steel, atomic energy, and materials. In the 1990's it gathered up most of western Europe into the *European Free Trade Association* and by 1994 the *European Economic Area* consisted of 15 countries. It culminated with the ***European Union***.

European Union (the *EU*)   -it's now a county, a little smaller, and a little more populated than America. Actually, the *EU* about half the size of America, but it has about half again more people. WWII ended in 1945, ***European***
Economic Community got its start in 1957, and they went on to have themselves various associations, treaties, & conferences. It's hard to say when it was finally unified, but 2002 is as good a date as any because this was when they unified their currency. They are still evolving by having themselves committees and by adding members from time to time. Today it has 28 member countries, a population of 510 million, and a nominal GDP of $19 trillion -$37,900.00 per capital. (America's GDP is $16.8 trillion and $53,000.00 per capita.)

The *EU*'s government is a little different from America's and for that matter, different from England's. The executive is the President of the European Commission. The legislative chores are handled by both the Council of the European Union, (economics, foreign policy, and security), and European Parliament, (budget and membership). The judiciary at the very top is the Court of Justice of the European Union, but it concerns itself with squabbles between the members and multi-national businesses rather than crime and punishment. Perhaps the most interesting bit is European Central Bank. It certainly seems to get itself in the news a great deal as they sort out member countries which have overdone debt.

This is all well and good, but England voted to exit the EU in June of 2016. This will happen over the next few years.

Exchange, The Royal   -dates back to the 16th century and was where merchandise could be bought and sold in London. In fact, many towns had similar locations. As the economy grew, commodities like grain, metal, and even money were exchanged. The New Exchange came along later in the Strand, and is now part of a fashionable place in London to spend lots of money.

Exchequer
Not quite the equivalent of the American Treasury, but close. It used to be little more than the nation's book-keeper, but about 1620, HM's Treasuries took over this function. Now the ***Chancellor of the Exchequer*** is very much like America's Secretary of the Treasury.

Exeter
-a town in the far south west corner of England famous for its cathedral. It may also be a college at Oxford that had J. R. R. Tolkien as a student.

Exeter
200 kilometers

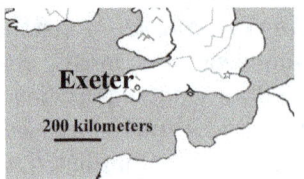

Express Most basically a daily paper, but over time, and in various iterations, the word has taken on shades of what Americans might call tabloid journalism

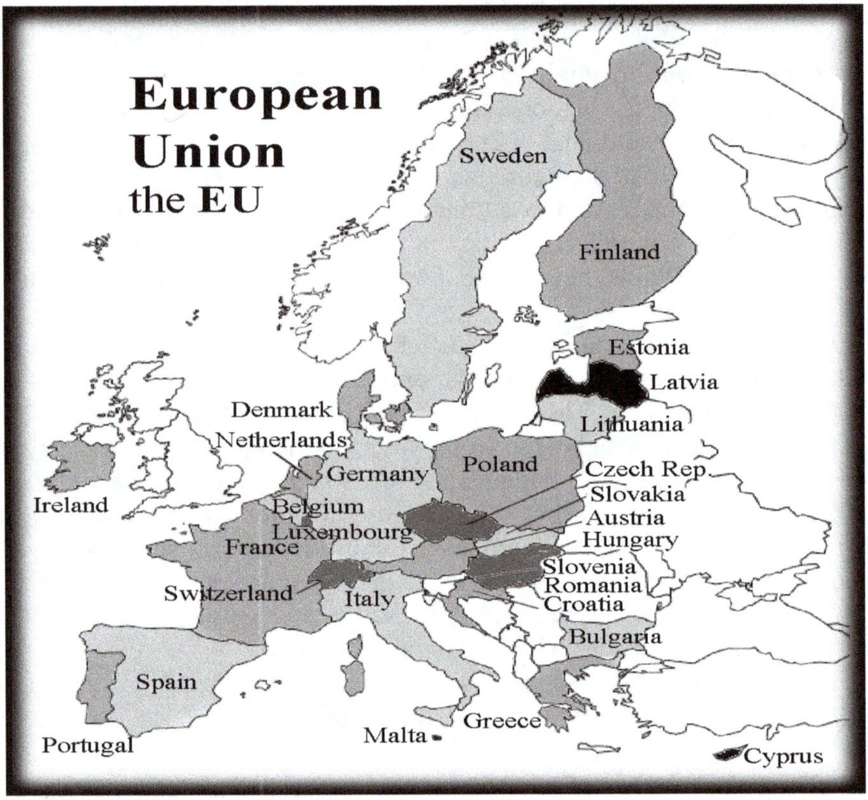

European Union
the EU
Sweden
Finland
Estonia
Latvia
Lithuania
Denmark
Netherlands
Germany
Poland
Czech Rep.
Slovakia
Austria
Hungary
Slovenia
Romania
Croatia
Bulgaria
Ireland
Belgium
Luxembourg
France
Switzerland
Italy
Spain
Portugal
Malta
Greece
Cyprus

F is tricky. In old Greek it is a vowel, but in Latin, it is the ancestor to U, V, and W. 300 years ago, it showed up in printing in place of *s*. But not really. The italic looking *f* is actually a double **ss**. In German, the ancestor of the English language, they use an *eszett -ß-* for the double **s**. In modern English, **f** can be pronounced as f as in *off*, like a *v* as in *of*, but in German, *f, v,* and *w* are all mixed up—at least to the minds of English speakers.

F

Factory Act   A rather grim bit of history, or an attempt to correct a grim situation, but one that illustrates how difficult life was for, for example, Dicken's poorer characters like Oliver Twist. In 1819, the first act forbade children under the age of nine from factory work and limited sixteen-year-olds to a mere twelve hours a day. In 1833, a second crack at the situation limited those less than thirteen years of age to no more than a forty-eight-hour workweek, and those under eighteen to only sixty-eight hours. In 1844 women could only work twelve hours a day, and children under thirteen could only work six and one half hours a day. In 1855, all textile workers were limited to twelve-hour days. see ***work, apprenticeships***

fag / faggot   Nothing whatever to do with homosexuality. A faggot is a bundle of sticks and twigs; it's kindling. Or it could be what Yanks might call a scare-crow or a cosmetic crowd-filling stand-in. Voter fraud sometimes involved *faggots*. A *fag* may also be a cigarette.

fair   There are lots of fairs in English literature. In medieval times, a fair was a big and more or less an annual ***market*** gathering while a market was smaller and happened more often. Fairs were often for a specific commodity like wool, sheep, geese, etc. These annual fairs often attracted sin and vice of every description, sometimes to such an extent that the original commercial purpose of the fair was eclipsed. *Pleasure fairs* or *fun fairs* came to be like American traveling circuses or the smaller and deicer carnivals. *Trade fairs*, however, still happen but these are now more like conventions in America held for assorted professions and / or industries.

family credit   Going back as far as 1909, this might be thought of as like America's Aid to Families with Dependent Children. It includes food stamps and tax credits etc. It has grown over the years much like America's welfare system.

farriers - looked after horse's feet.

FC   When you see the name of a city followed by F. C. or just FC, it refers to a football club. i.e. *Chelsea FC* or *Manchester United FC*.

Father Christmas

England's Santa Clause. He brings gifts and has a white beard like in America, but in England he wears a long white robe and doesn't do the reindeer or chimney thing.

feast   Up until the early 1700's a feast most likely referred to a given saint's day and only after that it was a big meal and / or celebration.

fellers   -were more than just trees chopper-downers. This they did, but they did so in fall and winter when the sap was down. They dried the wood very carefully, and shaped trunk & limbs into curved knees to make ships. Trees were important things and nothing was wasted. see ***barkers*** and ***charcoal burners***

FHB   -Family Hold Back -a warning to working class children not to take some item of food until the guest had made his or her choice.

fiddle to -cheat or avoid the tax-man.
fiddling -of trifling importance but not necessarily dishonest.
fiddley bits / naughty bits -a fairly polite reference to the genitals.

Fiddler's Green   -heaven for sailors -full of rum and tobacco.

fiefdom   -basically, the estate or domain of a feudal lord. A fief or fiefdom was inheritable and given to a vassal in exchange for 'fealty,' (*in fee*), by the king or other over-lord. Until it was taken away and given to someone else who the king liked better. A fief did not have to be land. It could also be a governmental office, or rights of exploitation, monopoly, or taxing authority.

Field Marshal   -top guy in the army -like an American Five Star General. Think of Field Marshal Bernard Law Montgomery, 1st Viscount Montgomery of Alamein, KG, GCB, DSO, PC, DL His American counterpart had a much simpler name; he was simply General Dwight D. Eisenhower (nick-named *Ike*). His job title was 'Supreme Commander Allied Expeditionary Forces' and he was more or less Montgomery's boss.

Financial Times   -much like America's *Wall Street Journal* but more international in scope. The FT Indexes are actually a number of indexes and are like the Dow Jones Averages that include industrial, utilities, and transportation etc.

fire   -a fireplace, furnace, or space heater of any sort burning wood, fuel oil, propane, natural gas, or even coal, at least up until about 1950 when coal was banned and replaced with natural gas. This ended ***pea soup*** fogs that were a mixture of fog and horrible pollution from burning coal. People actually died.

Fire   see ***Great Fire***

fishwife   -a loud and vulgar woman

fitted carpet -wall to wall carpeting.
fitted cupboard -built in cabinetry,
fittings -store fixtures.

flannel -washcloth
flannels -flannel trousers, casual wear usually, and just the thing for grouse hunting.

flashers -turn indicators on a car.

flat   -an apartment. A self-contained apartment on one floor of a building large enough to have several flats on that floor. Originally it meant all the rooms on a given floor. A *service flat* is one in which servants are provided by the landlord.

Fleet Street   -alongside the Fleet river which is a tributary to the Thames in London. It is now synonymous with printing and publishing. Fleet Street was also the location of a debtor's prison that shows up occasionally in literature, but it was torn down in 1846.

floors, building　　In England
the ground floor is just that,
but the next floor up is the
first and what would be the 3rd
floor in America, would be the
2nd in England and so on up.
BTW, England's elevators are
called 'lifts'.

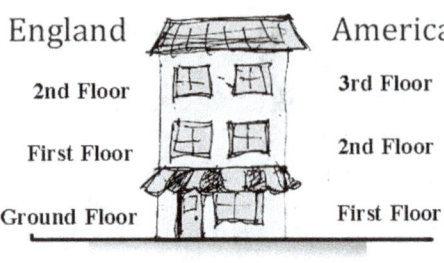

England		America
2nd Floor		3rd Floor
First Floor		2nd Floor
Ground Floor		First Floor

fog　　Yes, London has a lot of fog, but it turns out it was actually smog.
In 1952 it was so bad it killed people. In 1965 burning soft coal in **_fires_** was
outlawed and the fog / smog disappeared straight away.

foolscap　　-a piece of paper 11 x 17 inches -typically used by
accountants.

food　　The notion that all English food is bland
and boiled is perhaps undeserved. But only a little.
Every one of the many versions of the old _Lucky /
Unlucky Ambassador_ joke[1] always pairs the unlucky
ambassador with an English cook. Nonetheless,
basing judgment on such things as an old joke is

neither helpful nor accurate. Better to get scientific & historic and take an
objective look at it all.

　　Any large crowd of people going back centuries will evolve a cuisine
based on what the environment might provide that could be eaten. No great
surprise there. From the viewpoint of the 21st century, it is vital to remember
that thru most of human history, getting enough to eat from that environment
was no small thing. While starvation still exists and is not to be made light
of, we live in a time of wonderfully plentiful, healthy, and cheap food. Even
in my childhood (the 60's) a middle-class family might spend as much as a
quarter of its income on food. Today it's a little over 10% and now it
involves lots more meat and far less home-grown vegetables. As we look at
the history and evolution of English cooking, it is important to keep the
specter of starvation in mind.

　　For starters, England is an island and fish have been an important part of
their diet for millennia. Fish are easily dried and dried fish can be tucked
away for a rainy day. They are easily transported and therefore good for
trade. They are a good source of protean and protean is ever the tricky and
expensive part of any diet. During much of the Middle Ages, cod and

---

[1] (Not PC) The lucky ambassador has an Italian Cook, an English valet, French mistress, and
a German chauffeur. The unlucky ambassador has an Italian chauffeur, German mistress,
French valet, and -you guessed it- and English cook. You may mix, match, add, or subtract as
you like.

herring were northern Europe's single most important source of protean. Dried fish are naturally salty and salt is also important. Oysters were cheap food for the common man until the 19th century.

Consider this: cows provide beef, deer give us venison, pigs are chalk full of pork, but the stuff we eat that comes from fish is called 'fish' and when we dispatch a chicken, we eat 'chicken.' Why the disconnect between big animals and little ones? Remember the Norman (French) Conquest of 1066. The victors and anyone who wanted to hang out with them spoke French, (or Latin), and ate beef, venison, or pork. The little guy, who shoveled up the shit, still spoke the common language that would become English, and he ate fish or chicken if he was lucky.

Consider also the knight in shining armor. He is an expensive fraud. Far more likely to be a thug and a rapist than a rescuer of damsels in distress. Take his horse. A little horse weighs about 850 pounds and a big one, say one that was big enough to carry around a fat nobleman in his iron suit, might weigh north of 2000 pounds. People were smaller back then, (but not  as small as you might have thought), and a man weighed in at 160 pounds on average. Now a horse can eat hay, but the rich guys who had horses were more likely to feed them about 10 to 20 pounds of oats every day. Anyway you do the math, you could feed an entire family or one horse.

Porridge, (oat, pea, or wheat with maybe a nibble of chicken or fish) was what kept the Medieval common-man alive, at least till the next harvest. In
today's terms, think of life for the little guy back then as having hot oatmeal three times a day up until about 1589.

This was then that Sir Walter Raleigh came back from the new world with these astounding new things called *potatoes*. Much to be said for potatoes and a lot of what was to be said was that potatoes weren't porridge. The Irish were so keen on the potato and the Irish environment so potato-friendly that an entire Irish family could be fed on as little as a quarter acre and maybe a few chickens. At least up until 1845 when a nasty little organism killed all the potatoes. About a million Irish starved and another million left, most of them for America. Ireland was a NET EXPORTER of food the whole time and most of it went to England's breakfast tables.

The stereotypical English gentleman with his glass of claret was a long way off. Not a lot of grapes grew in England, particularly during the mini ice age from 1645 to 1710, so what to drink? Cider and beer. Drinking water was apt to kill you, but let apple juice ferment and you get mildly alcoholic cider, or toss a handful of grain in water and then let it ferment, and you got beer. Both were safe to drink. Make you a little tipsy, but you didn't die of cholera. If all you were doing was plowing the oat field, tipsy was not a big deal. And everyone was tipsy pretty much all the time -men, women, *and children*.

Louis Pasteur figured out how germs caused diseases about 1857, but old wives knew that boiling water made it safe to drink long before that. Ever had a nice cup of boiled water? Tastes filthy. Let it cool, put ice in it, and it will still taste filthy. But if you steep some leaves in it, it gets tasty. Or even better, roast and grind up some little coffee bean things and it becomes not only tasty, it keeps you awake. Actually coffee got to England a little before tea did.[2] Coffee came from places like West Africa where the English could not exploit it for economic gain, so they quickly found something upon which they could make a buck or a pound. Tea came from China and India, and the colony of India was the Jewel of the English Crown of Empire. Some Englishmen in another colony liked tea as well as the ones back in the Sceptered Isles, but got into a frightful twist about the price of tea so they decided they weren't going to be English anymore, but rather 'Americans.'

But tea is only half the story. Sugar is the real economic engine. Several big trends start trending about 1750 and sugar sits in the middle of a lot of them. First, the English little guy leaves the farm and comes into the city to work in factories around whirring buzzing machines. You get sucked into one of these machines and it will ruin your whole day. Of greater importance, at least to the rich guy who owned the machine, was that the worker's dead body messed up his expensive machinery. Being tipsy is not a good option anymore. As the industrial revolution unfolded, the English developed a taste for sugar. Follow this trend: in 1700 the English ate 4 pounds of sugar per head per year, in 1800 it was 18 pounds, 36 pounds in 1850, and 100 pounds by 1900. (BTW, in the US in 2012, the figure was 130 pounds of sugar and high-fructose corn-syrup per person per year.)

Sugar was a luxury product, but it was getting cheaper throughout the 18th and 19th centuries, and a lot of it went into tea. It also went into jams and jellies like never before, and candy became common and affordable. (Chocolate would come along later.) But a nice sweet cup of hot tea was just the thing to keep workers productive. England's sugar came from the West Indies with the help of slave labor. A byproduct of cane sugar manufacture was and is,. molasses and molasses makes rum. Furthermore, while England was starting to make things out of iron like railroads and steam engines, they were also making a lot of big gears and levers to use to crush sugar-cane, drive sugar mills, and run distilleries in the West Indies. By 1750, all of England's Navy was paid for with sugar revenue. All manner of history lies at the feet of sugar, slavery, the Industrial Revolution, and the English Navy, but let's stick to food.

As England got good at making things, it got wealthy and the population grew.[3] Agriculture, however, didn't keep up. No matter. England simply

---

[2] Lloyds of London -the famous old insurance exchange got its start as a waterfront coffee shop. Lloyd found a clever way to bring the customers in. He hired guys to go out and gather gossip about the ships which he would post on a chalk board in his shop, sort of a 17th century gossip web-site. This information was useful to rich guys who were willing to write their names under a posted insurance solicitation, (to *underwrite* a risk), as well as the ship owners who wanted insurance on their ships and posted these contracts, also in Lloyd's London coffee shop. The rest -as they say- is history.

[3] Despite legend to the contrary, Napoleon was actually about average in height for the French of his day, it's just that the English were taller than the French, about two inches on average and better nutrition was probably the reason.

imported food as well as cotton, lumber, and certain metals. Cotton came from India, (when it wasn't coming from the American South, like during the American Civil War), and India was also the source of the most English of all food. It's not roast beef. It's curry. Curry is not so much an Indian food as it is a complete Anglicization of something vaguely Indian and of minor importance in real Indian cuisine. No less a personage than Queen Victoria was mad for curry and now almost 180 years after her coronation, the English are still slurping up more chicken *tikka masala* than any other dish. According to their Food Standards Agency, today two-thirds of eating out in England is Indian food, or perhaps more accurately, what the English think of as Indian food. Real Indian food is so spicy that it would likely melt the faces of most Englishmen.

Before leaving India, we need to consider gin and tonic. Gin is a Dutch invention, that found its way to England when the William III from Holland was king. There are lots of recipes for gin, but juniper berries figure into them all. A little like drinking a Christmas tree to my mind, but juniper berries do an admirable job of covering up a poor job of distillation. The real story of gin and tonic is quinine which gives tonic it bitter flavor. Quinine is a medication to treat malaria and malaria is one of the diseases the English tripped over in India while colonizing the heck out of the place.

England was still an Empire when Queen Victoria died in 1901 and Edward VII became king. The Victorian Era was thought to be very proper and straight laced if not prudish. (In some homes, piano legs were actually covered in little pants so as not to be too suggestive of a woman's 'limbs.') Those of a psychological bent say that the Victorians were  repressed and given that their new and popular king was a big eater and an even bigger philanderer, the Edwardians really cut loose and had themselves a Dionysian Ball. The 14 years between Edward's coronation and the start of WWI were a good time to be a high-end chef. Dinner parties were competition and the winner was the guy who spent the most money. Eight courses and as many as 50 pieces of cutlery and china for twenty guests. Do the math. Meals often ran to five hours. Barely gave the Edwardians time to change clothes before the next meal. And if you have seen pictures of these people, you know how important fancy clothes were to women *and men*, but men went in more for uniforms, but very pretty uniforms.

It all ended with the start of WW I. One of the many causes of this war was England's terror of a naval blockade and starvation on a biblical scale. Thru out most of the 19th Century, (and all of the 20th century), England was a big importer of food. The importance of her navy is very clear. Things didn't improve much after Armistice. The Depression hit England nearly as hard as it did America.

German submarine warfare nearly fulfilled the English concern about starvation during WWII, but things weren't any better in Germany. During this war, the German pilots who were shot down over England were interrogated by a very smart and crafty Brit. All very polite and proper, it was more of a conversation than an interrogation that started the afternoon the pilot was brought in. The English officer would begin by apologizing for the fact that there were no beds available in the POW camp for officers. They would sort it all out in a day or so, but in the meantime, the pilot could bunk with the enlisted POW's. (While no one is more snooty and class-conscious than the Brits, the Germans, particularly old-family Prussian officers were no slouches at snobbism.)

But there was another option. If the German would give his parole as an officer and a gentleman, this is to say, a promise not to try to escape for the next day or so, he could come home with the English officer and have a nice bath, eat a meal with his family, and sleep in his own room, just until they sorted out the POW officer's quarters. Usually the pilot would choose this option and give his parole. They would drive off together in the Brit's car. On the way home, the guy would mention that his wife had asked him to do a little shopping and they would stop in at a little neighborhood grocery store to buy beef, butter, cheese, eggs, sugar and maybe even a little bacon for breakfast the next morning.

The next day, they headed back to the POW administration building to process the pilot and have a nice chat about the war and how things were

going back in the father-land. Now it is important to remember that for a good bit of the war, Germans were eating rye bread and little else. The meal he had so casually been given the night before may have been best food he had enjoyed in years. The pilot had to conclude that the war was going very poorly for the Germans while the English were only slightly inconvenienced by it all. The following chin-wag often produced more useful information from a sadly deflated and discouraged enemy than beatings and torture would produce.

Now the reality was that the officer did not have his own car. Nobody did except maybe some generals and they had drivers. The grocery store was a scam and only opened when this English intelligence officer was coming by with a German pilot. The other shoppers were actors and once they had 'bought' their food, they went around to the back door and returned it.

While the Germans were eating rye bread, the Brits were mostly eating oatmeal. Again. This reality would only become clear to the POW pilot when he was processed into the actual officer's camp and found himself eating oatmeal as well. To put food in perspective in England during WWII just a little bit more, in the eyes of the English, American pilots and soldiers were said to be "Over fed, over sexed, and over here."

When WWII and rationing ended, the Brits discovered Italian food but having just finished a war wherein the Italians were on the wrong side, they called it Mediterranean Food. They loved it, but not as much as curry. (Wiener schnitzel and sauerkraut don't show up on the English dinner table very often even to this day.)

The English language shamelessly borrows words from all over the place and no less do the English absorb food from everywhere. Besides India, they enjoy dishes from China, Thailand, Ethiopia, Greece, and France. The influence of French food goes way back, but it is ever at the high-cost end of the spectrum. What have the Americans contributed to the English table? Sadly, not much except the Colonel's Chicken, the fast-food hamburger, and the American version of pizza which is nothing like Italian pizza. Curiously, one hears from Yanks that it is nearly impossible to get a taco or burrito anywhere in England, but that may be changing.

All cuisines have sauces. The French, for example, have five mother-sauces which are used to make dozens if not hundreds of daughter sauces. The Brits have simplified this. They have three. First is a bland form of mayo called salad-cream for cold vegetables, (*salads*), a sweet custard sauce to pour over deserts like **bread pudding**, and finally, there is HP Sauce (for House of Parliament) for everything else, usually meat and potatoes; a little like a mild American steak sauce.

A final word on food in England. It isn't just the Americans who are getting fat, but they are leading the trend. In Europe, England is #5 for percent of the population that is merely overweight (49%) and #4 for obesity at 10%. This according to the World Health Organization. France finished in 10th place. The winners? Turkey and Andorra are tied. (Andorra is the tiny country in the mountains between Spain and France with ski resorts and tax-dodgers.)

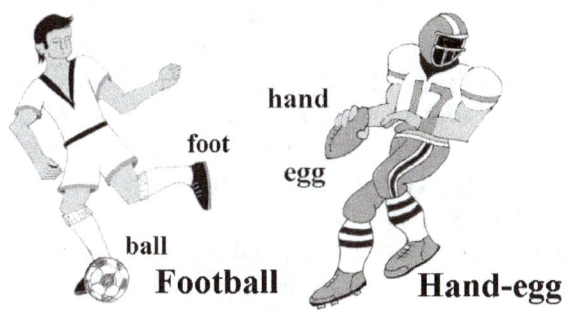

Football   **Hand-egg**

Football / association football (soccer)   Americans do not quite reach the level insanity and rabid *football hooliganism* the Brits do, but Yanks know enough about football / soccer. Even so, some history and statistics might be interesting.

- 250 million people play it in 200 countries.
- It is the most popular sport in the world.
- In 1863 the first game was played per written rules in England.
- The International Football Association Board was founded in 1886.
- It became an Olympic event in 1900.
- The Canadians actually call it 'soccer' like Americans.
- The Chinese played a ball-kicking game circa 200 BC.
- The Greeks played a kicking game that forbade use of the hands in 100 BC
- The Romans were playing a similar game by 200 AD

football hooligans   Rabid soccer fans who were often drunk and prone to beating on the other guys. They show up as far back as the 1970's and

England's fans are so bad that the rest of Europe is getting very tired of them. see *chavs*

Foreign Office   Up until 1968, this ministry stood alone when it was merged with the **Commonwealth Office**. Its job was to look after England's interests overseas. After '68, it became the Foreign and Commonwealth Office, (FCO), headed by the **Secretary of State** for Foreign and Commonwealth Affairs who might be thought of as like America's Secretary of State.

The **PM, Foreign Secretary, Chancellor of the Exchequer**, and **Home Secretary** are the four Great Offices of State. Like other ministries, this office has a professional un-elected Permanent Under-Secretary of State for Foreign Affairs. This particular chap is also the head of Her Majesty's Diplomatic Service.

Characters in the Foreign Office often show up in English literature in the 19th century and early 20th. It is a matter of faith, (or bias), that the best and brightest *civil servants* in the Foreign Office were sent off to India. The second string went off to various possessions and colonies, and the least capable civil servants were kept in England.

James Bond worked for **MI-6**, (Military Intelligence, Section 6) as a part of **SIS**, (Secrete Intelligence Service), and therefore worked under the auspices of the Foreign Office.

BTW, if you look closely at the crest you will find the words 'DIEU ET MON DROIT' at the bottom. It's French for 'GOD AND MY RIGHT.'

form   -close to what Yanks would call 'grade' in school as in first thru fifth form, but beginning a bit later than America's first grade.   see *school*

fortnight   -two weeks. It may used after the day of the week meaning two weeks later, i.e., I'll be back from holiday Monday fortnight.

French Fancy   -a wee pastry similar to, but much fancier than, the American cupcake.
French leave -desertion
French prints / novels -pornography
French *pox / gout / ache / crown / etc* -venereal disease
NOTE: The French return the favor. There are many French expressions for undesirable, unsavory, or detestable things that begin with "Anglish..."

frigate   The largest *small* ship in the Royal Navy; it was not a **ship of the line**. Frigates were typically 140 feet long and as long as bigger ships that had more decks and carried more guns. Frigates were fast, nimble, needed moderate crews, and had *long legs.* They could go longer distances without replenishing than the bigger ships could. They carried respectable firepower of between 20 and 40 guns and were the work horses of the Napoleonic Wars. The USS Constitution is a frigate.

frock   A useful word, 'frock.' In the medieval, a frock was a monk's habit and 'defrocked' meant he was no longer ecclesiastic. Later it came to mean a long man's coat, but by the Elizabethan era, it moved over to women's wardrobe, and even later, it was for children. Then it went back to men and in the 19th century, it went back to women's closet, but as a daytime dress. Finally, in the Mod Era of the 1960's, the frock became a kicky party dress for the trendiest of the trendy. see ***smock***

full stop -a period. This sentence does <u>not</u> have a full stop   This sentence ends in some *inverted commas* for no good reason""""

further education   -adult or continuing education often involving business or various trades.

funerals   Much can be learned about a society from its burial

ceremonies whether primitive tribes in some remote jungle or the historic English. Medieval cemeteries were sort of bone processing plants. When a small parish cemetery got too crowded, they dug up the old bones and piled them all together in a single grave. They also thought best place to be buried was to the south-east corner of the graveyard and facing that direction because the bodies closest to Jerusalem were the first to be resurrected.

During the Victorian era, the funeral became a fashion competition to see who had the nicest mourning clothes, who could spend the most money on the procession, and who had the most who's-whos show up to mourn. By comparison the ancient Anglo-Saxon practice of quietly burying people in tiny underground rooms with a few of their prized possessions seems relatively civilized.

fusilier - a soldier who fought with a musket and later a rifle. Unlike dragoons, lancers, and hussars, they actually took some actual risks and did some real fighting. see ***Army*** and ***military***

This is a comparatively modern letter. It showed up about 230 BC, much later than the Egyptians and Phoenicians dreamed up most of the other letters about two-thousand years earlier. The Romans decided **K** wasn't getting the job done so they invented **G** for the softer sounding **g** -words like *bridge* and *gaol*. This is the way the Brits spell *jail* but they pronounce it the way Yanks do. Despite the Roman's good intention, the hard **g** is still with us in words like *goat* and *golf*.

game pie   -a meat pie made with game. No great surprise here, but in time past, they were made with partridge, pheasant, or venison. Now they usually are rabbit.

Gaelic   -the ancient Scots and Irish languages, but now it usually refers just to the Irish.

Gaiety Girl   -a dancer in the old Gaiety Theater. In literature, she is not so much a loose chorus girl, as a woman intent on marry herself a rich nobleman.

gammon -either ham or nonsense. (A *gamine* is a sexualized little girl.)

gaol   -jail. Sound it out -soft G, long A, followed by 'ol'

garden   -another useful word with lots of meanings. Americans have front yards and back yards, the Brits have only the garden. They might have a wee kitchen garden way out back by the muse -the alley. The English garden is for flowers and other pretty things, with the important exception; during WW II when food was scarce and every possible scrap of dirt was used to grow food. Before that, however, gardens were a set-aside on a large manor for formal fussy geometry, topiary, and even an occasional maze on the very wealthiest manors. In the 19th century, gardens became more casual and natural. Other meanings of the word include:

garden variety -ordinary
everything in the garden -everything but the kitchen sink
lead up the garden path -sweet murmurings to influence or seduce
her garden -very old reference to a woman's naughty-bits

Gatwick -a back-up airport to the south of London. It is mostly for charter flights and minor league airlines and as such, it implies something just a bit second rate. On the other hand, **Heathrow**, the larger of London's two airports, is symbolic to the Brits of all that is hateful about modern life.

gas -natural gas is used for heating and cooking, as well as lighting back in the 19th century. Brits put **petrol** in their cars and use *paraffin* where Yanks might use kerosene.

General In general, a General was head of a general staff doing thing in a general way far from the action and not as exciting as colonels, majors, or even an occasional captain that make for exciting literature. Furthermore, there was no need for a general staff except at times of war. Finally, anyone high enough to be a general was also a duke or earl and therefore adding *general* to his title would be gilding the lily. For example, during WWII, England's highest ranking general was Field Marshal Bernard Law Montgomery, 1st Viscount Montgomery of Alamein, KG, GCB, DSO, PC, DL, For the Americans, it was simply General of the Army Eisenhower , but his job title was Supreme Commander of the Allied Expeditionary Force in Europe so he was really Montgonerry's boss. see **regiment, army, military**

General Strike
In 1926, the lingering austerity brought on by WW I, a growing Socialist movement, and the shrinking world economy made things fall to pieces in England. It started with the coal miners going on strike, and then spread to the dockyards, railroads, utility workers who also went on strike in sympathy. It lasted all of about ten days, but frightened the **middle class** and the aristocracy. The strike tends to show up in literature of the day as something of a turning point in the class struggle

genteel -another word with various meanings. Perhaps it can best be understood when followed with the word *poverty*. The merely *poor* could work and maybe improve their state. But to work was to cease to be genteel or of good birth. *Genteel* characters of the 20th century might have a little latitude in this direction because the word evolved to mean people who lived quiet, respectable, reserved and altogether the stereotypically dull English life. see **gentry** & **middle-class**

gentleman This is yet one more slippery term that tends to mean what the speaker or writer wants it to mean, and furthermore, one that changes with history. Before Shakespeare, it meant a man of good birth, but one who was not fortunate enough to have been the first born. After this, it came to mean any man who didn't have to work for a living, but rather spent his time hunting and riding horses and whatnot. He may have been in the army, but that wasn't really work. Gentlemen show up in government, the church, and the brightest of them sometimes became lawyers. By the 19th century, some gentlemen were doing science; they researched rocks, plants & animals, physics, history, and often went off to pester primitive tribes in various jungles. For example, Charles Darwin was a gentleman and went off to pester finches in the Galapagos Islands and we all know where that went. There were contributions made in all the other fields by England's educated but otherwise unoccupied gentlemen. A businessman, even a successful one, was NOT a gentleman. His grandchildren might become gentleman if they went to the right schools and waited until late in the 19th century to do it. After WW II, anyone with good manners and at least one suit, could claim to be a gentleman. See **schools, middle class,** and **aristocracy.**

gentry   -ne more of the many word the English use to separate themselves into *our kind of people* and *everyone else*. In the broadest terms, the gentry fit between the nobility and *middle class* -but England's middle class was very well off. The gentry owned land in the country, but didn't have titles, and they had to have inherited their wealth. There was none of that grubby business of actually making your own money like 'em *nouveaux riches*. see **middle class**

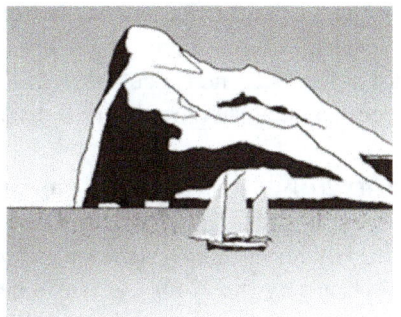

George III   King from 1760 to 1820. He was the third monarch from the House of Hanover but of greater importance, he was the guy who so thoroughly peeved the American colonists and lost that part of the British Empire. He was also thought to be mad toward the end of his life but it may have been he was severely depressed. He was also blind and deaf so perhaps he had good reason to be depressed.

Besides the American Revolution, George was king during all of the Napoleonic Wars, but toward the end, he may not have known it. His son, Georve IV filled in for him as Prince Regent during the **Regency Era.**

Gibraltar, the Rock of   At the very southern end of Spain, it is a huge rock mountain that forms a perfect fortress to guard the entry to the Mediterranean from the Atlantic Ocean. The distance between Europe and Africa is only eight miles at this point. In 1704 the Dutch and English took it away from Spain and never gave it back. It was an important naval base for the Allies during WW II. Gibraltar is also a city of about 30,000 people from all over the world. In 1967, the Spanish mentioned that they would like it back. They put it to a vote and the people made it very clear they didn't want any part of Spain. Same thing happened in 2002. Today Gibraltar is self governing, but the UK still handles its defense and foreign relations. It makes its living with on-line banking, gambling, tourism, and a little shipping. The Rock of Gibraltar and the White Cliffs of Dover are both very important symbols of England's invincibility and the difficulty of invasion.

gig　　-a small coach with one axle, one seat, and one horse, or it's a long narrow rowboat, (sometimes with sails), used to get important people between ships and shore. A gig is not to be confused with a rowing scull which would sink in a moment if there were any waves whatsoever or even a light breeze.

gin　　William of Orange brought a taste for gin to England about 1672 from Holland where it had been a medicine made from juniper berries going back to the middle-ages. It tasted filthy, but medicine was supposed to taste bad. The Brits fancied it up a little and slurped it up like it was going out of style. Gin and tonic actually was a medicine after the early 1800's but not because of the juniper berries. It had more to do with the quinine in tonic that was a treatment for malaria in the tropics the English bumped into in their tropical possessions. see *cocktails*

ginger　　-a redhead.
ginger up　　to give a little encouragement, as in "Ginger yourself up and get going."
ginger beer　　-ginger-ale, but with alcohol.
ginger nut　　-ginger snap.
(Ginger is perhaps the spiciest food the Brits enjoy, except for a little horseradish on their roast beef.)

Giro　　-an English post office that also operates as an almost-bank for the common folk who don't have checking accounts. Bills can be paid and deposits receipted to be delivered to ordinary banks. Social security payments are mailed to recipients as Giro money orders and cashed. England's post office is a far better thing than the American one in many ways, but ordinary mail does not actually come twice a day in England, but it might seem so because parcels are delivered separately.

Glasgow　　The largest city in Scotland and third largest in the UK, behind *London* and *Birmingham*. The University of Glasgow was founded there in 1451 and by the 1700's, it was a center of both the

Scottish Enlightenment and shipping. With the industrial revolution, it became a center of chemicals, textiles, engineering and -most importantly-shipbuilding. During the Victorian and Edwardian eras, Glasgow was England's second city. Sadly, the 20th century has not been so good to Glasgow. Its population peaked in 1939 at a little north of a million. Today it is about 600,000.

Glorious Revolution   Even after all the excitement of the English Civil War, beheading Charles I, Protestants killing Catholics and vice-versa, restoring Charles II to his dead father's throne etc, things were not as quite as settled as things might have been. James II was tolerant of the Catholics and this did not set well with the Protestants, so Parliament went to William and Mary and asked them to be king and queen in 1688. James took off for Ireland and the new team pretty much put paid to the Catholics, but they did sign a Bill of Rights that still serves to limit the monarchy to this day. This revolution was sometimes called the ***Bloodless Revolution.***

glovers / glove-making   This was a surprisingly fraught issue for what might strike Americans as a small unimportant thing. As a profession, it split off from tanning early in the 1300's and it became its own guild in 1349. It was also about the earliest industries to adopt a primitive form of the ***putting out system***. Gloves, unimportant things to the modern eye, show up as gifts throughout as well as in the fancy portraits of Brits well into the 20th century.

GMT   -Greenwich Mean Time -the most important time in the world -at least for people on ships who need to know what time it is in England in order to navigate anywhere in the world. see ***Greenwich***

go	-get, as is *go sick* in England is *get sick* in America
go-by	-pass.
go begging	-extra or left-over. It often refers to food.
go up	-enroll in school
go down	-leave school
go west	-die
go off	-spoil (as in food)
have a go	-try
go to the country	-throw a general election

gobshite   -someone who talks nonsense or is otherwise unpleasant with shite coming out of his or her gob (mouth).

going native   Given the Brit's adherence to doing the right thing, and given their fascination with the exotic east, *going native* is the ultimate rejection of all things dull and proper. This theme shows up vividly in a lot of the writing of Summerset Maugham and Joseph Conrad.

got the hump   -be annoyed for a perceived wrong "He got the hump because she didn't return his call."

Goodman / Goodwife   -a medieval address of respect for an independent householder and his wife. He was probably a master craftsman with ***apprentices,*** and his wife probably supervised some number of ***servants***.

goods   -freight
goods train   -freight train

goolies -testicles

governess   English literature has a lot of governesses because their sad state makes for interesting love stories and plot lines. A governess is the very picture of ***genteel*** *poverty*. She is concerned with the education of older children, while nannies or nurses are concerned with the health of younger kids. They were often the only education available on the Manor out in the country. They fell out of popularity after WW I except among the very rich. see ***servants***

Government, the English   Much of England's history has been a long and admirable march to democracy. They arguably lead the world in this direction with a little input from the Americans. This being the case, a comprehensive discussion of government would need an entire book if not a degree from a reputable university. While the history is important and interesting, for the reader, a brief comparison of the English and American systems <u>as they are now</u>, might better serve the non-academic reader.

Monarchy	
America	**England**
None. This is rather the whole point of what made some colonists into Americans back in 1776.	While the monarch -currently King Charles III. Queen ***Elizabeth II*** died in 2022 and was much beloved by her subjects, but she was largely ceremonial and mostly a figurehead. The Brits are not quite sure what to do with Charles and his sons. The Government is formally referred to as *His Majesty's Government* and the ***Prime Minister*** trots back and forth from ***10 Downing Street***, (like America's White House), to Buckingham Palace, (where the king lives), to advise him and get his (ceremonial) blessing on the government's goings-on.

Executive

The President -elected every four years from one of two parties by an electoral college.	***Prime Minister*** -selected by which ever party in Parliament has the majority. Lately, there has been no single party with a majority, so a ***coalition government*** is formed and they pick someone.

Cabinet:

The English has a cabinet like America to advise the PM and tend to matters divided up much like America's various departments and administrations. The English cabinet, however, is made out of ***MP***'s (Members of Parliament), and therefore political. They are advised by non-political experts in their fields, the ***Permanent Under-Secretaries***.

Legislative

America	England
Two houses: the Senate -fewer of them serving for longer terms, and the House of Representatives -more of them and serving shorter terms. The senate is presumed to be the wiser and more conservative crowd and the representatives the more rambunctious and more beholding to the people. It is, however, not at all clear either bunch gives a tinker's damn about the citizenry beyond getting re-elected	The ***House of Lords*** and the ***House of Commons***, but do not confuse these two bodies with America's division. The House of Lords is now largely ceremonial being as it was made up entirely of rich people back in the day. The House of Commons, on the other hand, is where it's at. The majority party in Parliament IS the government. The word *Commons* as in the *House of...*, does not mean it concerned itself with the common man, but rather that these legislators served everyone in a given district *in common*.
	As for the House of Lords, (more correctly the *House of Peers* -as in *Peers of the Realm*), being largely ceremonial now, is not unlike the Queen. They are not sure what else to do with these people, so the English just let the ole dears sort of putter along with titles, funny old clothes, and a fancy club-house in Westminster. There is, however, one important job for the House of Lords / Peers. They are the source of the Law Lords / Supreme Court Justices.

Judicial

America	England
FEDERAL: Supreme Court -9 justices appointed by the president w/ the consent of Congress.	It varies between England, Scotland, Wales, and Northern Ireland. In general, the hierarchy of English Courts is...

-hears cases at its own discretion.

US Courts of Appeal
-Justices are appointed like the Supreme Court justices.
-must hear all cases brought before them.

District Courts.
-94 districts and 3 territorial courts.
-also a court of appeals

STATE: (vary state to state)
State / Trial Courts.
-often held in county courthouse.
-judges may be appointed or elected.
-hear both criminal and large civil cases.
MUNICIPAL:
Large cities, (city & county cities) hear minor criminal and civil (small claims) cases.
Small city and town courts probably only hear traffic cases.

Supreme Court:
Like America's Supreme Court, it is the Highest Court of Appeals. England's Supreme Court the–*Law Lords*–only replaced the House of Lords Appellate Committee in 2005.

Privy Council:
The highest court of appeals for specialized **Commonwealth** issues.

Court of Appeals:
-two division, one for civil and another for serious criminal appeals.
-its decisions are final.

The High Court:
-civil court of the first instance and appellate court reviewing lower court decisions.
-3 parts: **Queen's Bench**, Chancery, and Family Court.

Crown Court:
-criminal court of both original and appellate jurisdiction.
-the **Old Bailey** is the famous criminal Crown Court that shows up in literature as a very bad place to be.

Magistrates Court:
-lay (amateur) courts, but specialized trained magistrates hear local cases involving licensing, minor criminal cases, youth crimes, and some family matters.

County Courts:
-district or circuit judges hear civil cases including divorce.

Despite the confusing list of courts above, the English use a wider variety of specialized courts and tribunals including military, ecclesiastical, maritime, and election courts. There is even one for chivalry, but this court hasn't convened in a long a while.

Regulatory

America	England

Consumer Product Safety Commission Environmental Protection Agency Equal Opportunity Employment Commission Federal Aviation Commission Federal Communication Commission Federal Deposit Insurance Commission Federal Reserve System Federal Trade Commission Food and Drug Administration Interstate Commerce Commission National Labor Relations Board Nuclear Regulatory Commission Occupational Health and Safety Administration Securities and Exchange Commission 	Over and above the following categories of authorities, England has to dance to the European Union's tune and its trans-national regulators. At least till they finish separating themselves from the EU. To England's credit, however, many of these organizations are made up more of practitioners within certain fields, than America's career bureaucrats. Charities -one each for England, Scotland and Ireland. Education -one for all three parts of the UK and two more. Environment -three for each of the three kingdoms plus a forth for the environment as a whole. Finance - six assorted authorities. Health -fifteen councils concerned with the various specialties and professions. Law -six including one for Ireland and another for Scotland. Social Care -four and one each for Wales, Scotland, and Ireland. Utilities -six somewhat overlapping regulators re. water, electricity, phones, gas, sewerage, and nuclear energy. Other -21 miscellaneous authorities covering everything from advertising to casinos.

It would be hard to say if England or America is the more regulated economy. England clearly has more regulators than America, and arguably it got a head-start after the General Strike of 1926 and the subsequent nationalization of coal and other industries, but this is pretty thin gruel. The pendulum may be swinging the other way now in England, while in America, regulation is still increasing.

Over and above the regular regulators, commissions, and authorities listed above, there are 25 *Ministerial Departments* under the purvey of the *Members of Parliament* who are also *Ministers* along with their *Permanent Under-Secretaries*. They include:

Attorney General's Office   Cabinet Office

Department for Business, Innovation and Skills

Department for Communities and Local Government

Department for Culture, Media and Sport. **(Sport?)**

Department for Education

Department for Environment, Food and Rural Affairs

Department for Exiting the European Union (!?!)

Department for International Development

Department for Transport

Department for Work and Pensions

Department of Energy and Climate Change

Department of Health

Foreign and Commonwealth Office

Her Majesty's Treasury

Home Office

Ministry of Defense

Ministry of Justice

Northern Ireland Office

Office of the Leader of the House of Commons

Office of the Leader of the House of Lords

Scottish Advocate General

Scotland Office

UK Export Finance

Wales Office

There are also twenty-one *Non-Ministerial* departments which somewhat overlap the regulators.

Charity Commission for England and Wales

Competition and Markets Authority

Crown Prosecution Service

Food Standards Agency

Forestry Commission

Government Actuary's Department

Government Legal Department

Her Majesty's Land Registry

Her Majesty's Revenue and Customs

National Crime Agency

National Savings and Investments

Office for Standards in Education, Children's Services and Skills

Office of Gas and Electricity Markets

Office of Qualifications and Examinations Regulation

Office of Rail and Road

Ordnance Survey

Serious Fraud Office

Supreme Court of the United Kingdom

governor   There are no states as such in England, but they get good use out of the word *governor.* He or she is not likely to be a part of any local government but such a person might be...

- the representative of the crown in colonies or dominions.
- the head of a prison.
- the boss as slang among employees.
- a respectful term used by Cockneys etc. 'guv'nor' or simply 'gov.'
- the head of a charitable organization -much like an American Chairman of the Board of Trustees.

gown   Much like an American woman's nightgown or evening-gown, but with a few exceptions and a lot more history. In England, a man might wear a dressing gown or what the Yanks call a bathrobe. The silly dress-like gown worn by professors and students at some universities have fallen out of favor except for graduation and such ceremonies. Of course, barristers and justices (judges) still wear them, but so do American judges.   see *wig* and *barrister*

Grace, Your   -a bishop or duke

graduate   -not from grammar, high school, or even colleges. In England, only universities make graduates.

grammar school   Before WW II these were more or less England's high schools. Student's were tested at age 11 and sent off either to trade schools, or tracked for college. They were funded by the government or church and were not boarding schools. Their students were local students. After the war, they were largely replaced by the *Comprehensives* or converted to fee-charging public schools. see *schools*

grant -scholarship

Great Fire   In 1666 most of London burned down. This was everything within the old Roman city walls. It missed Winchester and Whitehall, but burned almost 14,000 homes, and 87 churches. 70,000 out of 80,000 people were left homeless. There were surprisingly few deaths, perhaps because the common folk didn't count; literally, they weren't counted. It was rebuilt quickly, but this was because what burnt down were mostly *wattle-and-daub* timber hovels. It might have started accidentally, or by a retarded Frenchman who was supposedly an agent of the pope, or by Catholics. It was rebuilt fairly quickly, and rebuilt with the least little nod to what would much later become urban planning.

Great Vowel Shift   Among people who study how things were pronounced between Medieval English and the (almost) Modern English, the GVS is terribly important.   Think first of Chaucer whose writing needs some translation, and then Shakespeare who wrote and spoke more or less the way we do now. Between 1400 and 1600, the English went mad for long vowels. *Bit* was good enough for grandpa, but the youngsters pronounced it *bite*. So it went with all the vowels, except maybe *y* which no knew quite what to do. The GVS is also largely responsible for much or the hopelessly messed up spelling we live with today in English, but the fact that the English have taken more words from more other languages than any other language, (except maybe the Americans) has undoubtedly contributed.

Great War   Until World War II came along, this is what they called World War I. There are lots of great movies about WWI. ALL QUIET

ON THE WESTERN FRONT is old (1930) and from the point of view of a German teenage soldier. It is by no means an easy movie to watch, but something of a classic. It's all about the end of innocence and two and a half hours long. There are easier versions of the war from 1979 and 2022. There are also movies about the war that are less fraught and more 'heroic.'

green fingers   -a green thumb.

green gage   -an ugly little green plum used to make chutney and jam.

greengrocer   -seller of fruit and vegetables.

greens   -usually cabbage or sprouts in England.

green   -an open area in the middle of a medieval village. (The **commons** surrounded the town,)

Greenwich   -hugely important to navigation and therefore the Royal Navy. The Royal Observatory was built there in 1675 to sort out just where the navigational stars were and *when* they were there so ships at sea knew where *they* were. Greenwich in on the edge of London, and in addition to being historically important to the Royal Navy, it is the site of the Navy College, the National Maritime Museum, and finally, it was the site of one of Elizabeth's favorite palaces that was later turned into a hospital and home for Navy pensioners. see **GMT**

grenadier   -a soldier who threw grenades. The best grenadiers were strong and tall and hence the word came to imply a particularly big attractive soldier.

grog   -a mixture of rum and water given to sailors every day from about 1750 until 1971. Originally, the rum the Royal Navy purchased in the British West Indies in the Caribbean was of doubtful proof. As such, if it was diluted just before it was dolled out, it would spoil in short order, so the sailors could not be able save up a few days rations till they had enough to really tie one on. The officer who enacted this policy was Lord Admiral Edward Vernon. Vernon wore a grogram coat, (course wool -the word crossed back and forth between England and France and comes to us to day as *grosgrain* as in grosgrain ribbon). He wore this coat so habitually that he was nick-named 'Old Grog' by men who thought he was a pretty good guy. One of the people who admired him was a young cabin boy from the Colonies. The lad so admired his boss that he would later name his home Mount Vernon after the old gentleman. This man was George Washington's older half-brother and George would inherit the estate.

ground nut   -a peanut or goober

grouse   -a harmless little bird like American partridge. They were hunted in huge numbers far in excess of the amount necessary to bake into pies, but shooting was all the rage thru most of the Victorian era. Shooting was often a part of massive social affairs put on by the swells at their country homes. It required a very particular wardrobe and servants going out to flush the birds so the swells could blast away, and get back in time to change clothes for a huge meal that probably didn't involve grouse. *Shooting* was for grouse and other birds. The *hunt* was for bigger animals.

gruel -oatmeal cereal -on the watery side. see *food*

Guardian, The -a very old and popular newspaper published in London. Its primary customer is the educated elite or what Yanks would call a *liberal.*

Guards, the One of several elite regiments who originally stayed home to guard the monarch. (The Expeditionary Forces were for fighting outside of England.) By the Victorian era, they were better known for pretty uniforms and ceremony. see *regiments, army, commission*

guild From the medieval until well past the time of Shakespeare, whatever part of the economy that wasn't controlled by the crown, was controlled or regulated by the guilds of the various trades. This is to say that unless you grew it yourself, (and a lot of people did), you bought it, wore it, used it, or even ate it only after the guild dictated how much you paid for it, how the guy who sold it to you ran his business, and how he treated apprentices. see *work* and *apprentices*

guinea -£1.05 see *money*

Gunpowder Plot -an attempt by *Guy Fawkes* and friends to blow up Parliament in 1605.

Gurkha These were soldiers from Nepal who served in the British Army. They were some seriously dangerous soldiers. During WW II, there were stories of a Gurkha sneaking into a German camp and slitting the throat of a single sleeping man and leaving the rest of them in a given tent utterly frightened and demoralized.

gutter snipe Snipes are small marsh birds that are sometimes seen in the city eating out of the gutter so the term has come to mean an orphan or a street urchin.

Guy Fawkes (1579-1606) Guido "Guy' Fawkes was a devout Catholic at a time when this was a problematic religion. He had dealings with the Spanish who were also Catholics and were at war with the Dutch who were England's allies at the time. He and some friends, who were variously Spanish, Catholic, and / or just generally opposed to *James I,* rented a cellar beneath Westminster Palace and filled it with gun powder—the *Gunpowder Plot*. Fawkes was discovered before they had a chance to blow it up and he was tried, tortured, and executed about 90 days later.

Guy Fawkes Day Take this as an indication of the British sense of tradition and humor. November 5, (the day the Gunpowder Plot was discovered), is a day for riotous good fun, bonfires, fireworks, and burning poor Guy in effigy. Sometimes they would also toss a dummy of the pope on the fire just for good Protestant measure.

There are contemporary images of Guy Fawkes, but between 1982 and 1989 the graphic novels by David Lloyd, V for Vendetta drew a highly characterized version of his face. A 2005 movie of the same name then popularized this image and it became the Guy Fawkes mask. It is now sometimes worn as part of anti-establishment protests in England and elsewhere in the world. It is also called the 'Anonymous Mask' and thereby useful to protesters.

Bring to mind the scene in <u>My Fair Lady</u> wherein Professor Higgins is trying to teach Eliza Doolittle to pronounce her *haithces* correctly. (And yes, that is how you spell the letter H.) The problem arises that *aitch* is also correct -in Ireland, but in England, dropping the H is for the commoners. It also comes down to a Catholic (aitch) and Protestant (haitch) thing. It's a shibboleth. This means it's "a word or custom whose variations in pronunciation or style are used to differentiate members of in-groups from those of out-groups, with each receiving value judgments of superior or inferior." Who knew?

haberdashers   *c* In England, haberdashers dealt in what Americans would call *notions* like buttons, thread, ribbon etc. The best and fanciest of these items came from Milan, Italy, and a Milan haberdasher was a *milliner* and this word came to mean someone who made women's hats. It's not clear why. Furthermore, an American haberdasher dealt in men's clothing.

hackney / hack   -originally something rented out like a horse or coach. It would come to mean someone who rented out his labor, or her body. Later still, the word came back around to mean a horse and carriage, and finally, by the 20th century, it was a taxi.

Hadrian's Wall   About 120 AD, the Roman Emperor Hadrian financed a wall about 70 miles long to keep the barbaric Picts in Scotland and out of civilized Britannia. While it was military in origin, it also served in matters of commerce and customs -this is to say, taxes.

haggis   A traditional Scottish dish consisting of oatmeal, suet, spices, bits of mutton, and a sheep's heart, liver, & lung all packed in a sheep's stomach and boiled. It sounds disgusting. According to one French writer, "... its description is not immediately appealing...", but consider this, if you were to leave out the lung and cram it all into a pig's intestine, you would essentially have knockwurst.

Half-pay   During the comparatively rare times England was not at war, the crown kept officers in reserve and on half-pay.

hangmen   -were formally referred to as 'Finishers of the Law.' Enough said.

ha'penny   -half a penny or one 240th of a Pound. At its highest exchange rate with the dollar about 1835, a ha'penny would have the buying power of about $0.50 in 2010. see ***money***

hare   -larger and tougher creatures than rabbits. Their meat is also tough. Until the middle of the 20th century, they were a common food, but only after marinating and/or stewing. In the 18th century, the correct way to cook a hare was to roast the thigh and make stew from the rest of the meat with gravy made from its blood. They are also crazy fast so hunting them is a popular challenge. Finally, the hare's speed gives the Brits the expression *haring* meaning to run very fast or otherwise flat-out move!

Harrods   -a huge department store in London. Goes back to 1849 and now has 200 or 300 departments. The store sells everything wonderful in a one million square foot store covering 5 acres of prime London real estate. It had £ 796 million in revenues and pulled down a very respectable 16% profit margin. It is now owned by the Arabs.

Hastings   A village on the southern coast of England important for the ***Battle of Hastings*** where ***William the Conqueror*** defeated the Anglo-Saxons and brought the French & soufflés to England. Today it is yet one more resort town on the seaside.

hatch, match, and dispatch   -a lovely bit of British humor. It refers to being baptized, married and finally eulogized in church and in a newspaper. The expression is related to what they call a *four-wheel-Christian* -someone who is wheeled in on a pram (stroller) as an infant for baptism, and does not come back to church until his / her funeral service when wheeled into church in a coffin. (The analogy rather breaks down surrounding marriage.)

hatters   -made hats, but just how mad was "mad as a hatter"? Pretty mad indeed. It turns out that beaver pelts were cured and tanned with mercury. There were some processes in making hats that involved a little chewing on the pelt. No one made the connection in the day, but the symptoms of mercury poisoning were facial deformity and insanity.

hauler -a trucker in America. His truck is called a lorry.

have a butchers -an example of *Cockney rhyming slang* It starts out with 'have a butcher's hook' which rhymes with look, so hook and look are left out and they are left with 'have a butcher's' means to *have a look*. Yes, it's silly

have it off	-sex (vulgar).
have on	-tease or play a trick on someone.
have a go	-do or try one's best.
have up	-haul into court or the police station.

headmaster	-school principal.
head boy	-a senior student used as a good example and usually roundly hated by the other students.
head lad	-head stable man / woman.

headlamps -a car's headlights.

heath -originally a large open area where heather grows. Sometimes it refers to a large flat commons, or to a soggy forbidding moor.

THE SAVAGE CLUB   SIR JAMES JEANS THE GUEST OF THE EVENING
FEB·12 1938
THEODORE HOLLAND IN THE CHAIR
AN EARLY ATTEMPT TO SPLIT THE ATOM

Heath Robinson -a popular cartoonist for Punch and other publications. During WWI his name became synonymous with anything unnecessarily complicated -a *Heath Robinson Contraption*. On the other side of the Atlantic, a Yank named Rube Goldberg did similar work and his name became synonymous with things similarly complicated and useless -a *Rube Goldberg Machine*.

Heathrow -London's largest and most important airport about 16 miles to the west of the city. Traveling by air is not without its vexations anywhere, but to the mind of the Brits, Heathrow is *hell's waiting room.*

hedgers -grew, pruned, intertwined, and just generally made hedges that were proof against cattle and sometimes even people. Hedging got to be big business after the *Enclosure Acts* starting in 1604.

Henry VIII (1491–1547) Henry was crowned in 1509 at age 18. By all accounts, he was a pretty decent young man; well educated, funny, keen on music & dancing, very tall for his day and considered handsome. Early in his political career, he took council from some of England's best. This would change as he came to dispense with anyone who disagreed with him or displeased him or failed to provide him with a male heir. By the end of his life, he was a total autocrat. He was also a sad figure of a man. He was isolated except for toadies who agreed with him. When he died at age 56, he was syphilitic, bloated, probably diabetic and possibly had a gangrenous foot that stank. He weighted 28 stone (398 pounds / 181 kilos) Along the way, he fought an assortment of wars -usually unsuccessfully, against the French in 1513, 1515, and 1544, and against the Scots in 1547.

Nonetheless, he deserves some credit; among his achievements are the establishment of England's Navy which would be come the greatest in the world, if perhaps not in his time. Whatever his reasons might have been for starting the Church of England, the dissolution of the monasteries freed up a lot of capital for better use than the pope in Rome might have used it for. No less than Winston Churchill said of Henry VIII "Henry's rule saw many advances in the growth and character of the English state. . ."

Perhaps Henry Tudor can best be understood by his enemies, real or from his paranoid imaginings. Here are the more famous unfortunates.

Anne Boleyn
Robert Aske & 200 of his Catholic friends
Thomas Wolsey
Thomas Cromwell
John Fischer –a Catholic Cardinal opposed to the Church of England
Thomas More

His marriages ran as follows:

Catherine of Aragon -married in 1509 -she died 1533
Anne Boleyn -1533 - beheaded in 1536
Jane Seymour -died after child birth
Anne of Cleves -married in 1540 divorced 6 months after marriage
Catherine Howard -executed for adultery -with younger men and
Katherine Parr 1543 - widowed 1547

Henry VIII: His Predecessors, Wives, and Children.

	1470	1475	1480	1485	1490	1495	1500	1505	1510	1515	1520	1525	1530	1535	1540	1545	1550	1555	1560	1565	1570
Edward V																					
Richard III																					
Henry VII																					
Catherine of Aragon																					
Henry VIII																					
Anne Boleyn																					
Jane Seamore																					
Mary I																					
Elizabeth I																					
Edward VI																					

Legend:
— lifetime
▬ reign
| marriage
- - - childbirth

Henry's Later Wives:

	1470	1475	1480	1485	1490	1495	1500	1505	1510	1515	1520	1525	1530	1535	1540	1545	1550	1555	1560	1565	1570
Anne of Cleves (born 1515, married and annulled in 1540 (6 months), died in 1557)																					
Catherine Howard (born 1521, married 1540, 1541 beheaded)																					
Catherine Parr (born 1512, married in 1543, widowed in 1547, died 1548)																					

Other Figures in Henry's World:

Lady Jane Grey: born 1536, Queen for about 90 days in 1557 (between the 15 year-old Edward VI and (Blody) Mary I. She was beheaded at age 17 mostly because she was Protestant.

Philip of Spain: Married Mary a year into her reign but was out on his ass when she died in 1558. He married three times and died in 1598.

Thomas Wolsey: born 1473, Lord Chancellor 1515 to 1529, died on the way to trial for treason in 1530.

Thomas Cromwell: born 1485, Minister from 1432 to 1440 when he was beheaded for treason.

hereditary property / title   The number of rich guys who owned their stuff so completely they could give it to their kids was limited to the highest layers of the peerage. Knighthoods, for example, were pretty keen things, but their titles were non-hereditary. Upon their deaths, it all went back to the king. In the medieval, knights were supposed to gather any yeoman volunteers they could from the countryside, go fight the king's wars, and in between times, make sure that countryside was productive and paid taxes to the land owner who was probably the king or a duke.

heriot   a death tax paid by a tenant to the local noble. Originally it was military equipment the king lent to his villeins to be returned to the lord and presumably of no value to the widow, but over time it came to be way of taking the best horse and still later, stripping the surviving family of everything. Pretty nasty practice.
The veterinary writer, James Alfred Wight used *James Heriot* as his pen name after a Scottish football goalkeeper he admired.

herring   -the fish, but an important source of protein for the common man thru the medieval and beyond, When kippered (dried and smoked) kippers are breakfast food.

Highlands, the Scottish

The *highlands* are the northern half of Scotland and the *highlanders* are the people who live there. It is beautifully mountainous, rugged, and desolate, but averages only about 1000 feet above sea level and its highest point, Ben Nevis, is 4409 feet high. (America's Georgia is higher on average and has higher mountains.) The highlanders, however, are not to be dismissed so easily. They gave the Romans fits, the Norman French didn't even bother with them, and it took the Brits until 1707 to gather the southern end of the place into its bosom, but the

highlanders to the north were having no part of it. They wore kilts, played bagpipes, made great liquor, (and still do), and spoke their own flavor of Gaelic until the 1850's. Throughout, the English thought of as them as somewhat barbaric savages. For example, 100 years ago, when Americans advertised tobacco with the *cigar store Indian*. The Brits used a kilted Scots to the same end.

hire -to rent. A hire car is a rental car and a hire firm is a rental place. *Hire-purchase* is to buy something on the installment plan. This last is sometimes referred to as the *never-never* plan.

History, English: A VERY Brief Overview:

Sometime around 25,000 years ago some maybe-not-quite-modern-humans carved a little fat woman called the Venus of Willendorf in Germany, and then about 17,000 years ago, some probably-humans painted horses on the walls of a cave in Lascaux, France. Not much else happened till the Romans spread themselves all over Europe and made the Mediterranean Sea a "Roman Pond." This was about at the time of Christ. This period is very interesting to the people who study language but was otherwise rather dull. The Romans petered out about 450 later and the Ages got very Dark. The Four Horsemen of the Apocalypse rode rough-shod all over Europe for about a thousand years. As unpleasant as it must have been for the people, not much big history happened till about 1400 when the Renaissance kicked off. A very important thing, this *re-birth*, but it may best be studied in an art-history class.

Long about 1600 the Spanish ran things with a little help with the Portuguese. It's about now that America is mentioned, but the really exciting things were some islands south of China where spices could be gotten and South America where gold could be stolen. North America was good for cod and not much else. Yet.

In the 1700's the English fought with everyone, particularly the French, and in the 1800's, things were fairly calm, largely because the English were in charge. In the 1900's the Germans fought with everyone and Russia went crazy.

A Slightly Less Brief Overview:

People -or something very much like people, came to England about 40,000 years ago. Then they left because glaciers covered up everything, but the glaciers went away again about 13,000 years ago and the people came back. They had themselves some "ages" -Meso-lithic (middle stone age), Neo-lithic (new stone age), and bronze age. Stonehenge was built in about 3000 years before Christ and was built with big stones but built during the early bronze age.

The Celts, (who would only become English much MUCH later), were just getting started on their Iron Age when the Roman came. Things were fairly quiet when the Romans were in charge, but language got very confusing. The native Celts, occupying Romans , and German(ic) Angles & Saxons all contributed to the mix that would eventually come to be the English language. The Romans left with more of a whimper than a bang along about 450 AD.

It's about now that the legend of King Arthur, Merlin the Magician, and Excalibur etc. were supposed to have happened. It's hard to say for sure. The native Celts, Angles, and Saxons muddled along with occasional visit from the Vikings until the French came in 1066, but they were called the Franks and another language got stirred into the mix. William the Conqueror might be considered England's first king and his 'dynasty' did a reasonable job of running things until it all fell to pieces in 1135. The next ten years were knows as "The Anarchy". Interesting word *anarchy*; it implies mayhem, tumult, and turmoil, but it really means *no king* . A **monarchy,** for example, means one king.

After the no-king period, the House of Plantagenet came to be in charge, and it was off to the races with kings, and their thrones, intrigues, wars, and all manner of the stuff that makes for great literature. Confusing as all hell too. see *Monarchy, Norman Conquest, Protestant Reformation & Restoration, Colonies,* the *Commonwealth, Government, Napoleonic Wars* and battles of *Agincourt,* the *Atlantic, and Britain*

HGV -heavy goods vehicle -an American semi-tractor trailer. Trucks in England are generally smaller than in America being that it's a smaller place with lots of Narrow 500-year-old streets. The Brits may also refer to a HGV as an *articulated lorry.*

High Court -usually deals with tricky civil matters, slander, and appeals from county courts. After 1873, it divided itself into *Chancery* for probate matters, *Family Court* for adoptions, divorce & the like, and the **King's / Queen's Bench** for commercial & maritime law.

hiking -an expression borrowed from America to replace *rambling.* While Yanks are busy sliding down snowy mountains, driving all manner of motorized two and four wheeled vehicles everywhere, throwing balls, (without using their feet any more than necessary), and just generally making a lot of recreational noise, the British have always been quite keen on are having a quiet casual *constitutional.*

HMS His / Her Majesty's Ship / Submarine

hoarding -originally, a fence around a construction site which was often covered with placards. An American billboard would be called a hording in England.

hockey -American *field hockey.* Girls in knee-socks and plaid skirts running up and down a field using funny looking sticks to hit a ball and occasionally one another. The English think this is more feminine than kicking a ball. It is not clear why this is so.

Hogmanay -New Year's Eve. It's very big in Scotland and more important than Christmas. Gifts are given, visitors are fed, and *Auld Lang Syne* is sung.

Home Counties -towns surrounding London where rich people had homes when they were not in town on business or for parties and balls

Home Guard -during WW II, the home guard was a volunteer force made of men too old or otherwise unable to serve in the armed forces. They were considered the last line of defense against the Germans.

Home Office -the ministry in charge of domestic affairs. It is headed by the Home Secretary and deals with police, prisons, fire, immigration, and elections.

home rule -independence for what would become the **Republic of Ireland.** It was a long time coming; it almost happened in 1886, again in 1896, was approved by Parliament in 1914, but was postponed until 1920 because of WW I.

Home Secretary Along with the Prime Minister, Chancellor, and Foreign Secretary, the Home Secretary is one of the Great Offices of State. This Cabinet Level position is responsible for internal affairs. Like much of the UK's government, the Home Secretary's duties slice and dice up differently between England, Whales, and the rest of the UK. National or internal security is the Home Secretary's responsibility. MI5, (Military Intelligence Section Five), is also a part of it. Think of England's Home Secretary as the American's FBI, Secrete Service, and Homeland Security all mixed together.

Usually, but not always, the Home Secretary was of the same party as the Government and the Prime Minister who appointed him or her. Winston Churchill was the Home Secretary 1910 -1911 as well as Prime Minister from 1940 to 1945 and again 1950 -1955.

homely -not ugly as in America, but comfortable and domestic.

hops -a little green flower that is dried and used to flavor beer.

horners -made things out of cow horn or occasionally, ram, goat, or deer horns / antlers. Horn is pretty malleable stuff when heated or boiled and can be made into book covers, powder flasks, combs, shoe horns, drinking cups, snuff boxes, spoons & ladles, jewelry, and parts of other tools like looms. Think of horn as medieval plastic.

horses for courses -different strokes for different folks. Different horses are better for different courses.

horsehair workers -used horse and ox hair as well as pig bristles to make an astonishing variety of things including brushes, violin bows, wigs, military plumes, whips, fishing nets, and even window blinds. It was woven to make linings, or curled and used to stuff mattresses & upholstery. The funny looking costumes from olden-times where people had big hips, arms, bottoms etc. are all stuffed with horsehair.

hosepipe -hose or more currently, a garden hose.

hot cross buns -an Easter treat -a sweet bun with a cross on the top.
hot ice   -dry ice
hot pot   -mutton stew

hounds -the dogs used in fox hunting. Retrievers are called *dogs*.
hounds, following the -riding horse across field and glen while wearing
funny clothes. A fox may be involved but one is not entirely necessary.

householder   -head of the household, but only after about 1832 when
men–and only men–who owned a house could vote.

house / home, the English   To understand what the Brits mean
when they describe the various parts of their houses, it is necessary to go back
a long ways. The oldest castles were fortifications, administrative centers,
and storehouses. If you didn't live, (and work), in the castle, you probably
lived in a **wattle and daub** cottage. As homes got bigger, they kept some of
the vocabulary from earlier times.

Halls were a central large room in a castle where most of the indoor
goings-on went on. There might have been a throne, feasts, dancing etc. but
most of what went on here was household work that was not otherwise done
in the kitchen, stables, or armory etc. There were often
little chambers along the sides where people slept behind
curtains.

As time went on, the word *hall* came to mean any large
room with or without a castle attached. Later still it meant a
large home -with or without a large room, and still later, it
was a place where England stored its students. The American idea of a hall
-as in *down the hall and second door on the right*, would be a *passageway* or
hallway in England.

To understand the English need for **conservatory** which originally were
what Yanks would call green-houses, Americans need to remember that nearly
all of England lies north of the American / Canadian border. London gets
about seven and one half hours of sunlight on the winter solstice. (Northern
Scotland gets just over six.) By the 18th century, conservatories were
attached to nice country homes often as part of the **drawing room** and were
for ornamental plants and daytime entertainment. During the sixteen hours of
summer days, the conservatory was for after-dinner doings.

The **parlour** or **parlor** is another confusing room in an English house. It
comes from the French *parler* -to talk. For a good bit of domestic history, the
parlor was a smallish room for quiet family conversations and the drawing
room was for larger gathering. Among families that couldn't afford so large a
house, and didn't have a drawing room, it was just the opposite. The parlor
was for guests but not for the family. The family gathered in the room
between the parlor in the front, and kitchen in back which was sort of a
combination of dining room and what Yanks might think of as a family room.

To complicate the whole thing even more, under the Norman (French)
influence, the parlor was the second room in a two-room cottage–the one
without the kitchen and fireplace. It may also have been the room where the

family lived when work was done in the other room. (Bedrooms just for sleeping etc., were a long way off for the little guy.) The word *parlour* is now old fashioned -it's been replaced with either **lounge** or the American *family-room*. The **lounge** was originally a separate, (more expensive), room in an inn where guests could enjoy a little more privacy than in the public room.

The **sitting room** was for sitting not dining, and not much different from the drawing room, parlour, or lounge, except it often applied to a comfy little room for the family in poorer homes. In wealthy nineteenth century homes with the full compliment of other rooms, the sitting room was probably for women and probably a morning room that caught the morning sunshine.

Finally, there is the **drawing room** which has the longest and most confusing history. Originally it was called the *withdrawing* room where the family withdrew from the public goings-on to enjoy some privacy. Later it would be where the women withdrew after a dinner party, and then it became simply, the *drawing* room. The confusion arises in what the word means in homes of various levels of wealth and status. Among the wealthiest, the drawing room became the most public room in the home for afternoon tea among the women and then it was where men rejoined the women after they did the after-dinner cigar and port thing. In the royal household on the other hand, the large drawing room in a palace was where women were formally and ceremoniously presented to the monarch, but this room was by no means a *room-of-state*. These days, when a contemporary character refers to his or her drawing room, the author is probably implying he is a pretentious ass.

House of Commons   -the theoretically lower of the two legislative house that make up Parliament. It does not mean it represents the commoner, but rather these guys represent various communities *in common*. Originally, they met only when the king needed to come up with a new tax but they were made to meet in the much simpler room that was quite separate from the *House of Lords* fancy club-house.

England's long march to democracy, or what Yanks think democracy ought to be, arguably began with the **Magna Carta** (1215), and then bumped along thru the Civil War & the Reformation, and picked up a little speed with the R**eform Act of 1832**. As it did, government got bigger and more complicated and the House of Commons became increasingly important. It also came more and more to represent the common man. Even so, most of its members were rich up until the 20th century when Labor Party started showing up and then it was largely made of lawyerly types as it is in America and, like in America, pretty rich types too.

House of Lords   -the upper legislative body. This is the original Parliament and originally, they actually advised the king when he asked them. One king, **Charles I**, didn't ask them often enough and look how it ended for him. It is also called the House of **Peers** -as in Peers of the Realm. It was originally 80 *Lords Temporal* and

25 *Lords Spiritual*. They pretty much amounted to everyone who owned all the land in the England. (For a long time, a lot of what a Yank might of as owning a home or building, meant someone owned the building but paid a ground rent.)

In 1909 King George sided with the little guy and the **House of Commons** on a tax proposal. He threatened to appoint so many liberal Lords it would ruin their conservative majority. The exclusivity of their club proved to be more important to them, so they gave up their right to veto the lower house and their role has been mostly ceremonial ever since. Today they have some involvement in the courts, and they review proposals from the House of Commons, but the lords can only advise the lower house and slow things down a little. In 2016 they were surprisingly balanced; 252 conservative members, 202 labor, 178 independent *cross-benchers*, 146 other affiliations, and the 26 bishops. see **House of Commons, government, political parties**

HP Sauce   -named after the House of Parliament and a very popular steak-sauce sort of condiment the Brits pour over everything, maybe even more than Yanks pour ketchup.

Hoyle, According to   -according to the rules of the game from the highest authority. Edmund Hoyle (1672 – 1769), was a lawyer and big fan of card games. He wrote <u>A Short Treatise on the Game of Whist</u> wherein he listed both the rules of the game along with some how-to. (M**arquis of Queensbury** rules apply to boxing.)

hulk   -an old ship with its masts removed and moored in a harbor somewhere. They often stored prisoners on hulks; both the ones they decided not to hang, and sometimes French prisoners of war. Once they had collected up enough of them, they put them on real ships and **transported** them to barbaric places like America and Australia.

Humane Society   -volunteer life-guards by the water.

hunt   -riding horses all over the countryside presumably after some poor fox. Hunting birds is done with shotguns and without horses, and is called *shooting*. In the past, when only the rich had horses and fox were more plentiful & bothersome than now, it was great sport. A *hunter* is a special fast horse that could jump fences. see **hound**

Hussar   A mounted soldier who fought primarily with a saber. A saber was worthless against muskets and such, so hussars were most useful in crowd-control. Less risk of getting hurt and missing the next party if you were riding a house thru unarmed peasantry and swinging a heavy sword.

The letter i is closely related to the letter *j* and both were used interchangeably until the middle of the 1500's. The dot over the i? Called a ***tittle***. Why is *I* as in *me, myself, and I* always capitalized? Goes back to about 1250 in England's written manuscripts so it wouldn't get lost. Same reason the lowercase *i* was given its tittle.

ice -ice-cream. England's *water ice* is sherbet, and *dairy ice* is ice-cream made with actual cream -rather than vegetable oil. The American practice of putting ice in drinks is increasingly popular in England, but it must be remembered that 'room temperature' England is the temperature of a stone castle and much cooler than a snug American home in the suburbs.

incapable -drunk, but not causing any problems, Drunk *and incapable* is quite different from *drunk and disorderly.*

Inclosure Acts see *Enclosure Acts*

income tax The English have been paying income tax longer than have the Americans. Their first crack at it came in 1799 to pay for the early Napoleonic Wars. The tax ran two shillings a pound, or 10%. The American first got to pay a smallish (at the time) portion of their income during WWI, and it was at about this time that England came up with a two-tier system, a higher one for the rich and lower for the not-so-rich. Thereafter it was off to the races with progressively higher and higher taxes for the rich. It is to the credit to the Brits, however, that after 1980, they closed all the silly loop-holes so dear to American politicians and reverted to a simple four tier system as follows:

Polite Name	Taxable Income	Tax Rate
Personal Allowance	Under £11,000 ($13,420)	-0-

Basic	£11,001 to £43,000 ($13,421-$54,460*)	20%
Higher	£43,001 to £150,000 ($54.461-$183,000)	40%
Additional	Over £150,00 ($180,000)	45%
* Dollar values as of 2016.		

India   "The Jewel in the Crown of Empire." In chronological order, the history was about spice, opium, tea, cotton, soldiers, and finally, math & computer majors.

In 1623 the Dutch kicked the English East India Company out of the Spice Islands further east. The company then set up trading posts in Bengal and fought a war with French merchants and traders. The company,

being a for-profit organization, hired merchants to fight for them and finally finished with the French in 1763. By this time *tea* was a huge money maker. It was so profitable not because the English were particularly good tea farmers, but because they controlled the sea trades and had the better military. Only half of the country was controlled by the Brits and the half they didn't control directly, they controlled by making the local rulers richer.

Mahatma Gandhi was an Indian educated as a lawyer in London and an entirely loyal subject of the crown, at least originally. He would begin leading India to its independence with passive resistance in 1915. England packed it in 1947 under Lord Mountbatten, and left behind two countries, Hindu India and Muslim Pakistan. It has not gone well between the two ever since.

The 1982 movie GANDHI is an excellent picture of India and it's struggle for independence from England. What is more, it shows the fundamental decency of the English at the time.   But set aside some time; it runs just over 3 hours. For an even deeper dive into it all, there are several TV mini-series and documentaries on Mountbatten.

Inland Revenue -England's IRS see *income tax*

in ordinary a somewhat old fashioned expression that applies to naval ships that are put out of commission -in America it would be to *mothball* a ship. It also refers to a professional or government position that is both permanent and full time. When you find it in you reading, it suggests an individual of some importance, but not one of the noble swells.

inns & taverns These show up in literature of many eras because the neighborhood inn was often the center of news, gossip, commercial dealings, as well as the place to catch a coach to the next town or even to London. Over and above their commonality among the common people in the surrounding community, they were useful settings for intrigue, romance, and drama.

From the 15th century onward, they were licensed to sell various sorts of things. It worked out as follows:

Inn -lodging, food and all sorts of liquor. If a town had only one place, it was an inn and it was *the* place to be on Saturday night.

Tavern -sold food, ale, beer, and wine

Alehouse / Tippling House: -brewed and sold ale and beer, but not liquor

Beer House -sold beer and ale, but didn't brew it, and were not licensed to sell liquor

Public House / Pub -(modern) food, all sorts of alcohol to be consumed *on* premises and sometimes lodging.

Off-License -retailer of liquor to be taken off premises -England's equivalent of American liquor stores

Inspectors of Nuisances -not a form of the constabulary rousting the town drunk, but rather they were more like sanitation health officers. 'Nuisances' were garbage dumps with their attendant smells and vermin. Cholera came to England in 1831 and in 1841 the *Nuisance Removal and Prevention of Disease Act* put these inspectors to work.

Inverness -a city and port in north-eastern Scotland. Also a long coat like the one Sherlock Holmes wore. And the goofy hat he wore, at least in all the old movies? It's called a *deerstalker*, but it's doubtful the author, Arthur Conan Doyle, ever intended him to dress this way. Holmes was far more likely to ware a silk-hat or what Yanks would call a top-hat.

Ipswich A port town on the east coast of England that during the restoration era was important for the wool trade with Germany and Holland. Cardinal Thomas Wolsey was born there.

IRA The *Irish Republican Army* is not to be confused with the legal army of the **Republic of Ireland.** The IRA was an armed militant force resisting what they felt was England's occupation of Ireland. see **Ireland** and **Orange, the House of**

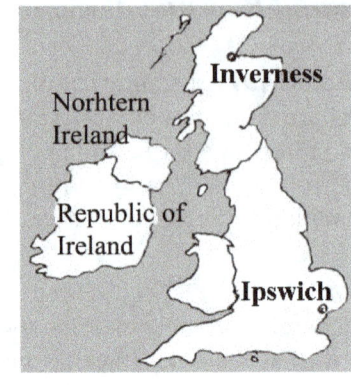

Ireland People came to this island about 12,500 years ago and by about a hundred years after Christ, were the Gaelic subset of the Celts. The Roman did not have a lot of luck colonizing the Gaels, nonetheless, Ireland was thoroughly Christian by 500 AD. (**Saint Patrick,** a real person, had much to do with this.)

Normans were not much more successful than the Romans, and the English took a shot after the Norman's left. It didn't workout too well for the Brits either until about the 1500's and even then, sovereignty was a dicey thing. In 1690 the Protestant's came and that's what finally did it. They simply kicked the Catholics off their land. Rebellions, occupations, battles, a horrible famine, the ebb and flow of rights & the vote for the Catholics followed.

In 1920 Southern Ireland separated itself from England and became the *Irish Free State* and later, the *Republic of Ireland.* (This end of the island actually sat out WWII as a neutral nation.) Northern Ireland was more Protestant than the southern end and remained a part of England, but not a peaceful part. Between 1960 and 1990 there were *The **Troubles*** which were some serious civil unrest and more occupation by the Queen's soldiers driving about in combat vehicles which the **IRA** occasionally blown.

During the potato famine between 1845 and 1852, some million Irish Catholics died, but the protestant English did just fine. Another million left mostly to come to America. The contribution to America by the Irish is very important, but out of the scope of an explanation of the English to readers. What is, however, well within this scope is Ireland's contribution to English literature. This goes way back to the medieval times when the Catholic monks living in Ireland were about the only literate people outside of Persia. The following is a brief representative list of important authors and poets born in Ireland. Whether they are *Irish* writers, or really English writers born in Ireland, is best left to the literature professors.

Jonathan Swift	1667 - 1745	A Modest Proposal
Edmond Burke	1729 - 1797	On American Taxation
Bram Stoker	1847 - 1912	Dracula
Oscar Wilde	1854 - 1900	The Importance of Being Earnest
G. B. Shaw	1856 - 1950	Pygmalion (aka My Fair Lady)
W. B. Yates	1865 - 1939	Lake Isle of Innisfree
James Joyce	1882 – 1941	Ulysses
C. S Lewis	1898 - 1963	The Chronicles of Narnia
Edna O'Brien	1930 - ~	The Country Girls

ironmongers   -not so much individual people, as the department stores of the day, and the day was the comparatively modern Victorian Era. You would go to the ironmonger's because you wanted some metal hardware or machinery for the home as well as china, pottery, glass, wallpaper etc. Moreover, they would not only sell it, they would install and repair it as necessary. The important take-away here is that the ironmonger crossed many of the responsibilities and *protected territories* of many guilds. They were evidence of the economy moving from the guild / apprentice system to the more modern merchandizing economy.

Isle of Man   -an Island of about 220 square miles, sitting between England and Northern Ireland. It is self governing, but the Queen is the head of state and the UK is responsible for foreign relations and defense. Its history involves Celts, Vikings, and some back & forth between the Scots and English until the Battle of Neville's Cross in 1364 when the English won out. In 1866 they more or less gave it back and the Isle got got limited home rule.

   It's about the soggiest place in all the British Islands and a tax haven besides. Banking, tourism, and a little manufacturing have surpassed fishing as economic forces. The old timers on the island speak Manx and 'Manx' is the word for people who live on the Island of Man whether they speak Manx or not.

Isle of Wight   A wee island off the southern coast of England and a historic vacation spot and summer home for the wealthy mature crowd. (Queen Victoria loved the place.) It also contains lots of history as a staging point for various wars. In chronological order, the Jutes & Saxons used the island as a jumping off point for their visit to the mainland. Then the Normans hung out there before their conquest. Henry VIII built his navy just across the **Solent** in **Portsmouth**. During the English Civil war, **Charles I** literally missed the boat to France but made it to the Isle of Wright. (Sadly for him, the island's governor tossed him in jail and turned him over to **Oliver Cromwell**.) Early in the Seven Years War (1756-1763), the English began staging there for an invasion of France, and later in the war, they did much the same thing, but as a defensive measure against a French invasion that never came. The 19th century was calm enough for the English royals to sail their yachts around the island, but the Germans bombed the daylights out of it during WWII. Yachting and ship building has been there for a long time as well as hovercraft, rocket ships, and before that, flying boats during WWII. In 1970 they had a rock festival that 600,000 people attended. Only about 400,000 attended Woodstock the year before.

it's monkey's balls / brass monkey   -dang cold. The term derives from the British Navy. Iron cannon balls were stored on monkeys which were brass rack things. When it got cold enough, the brass metal contracted and the cannonballs fell off. see **CANOE**

English has no respect for *j*. It is more popular than z, q, & x, but other than showing up in names like Jack and Jill, *j* is a sad bastard child from other lands. Words like fjord and jalapeño have a *j*, but England has neither fjords nor jalapeños and so they don't bother with pronouncing the *j* in such words. In words like *hedge* and *budge*, the *-dge* serves as well as *j*. In fact, it was only in 1633 that any English book on the language even makes a distinction between *i* and *j*.

Jack   This perfectly fine first name shows up a lot in English fables and fairy tales. This is because it is the iconic common name for someone who is clever but lazy. Consider Little Jack Horner, Jack the Giant Killer, Jack and the Bean Stalk, and the House that Jack built. Jack Nasty is a man who is nasty & rude. Jack Saucy is insufferably saucy. A jack-a-napes is even worse. Every-man-jack is every last man. The Whitechapel Murderer killed and mutilated five prostitutes in London's East End in 1888. He was never caught and so no one knows what his name actually was, but Jack-the-Ripper seemed to suit.

James I   -the king who wasn't killed by **Guy Fawkes** and friends. By most accounts, he was a pretty good king and probably the smartest one ever. James was bi-sexual and this lead to some minor friction with the church. The joke at the time was that Elizabeth was King and James was queen. (His immediate predecessor was his cousin Elizabeth I.) see **quing**

jelly   -American Jell-O. American jelly is called jam in England, marrowbone jelly is American aspic, and a *jelly baby* is a fruit candy favored by Dr. Who in one of his incarnations.

jersey   -a long sleeve pullover type sweater, warm and rugged, usually with a high collar. An English *singlet* is a sleeveless undershirt sometimes called a *wife-beater* in American slang, and a *doublet* is a short-wasted snug jacket worn from the 1300s' to about the time of Shakespeare.   see ***clothes***

Jersey   -a tiny little island off the coast of France's Normandy. It's the same Normandy of WW II fame. While it's not technically a part of the UK,

nor is it a part of France, but it is far more English than French. Technically, it is self-governing bailiwick, (a *bail* of authority granted by a monarch), and Crown Dependency. The government of this island is a hugely complicated civics lesson and there's an even more complicated history lesson about why Jersey and ***Gurnsey*** are English rather than French. Today it is an important center of finance having to do with a lot of tax and tariff advantages. Tourism and some great farm land round out the economy. It's home to about 100,000 people, but only half of them were born there.

Jews   Clearly a fraught issue, but Shakespeare's Shylock form *The Merchant of Venice* is not the only Jew to show up in English literature. Jews were expelled from England in 1290. (Spain did much the same thing between 1492 and 1502.) They began trickling back in from Holland during the Civil War. Cromwell, of all people, rescinded the 1290 expulsion law in 1656. ***Charles II*** was protective and supportive of the Jews because he "seemed to be happy to find one group that did not want to convert him to their religion."* There were still significant restrictions on them until the mid 1800's. As to an objective analysis of the English subjective thoughts on Jews, anti-Semitism has long been a part of England, Europe, and most of the world to one degree or another. Fortunately this sort of thinking has been decreasing in most of the world and England for a some time now, but it lingers, if only as anti-Zionism or *mild and cautions bemusement* for want of better words.

   *British English for American Readers. Grote, David, Greenwood Press, Westport, Connecticut, London 1992. This is a great reference for more in-depth study on the subject of the English.

Jock   -a nickname for a Scott -not an athlete like in America.

Jockey Club   No jockeys but lots of rich guys going back to about 1720. They used to govern horse racing and betting, but now that chore is handled by the government and the Jockey Club contents itself with owning most of England's race tracks which is good for about Ł150 million a year in revenue.

John Bull   A little like America's Uncle Sam, but while Uncle Sam is the government, John Bull represents the citizenry -hale, hearty, and patriotic. While he goes back to the 1700's, he shows up a lot in recruiting posters during WW I much like Uncle Sam at about the same time.

johnny -a putz -as in "Some johnny really bollixed this up."

John Thomas / JT   A woman or mother's expression for a man's or her wee son's tally-wacker or Willy.

joint   -a roast. It is usually made with all the fix'ens and carved at the table with some ceremony. A steak, on the other hand, was easier to prepare & serve and was not at all the same thing as a joint for a proper Sunday supper.

joint-stock company   an old-fashioned version of a publicly held company. Now they are called *limited liability companies*.

jointure -money the inheriting son gives to his mother.

jolly   -a wonderfully useful word, but one whose meaning changes with time and use. From Shakespeare's time, 'Jolly good.' meant pretty good indeed. By the 20th century, this use is more common among Yanks trying to sound British than actual Brits. The word *jolly* in the sense of "You will when I jolly well say you will.", is more like *damn* as in "You damn well will..." Today, a jolly is an expense paid business trip with little work to be done. It would be a boondoggle or congressional junket to Paris to study the lack of rain in Arizona. Finally, to jolly someone in England is to *suck up* to them in America.

Judge   Higher than a Justice of the Peace (a *JP*) or Magistrate. Judges as professionals are appointed for life and preside over complex civil cases, and serious criminal cases.

JP's   =-a Justice of the peace. They are not necessarily trained lawyers but are elected or appointed for intelligence, common sense, integrity etc. They may have assistance from a Justice's Clerk who probably is a lawyer. Judges in highest courts may also be called Justices of the Peace, but are trained as barristers or solicitors. As with all of England's local governments, it varies between boroughs, counties, municipalities and England's possessions. For American readers, think of JP's as slightly more sophisticated than Andy Griffin in Mayberry, but without the sheriff's duties.

It is Greek (Kappa) and stands for kilo or 1000. English is the only Germanic language wherein the **k** sound is always hard -except when followed by **n** in words like knife, knight, knot, etc, when it is ignored altogether. I don't know why.

Kensington   -a wealthy suburb of London. It is so wealthy that in 1901 they split form London and are now a self governing borough. *Kensington Palace* is a comfy royal

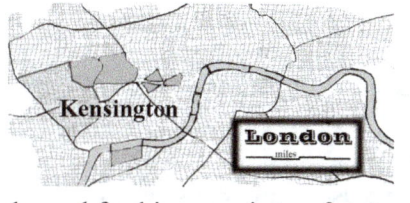

residence for the royal family and not much used for big occasions of state. *Kensington Gardens* is a street. The whole place is very elegant, snooty, and expensive.

Kent   A *county*, (a shire actually), in the far southeast corner of England. Given its proximity to the continent, lots of history happened there. Invasions, preparations for invasions (including D-Day in WW II), shipping first of wool in the Medieval days, and later tourist via the Channel

Tunnel. At various times in history, smuggling tobacco, salt, and liquor were profitable industries. London is just to the west, the channel and France to the southeast, and the River Thames is to the north. The *Canterbury Cathedral* and its Arch-Bishop are in Kent. *Chaucer* wrote the Canterbury Tales, and Charles Dickens set many of his works in Kent. Lots of fruit, beer flavoring hops, and other agriculture make it the 'Garden of England' (But it must be said that a few other places in England claim to be *the* garden spot.) Today 1.7 million people live in, and make their livings from the usual blend to occupations with tourism and agriculture being larger categories than usual for the rest England.

Kew Gardens -a 300 acre park* with lots of exotic botany to the southwest edge of London. It started as a park in 1759 and was formally made into the Royal Botanical Gardens in 1840. It has some 30,000 different plants including some James Cook brought home from Hawaii and other tropical islands. It will occasionally show up in literature for horrible crimes in an otherwise quiet and peaceful setting. Today it's a very important tourist attraction.
*San Francisco's Golden Gate Park is a little over 1000 acres.

kilt Yes, it's a man skirt, but with history. Originally it was just a long woven rectangle of dyed wool wrapped around the waist with the loose end thrown over the shoulder. Useful as a warm raincoat, small tent, or even as a 17th century sleeping-bag. After the English finally defeated the Scot Clans in the Battle of Culloden in 1746, the kilt was outlawed -in Scotland. The Scottish Regiments in England, (and they were not necessarily actually Scotsmen), were allowed to continue wearing the kilt. It's about now that the kilt turned into just a pleated skirt. BTW, a kilt is properly worn with a tasseled sporran and dirk which is a wee dagger. A sporran was essentially a purse worn on a belt around the waist and hanging down over the man's John-Thomas because the kilt didn't have pockets. See ***plaid***

king For so common a word, it's complicated. King comes to old English from the Germanic, no great surprise there. King, queen, and simply *monarch* are all more or less interchangeable. (*Your majesty* is not actually used in England to address the monarch and *your highness* is for prince or princesses. It's much more complicated than this, but if you find yourself waiting to be presented to the queen, someone will explain it all to you first. Otherwise, Americans needn't worry about it.)

In the very oldest literature, a king might be little more than a tribal chieftain particularly in Ireland and Scotland. This explains why any Irish or Scots American doing genealogy inevitably finds they are a descendant of a king somewhere along the line.

The notion of an all powerful king is misleading. They were perceived as filthy rich, but even this is misleading. They were often in debt and sometimes hugely in debt. War is an expensive undertaking which when lost, was also unprofitable and even sometimes unprofitable when the war was won. European history is full of wars and kings playing games with private property, tax system and debasing the currency (coining bad money) to pay for those wars. The ascendance of Parliament did some interesting things; it began to pay some small notice to the little guy (who paid taxes) and limited the monarch's power. Most importantly, it controlled the national purse-strings. During the 1800's nationalism even put government in charge of fighting wars, or more accurately, paying for wars. Kings were increasingly now able to enjoy simply being rich because they owned all the land.*

Even this would change. Going back as far as ***George III***, (1760 – 1820), the crown began to give royal land, which is to say *hereditary property†,* back to the 'government' in exchange for a fixed but very generous salary and expense account. As expensive as the queen is today, by some measure she and her family are a bargain for the UK. She has terrific diplomatic and PR value. (If you doubt this, pick up a super-market tabloid in any American grocery store and note the doings and misdoings of the royal family. And this is in America; imagine how it read in England!)

  * Owning land is all fine and well, but its income comes in over time. Soldiers etc. need to be paid right now. The history of borrowing to fight wars is not as interesting as the history of fighting those wars, but those who study such matters and think it is very important indeed. Perhaps even some of these lessons might apply today.

  † In some sense, property and land–even royal land–belongs to someone. Someone who might reasonably want to pass it on his or her children. see **heritable title, property**

King's Bench   -not to be confused with the king's court filled with courtiers and hangers-on. When someone was sent off to debtor's prison in an 1800's story, they were there because things went poorly for them in the King's Bench. This court concerned itself with common criminal law up until about 1870 when it got stirred up with some other courts and ministries and became the *High Court*. Thereafter, it tended to large civil matters like suing newspapers for libel and big personal injury cases. It is not the ***Supreme Court*** -but right up there.

King James Version / Bible:
In 1604 King *James I,* an author himself, authorized and financed a project to translate the Bible from Latin into English, the King James Bible. The job was finished by 1611. People who study such things, insist that this bible is responsible for an upward trend in English literacy, and their literature arguably becoming the best in the world, but such people are usually English speakers. *Shakespeare* probably deserves some credit too.

kipper   Kippered (dried and smoked) herring and tea are a classic English breakfast usually among the urban the working class.

knickers   -woman's underpants of the same era of American woman's *bloomers*. (What Americans think of *knickers*–the knee length men's pants worn by Nordic skiers and football players–are called *breeches* or *britches* in England.) see ***combinations***

knights / knighthood   You will bump into knights in almost all eras of English literature. It's worth trying to get a handle on the subject, but it is a subject of huge complexity and confusion. It really only matters to the Brits and it confuses them too. To really sort it all out, go get yourself a Ph.D. in English History. Otherwise, the following will get you through most English writing, but don't use it to settle an argument with any British nobility you happen across.

The most valuable and expensive fighters in the early middle ages were mounted and armored. They all were more or less mercenaries, but some of these warriors were knighted if the king felt they were loyal and capable enough to be sent off to look after things in the countryside. This was in consideration for the knight's willingness to fight. It was only in the 14th and 15th centuries that Christianity and a courtly code of honor get stirred into the minor nobility that were the knights. The Knights Templar personified these virtues, but they were more French than English. But even these knights had more in common with thuggish security guards than heroes of medieval literature.

Historians say that the term *blackmail* comes from armored fighters who couldn't afford a full-time servant (a **page**) who did nothing but polish his armor, so they burnt oil into it to rustproof it much like a cast iron skillet is seasoned. These guys were known as the *black-mail knigh*ts from the color of their armor and chain mail. They were not likely to have a manor to look after and made their livings between wars by jousting. In a tournament, if you knocked the other guy off his horse, you got to keep the horse. Now if the guy went home without his horse, it would be clear that he was a looser. It was likely that he was a rich old guy who *could* afford a full-time armor-polisher but was too old and fat to do well in the joust, so the black-mail knights would ransom his horse back to him at an excessive price. 'Black-mail'–then as now–means extracting money from someone who wants an embarrassing secrete kept secrete. These knights were probably closer to reality than the evil 'black knight' vs. the white knight or knight errant. *Errant* means an itinerant or wondering knight searching for adventure and damsels in distress, or more likely, out looking for a job and his next meal.

By the time, Columbus took off for what he thought was China, the knighthood had become obsolete. There were a few interesting reasons for this: first were national professional armies that were cheaper to train and outfit, as well as easier to mobilize. Second were improvements in guns that were powerful enough to pierce armor. Teaching a soldier to use a gun was faster and cheaper than teaching him to ride around on horses and kill people. Finally, they figured out that a bunch of relatively unskilled guys armed with pikes could mess up mounted knights quite thoroughly. The trick was to have everyone stand close together, jam the tail end of a pike into the ground, and stick the pointy business-end of the pike outward. A pike was a wooden spear that you didn't throw. It had a steel tip and could be up to 25 feet long.

None-the-less, England keep knights around and makes more of them every year to this very day, but now they are ceremonial rather than military. These days, people get knighted for things like being a good actor, writing popular songs, or discovering penicillin. They are then addressed 'Sir So and So'. (There are even lady knights, but they are called "Dames.") Like all things British, there is a lot of pomp, circumstance, and tradition surrounding the knighthood, and a lot of *this* guy being more impressive than *that* guy.

Orders of Chivalry*: Order of...* refers to the club, *Knight of...* refers to the person. For example, the individual *Knight of the Thistle* would be part of the *Order of the Thistle*. In general order of snootiness, knighthoods run from coolest to most ordinary as follows:

Knight / Order of the Thistle

The thistle is the national flower of Scotland and entirely appropriate given that a thistle is a prickly thing not to be messed with. **Knight / Order of the Garter**

A garter is a belt presumably to carry a sword, preferably a sword blessed by the pope, at least until Protestantism came along.

Knight / Order of the Bath

Yep, bath as in bathtub. Before the ceremony conferring knighthood, the guy took a bath as a symbol of purification, but he undoubtedly needed one anyway, at least by today's standards

Knight / Order of Saint Michael and Saint George

A comparatively modern order for diplomats and people in the colonial service.

Knight / Order of St. Patrick

This order is 'obsolete.' When Northern Ireland joined Great Britain and the Southern Irish were either starving or leaving for America, the need for mercenaries stomping around disappeared. So, while the order still exists, it has no members. I do not know why.

Knights Bachelor

The Bachelors are not strictly a Chivalric Order. This is to say you are a knight, and can call yourself "Sir." but you can't join a specific order. You aren't in a club.

Chivalric Orders are a little confusing. All are either 19th or 20th century inventions. They include:

Distinguished Service Order	-military.
Royal Victorian Order	-general services to the crown.
Order of Merit	-military, art, science, literature, culture.
Order of Imperial Service	-staying in the civil service for 25 years. Yikes!
Order of the British Empire	-miscellaneous military and civil.
Champions of Honour	-arts, science, politics, religion, and industry.

Orders of Empire This is the second broad category but a small one. It is separate from the Chivalric Orders. There are three Orders for India and one for Burma.

Decorations This is a separate category altogether, but it deserves mention here. Readers will meet people proud of things like The Victoria Cross, Military Cross, Distinguished Service Medal etc. They are pretty much all 20th century and all military.

There is an important point to remember about knights going back to the day when the king gave them a manor as payment for military service. These holding were not 'hereditary'; the guy's kids were more or less out on their butts when dad died unless they were knights too. This is unlike the dukes and earls who had stuff to pass on to their heirs. This was not the case on the continent -French, Dutch, Swiss, etc. knights usually got to pass the manor on their heirs. All of Europe and a lot of Asia was feudal for a good long time and as such, the king needed knights to keep the taxes coming in.

What is the American reader to make of the knighthood? In the whole hierarchy from common man up to the monarch, knights are somewhere in the middle. In modern literature, authors use them as self contained and handy characters to spice up a plot line. When the American reader bumps into a knight, he or she is probably meant to be an impressive figure. The relative status of, for example, a Knight Bachelor and a Knight of the Bath, is likely only to be meaningful to the chaps in question.

In 17th and 18th century literature, a knight straddled the line between strictly military and courtly. Going back further, for example the Knights Templar and the Crusades, knights were strictly military men or mercenaries.

The romantic chivalrous knight, Sir Lancelot for example, was a fixture in the oldest literature back when literature was either spoken or written in Latin because no one but the clergy could read. Geoffrey Chaucer's *The Knight's Tale* is an important exception, because Chaucer wrote in the vernacular that more people could read, rather than Latin. Furthermore, the tale was a story told by a knight, and not about knighthood in any way.

know (his / her / your etc) onions   -to understand.

L is a very vexatious letter. Everyone, except for some of the good people from the Orient know how to pronounce it, but the problem arises as to how many of the darn things to use, particularly at the end of words. As is the nature of spelling rules, there are as many exceptions as there are rules. In general, the Brits are in favor of using *ll* while the Yanks often get by with just one *l*. But not always. Best to rely on spell-check, or avoid writing to people who care about such maters. L is also the abbreviation for 10 in Roman Numerals, and liter for the metric crowd.

lace makers   -some of England's best paid working women. Lace came from Holland when the Flemish came to England in the 1560's for religious freedom and all. It took hours and hours to make and the stuff and it served to show the world just how rich you were. Lace can be seen in rich women's portraits on their gloves, aprons, fans, hats and festooned hither and yon on their clothing. Men often had a little lace peeking out of the top of their high boots. Those silly looking neck-tutus you see in their portraits? They serve some small purpose. They kept your fleas from jumping from your body to your head or vice-versa.

Labor Party   -England's new *Liberal Party*. When the *Liberal* party fell apart between 1905 and 1918, the Labor party emerged by aligning itself with labor unions. They would oppose the Conservative party between the two the wars, and after WWII, they supported nationalizing many of England's industries (notably coal) and National Health. This worried the middle class and thoroughly annoyed the upper class. see *political parties*

lacquer -hair spray.

Lady   -either the wife of a Lord or more recently, simply a term of respect for any woman.

Laird   -a Scottish Lord. The chap who occupies a Lairdship or a Scottish manor.

Lake District -the *"Most Beautiful Place in all of England"* but there are three or four of the *most beautiful places in England* in England. It lies in the north-west corner of the country amid mountains and lakes. The Lake

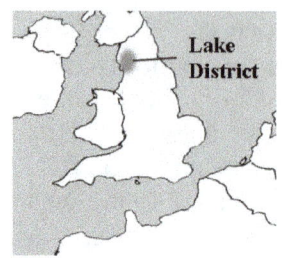

District has both, (all), of England's 3000 foot plus mountains, and its deepest and longest lakes. It also has lots of both deciduous and coniferous forests, red dear, working ponies, and vacationing families.

Lots of literature grew poetry grew there too, or it did after about 1850 when the poetic and artistic crowd discovered it wasn't full of ravening beasts, but rather nature and some nice nature at that.

Anyone used to tromping around in America's the Rocky Mountains or the Sierras would find the Lake District pretty tame, but to be anybody of an educated and enlightened sort in England, a long holiday in the District was a requirement.

Lancashire -a county to the northwest of England. In the medieval, it was all about wool, but with the industrial revolution, it came to be about coal, industry, and cotton mills. Cotton that came from the American South before the Civil War.

Lancer A mounted soldier who fought with a lance which was a rather primitive weapon that wasn't much used after the 1600's, but one that allowed lancers to ride around on a nice horse and wear a pretty uniform when they weren't seducing governesses.

Language, History of the English There is lots of it. First there were the Celts who didn't write anything down, or anything that survived anyway. Then the Romans came speaking Latin. In short order, the Angles and Saxons came from West Germany, the Norse Vikings, and finally the French all tromped thru England before the locals would be able to get on with building their own language. They did this a little haphazardly particularly as involves spelling, by stirring it all together into Middle English. (Old English was more German that any recognizable form of what we might think of as 'English.') Middle English was all the rage from the **Norman Conquest** about 1066 till the 15th century. This was the language of **Chaucer** but the rich people spoke French and the clergy spoke Latin or at least did so during services and ceremonies.

The transformation from Middle English to Early Modern English, the language of Shakespeare, happened at about the time of the **Great Vowel Shift**. The GVS was the invention of long vowels. Words that once sounded like 'fat' came to be pronounced like 'fate.' There were various reasons for this, but most had to do with people wanting to sound all educated and high-class. That 'e' on the end made all the difference and led to even more irregularities and confusion in English spelling. This sort of thing is important only to a certain flavor of experts.

Some other similar experts insist that the publication of King James's Bible in 1611–in **English** no less, rather than Latin, lead to increased literacy in England and thereby contributed to England's wonderful literary history. Shakespeare deserves a little credit too.   see *accent, English*

larder -the pantry.

lashings -lots, as in *lashings of clotted cream.*

Laudanum   -alcohol and opium. It was a good pain reliever. So good that for a good bit of the 1800's, a lot of people, particularly women, were addicts.

laundresses   It may have been a lifetime's work for a woman, but it was as likely to be part-time work done to supplement the family's income. The people who study this corner of history suggest that laundresses were under-reported in the census data. Mechanization to clean fabric came surprisingly late, (1860's thru 1890), but a woman who 'kept a mangle' (a wringer) per parish records, probably did laundry.

Law Lords   -England's supreme court from 1876 till 2005, but this is an over simplification. These Lords were correctly called the *Lords of Appeal in Ordinary* and acted as the supreme court in domestic matters. They were also members of the *House of Lords* until 2005 when England followed America's example by setting up the *Supreme Court of the United Kingdom*. Originally, there were only two Lords, but there were twelve by 1994. Once appointed to this court, the Lords gave up their right to sit in the House of Lords for as long as they were justices of the new court.

laying in hospital   -the maternity ward

lease / leasehold   Because almost all land was owned by a very few people up until recently, most property was rented rather than bought & sold. A *leasehold* was a rental for as much as 99 years. At the end of the lease, it all went back to the owner. Sucked for the tenant who may have built a nice house or farm. After WW II, *freehold* properties came to be more common and ownership was more or less forever.

Liberal Party   -generally opposed to the Conservative party. The Liberal party grew out of the much older *Whig* party circa 1850 which was in favor of free trade, social reform, and welfare. It all fell apart during the 1910's when it was replaced by the *Labor Party* which was a political view in favor of even more social reform. see *political parties*

license   Reference to a license in English writing probably refers to selling beer or liquor in one way or another.

Life peers   This crowd rather straddles the line between the old hereditary *Peers of the Realm*, and the people who actually have knowledge or experience to offer to the ***House of Lords***. Now having a fancy title is no longer automatic entry to this House.

line   -a regiment in the army or, in the Navy, wooden men-of-war all sailing into battle in a line.

line-out -in ***rugby***, after the ball goes out of bounds, the teams form two opposing lines, the referee throws it back in, and they push, shove, and just generally fight over it.

lines   -punishment in school, i.e. writing 100 lines of "I will not hit girls."

lightermen   Lighters were shallow-draft cargo barges that were used to unload—or lighten—ships that were not brought to a wharf because they were too deep, or the docks were too crowded otherwise.

literacy in England   In 1500, pretty much everyone was illiterate. This is no great surprise. It ran about 99% for women and 95% for men. The 5% of literate men were either the king, very rich, or in the church. Literacy trended upward slowly but pretty steadily from then on, with more men being able to read than women throughout. Between about 1725 and 1825, the gap between men and women widened.* In round figures, 65% of English men could read, but only 35% of women could. This gap closed up completely in 1900 to only 4% illiteracy among both men and women.

Around 1700, England lead France in literacy, (40% to about 30% in France), but well behind Sweden, (90%). Amsterdam & the New England colonies both ran at about 70%.

To put things in perspective, in America toady 14% of the population is illiterate and 21% read below the 5th grade level. In England, 16% of adults are 'functionally illiterate,' but it must be remembered that these numbers all come from different definitions of exactly what is meant by literacy and grade level, etc.

*Jane Austen published her first book, <u>Sense and Sensibility</u> in 1811 and died in 1817 with one book unfinished, (<u>Sandidton</u>) and two to be published after her death, (<u>Persuasion</u> & <u>Northanger Abby</u>)

Liverpool   -an important harbor city to the north-west on the River Mersey. Liverpool was particularly important for travel and trade with America, but has been in decline for some time. It does not show up in literature very often because it is thought of by the English in rather the same way Americans tend to think of as blue-collar rust-belt Detroit in the 21st century. Its greatest claim to fame is as the "World's Capitol City of Pop Music -or so says *Guinness World Records*. It is where the Beatles got started, and has a gay population that rivals that of San Francisco. There are now some half a million Liverpuddlians.

living -the income form a parish paid to a rector derived from the 10% tithe. It was a lifetime income that didn't even require him to live in the parish. see ***see***

local -one's favorite pub. It may not be the closest but it is the favorite.

London The *City* of London is a tiny little part of the whole thing. The city is about a square mile that was actually the Roman fortress of Londinium, and later, the medieval walled town of London. This is to say that you might have read that someone who was **in** London but was about to go off to 'the city.' Americans might say 'I'm going downtown'. Or up-town as the case may be. This little square mile was all there was of London and the rest of London was what Yanks think of as suburbs. At least until the middle of the 1800's when London started gluing itself together in various ways. Today it has formed into an independent county. The political ***divisions*** of England are terribly confusing, even to the English. An American might think of it as a combined city and county much like some big cities in America, but with one more combination added to get to city-county-state.

It is also the national capital of the UK. London has both a Mayor and a ***Lord Mayor***. The former is political, the later is kind of a one-man chamber of commerce at least today, but the Lord Mayor is also the oldest elected

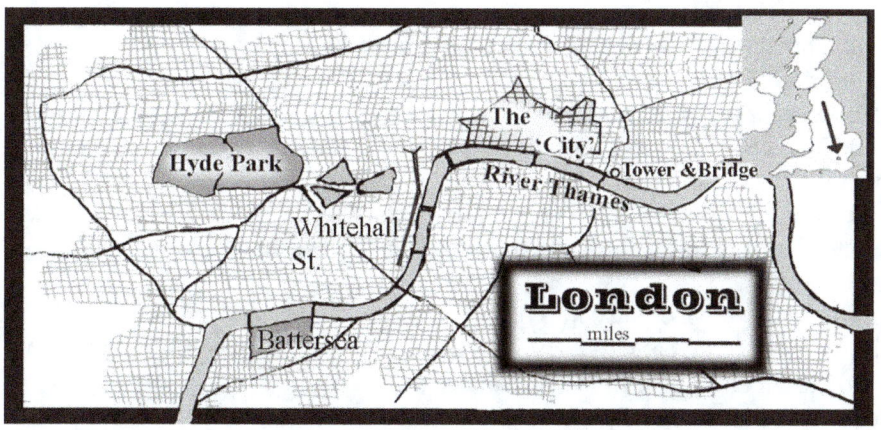

position in all of England. He or she is one of the oddly dressed people in the parade behind the queen's carriage. The regular, (political), mayor may be in the parade too, but toward the back and dressed in a regular suit.

London is so central to all things English and English writing that references to, and places within London, are scattered throughout. It goes back to the Roman era as fortified *Londonium* and might be named after King Lud, but no one is sure and for that matter, King Lud himself is a little hard to pin down historically. London became an important center of trade, (wool mostly), until Queen ***Bodecia*** burnt it down sometime around AD 61. When the Romans left in about 450, Londonium went down hill largely because it was a good target for the Vikings. This changed a little bit when the Vikings dreamed up Dane Law starting about 800. Dane Law is entirely English and is all about Viking raiders becoming more or less law-abiding English farmers.   By about AD 1000 owning valuable things like houses and farms, (things that could not be hidden when the Vikings came along), got to be a reasonably good bet once again and so London started growing again. The *Normans* came and built drippy ornamental cathedrals, the *Tower of London*, and started what would become *Westminster Palace*. They left in 1066. London bumped along thru assorted wars, religious upheavals, plagues starting in 1348, a big fire in 1666, lots of doings of kings and a couple of queens that history teachers go on and on about. It grew the whole time.

It was the largest city in the world until about 1925 when New York surpassed it. Today it is a little like Yanks might think of it as New York, Washington DC, Boston, and Hollywood all rolled into one. It had a population of a million as far back as 1800, more that two million in 1850, six and half million by 1900. In about 1939 it peaked at a little over eight and a half million but this had to do with WW II. It declined to under seven million in 1981. It has since recovered to eight point six million now.

London Bridge   The original one is now in Lake Havasu City, Arizona. It got taken apart, put in big boxes and sent there to be a tourist attraction in the desert with palm trees and college students getting sunburns, drunk, & disorderly during spring break. The new London Bridge is now a bland concrete thing. Do not confuse London Bridge with the *Tower Bridge*.

London Library   -the biggest and oldest library in England.
London School
   of Economics   -with a socialist leaning.
London University -a good school. It admitted poor kids throughout, and
      even women starting in 1878.
London Zoo   -among the oldest and biggest in the world. It's also
      reputed to be the most humane toward its animal residents.

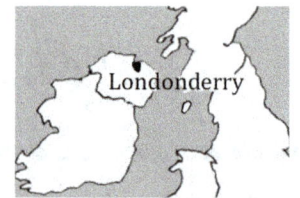

Londonderry   -a county in Northern Ireland. It used to be called Derry which was a nice little town and home to the O'Cahans and O'Niells. In 1613 *James I* granted what was essentially a bunch of London businessman ownership of the whole place to "undertake a plantation." Too bad for the Irish citizens. About 350 years later, they were still trying to sort it out, often violently, and recently by having the thoroughly violent *troubles.*

loo   -a polite word for the toilet. Probably from French *l'eau* -the water.

Lord, (the word)   Usually followed by "of the Manor" The rich guy in charge of the farm's workers and tenants. A somewhat slippery generic term, but not necessarily a member of the peerage. Barons -the bottom of the peerage heap are often addressed as Lord. The *House of Lords* might more technically be called the *House of Peers* and its members might be addressed as 'Lord,' but there are Lords who are not member of either House of Parliament nor are they peers. It gets more confusing when the judiciary is considered. England's Supreme Court is made out of **Law Lords** and the chaps in charge of the Her Highness' Navy are various **Sea Lords**.

Lords, the people, (assorted)   Lords are made out of both the nobility and the gentry. The nobility were guys who could pass their estates on to their kids. In order of the peerage they run dukes, marquises, earls, viscounts and barons. Barons are at the bottom of the nobility but they were eligible for the Parliament. Scottish barons, were non-peers. Below the nobility, were the gentry. These included Baronets, the hereditary knights who *could* pass their estates on to their kids, and regular knights who could not. There were also Scottish clan Chiefs or Lairds included at the bottom of the lower pile of Lords.

There are a whole series of Lords of historically important matters, but now they are usually ceremonial, honorary, and a sinecure. (This means a well-paying job with no actual work to be done.) In general order of importance (or status), they are...

> **Lord High Stewart:** Used to be first of the Great Offices of State, but today exists only for coronations. This is the guy who does the thing with the crown when the time comes for a coronation.
> **Lord Chancellor:** -the second highest Crown Minister and responsible for running the courts.
> **Lord Chamberlain:** Looked after the King or Queen, particularly the private *chambers* upstairs where only the special people could go. Curiously, the Lord Chamberlain also censored theater from 1737 to 1968.
> **Lord of the Privy Seal:** In charge of the monarch's seal for official documents. (The *Seal of the Realm* is kept by the Lord Chamberlain for agreements outside of the monarch's purvey.)
> **Lord Chief Justice:** Second to the Lord Chancellor in judicial authority. He, (or she), wears an extra silly *wig* and bright red dressing gown.
> **Lord(s) of the Admiralty**: No surprise here, in charge of the Royal Navy. They go back to 1628.
> **Lord High Mayor:** The mayor of London and the oldest elected office in England. see ***London***

Lord Haw-Haw   -an Irish American radio personality, but one working for the German's propaganda effort during WW II. He was captured as the war ended, tried, and hanged for treason in 1946.

Lords Lieutenant   Back in the day, he was the monarch's local representative. If you encounter one in your reading, he is likely a retired military office or some other old big-wig who is largely ceremonial but who may organize the county militia in the event of invasion. Going back to ***Henry VIII's*** day, the Lords Lieutenant took over the military functions and the local *yeomanry.* This was formally done by the ***sheriff,*** but with when the Lords Lieutenants came along, the sheriff was able to concentrate on maximizing agricultural output and tax revenue.

lose the plot -be exceedingly confused.

Luddite -angry workers whose jobs were displaced as the industrial revolution brought machinery and mechanization. Between 1811 & 1816 self-employed and highly skilled wool and cotton weavers were pushed out by power looms operated by less skilled and lower paid factory workers. They organized, broke into factories, and destroyed the machines. It all had more  to do with the austerity brought on by the ***Napoleonic Wars*** than a genuine hatred of machines. It got so bad in the northwest, (England's manufacturing center), that the military was called out to put it down. Similar things happened in the agricultural field surrounding threshing machines.

   The word survives in common lexicon meaning someone who is opposed to, or annoyed by, fancy machines and electronic do-dads, not to mention computers. see ***work*** and ***police***

lumber -stuff that should have been thrown out, but wasn't. (*Lumber* in America is *timber* in England) A *lumber room* is a large closet. It is also the place the bodies are hidden in a certain genre of English mysteries. That may be called a *box room*.

lunch Yes, now it's a comparatively light mid-day meal, but it hasn't always been so. It had to do with candles. Lunch didn't require them, but dinner did so lunch was the larger more elaborate meal. With industrialization, workers couldn't go home for a full midday meal and so they started bringing a portable light meal to the factory. see ***meals***

The letter *m* comes from the Greeks by way of the Semites by way of the Egyptians. Draw a wavy line and you have water. Chop off two waves and you have *m* -and this is probably how *m* came  about because the word for water began with *m* in one of these languages. BTW, the use of the Roman numeral M to mean 1000 is a modern invention. The Romans never used it this way. It's doubtful they could count that high anyway, math not being a favorite subject among the Latin crowd.

M   -the designation for motorways like America's freeways. They have limited access, a 70mph speed limit or 112 kilometers per hour, and are bigger than the *A* roads.

Mac   -Scottish for descended from...

machinists   Up until the industrial revolution, the blacksmith, founder, and carpenter made the tools people used in their work, usually on the farm. As manufacturing mechanized, the increasingly sophisticate tools and machines required a different set of skills.

Magna Carta   In 1215 England's nobility, barons actually, had it up to here with King John so they got the Archbishop of Canterbury to write up a set of rules. It covered some protection of the church, protected the barons from imprisonment without a little due process, (the king could still do whatever he darn well pleased to the peasantry), some limitations to taxation, and just a hint of what would come to be England's legislative body, the Parliament. Both sides pretty much ignored it and the pope back in Rome annulled it a year or so later. There were some wars. King John died and his son's regents, (the boy was so young he needed grown-ups to tend to matters for him), edited it and re-issued The Magna Carta -Mark II. There were some more wars, and the agreement was ignored slightly less than the first time around, but it would not be until 80 years later in 1297 that it became a real part of law. Throughout, it was just for the nobility -the little guy was still unimportant and expendable.

Manchester -a middling to large city in Northwest England with not one, but two ***FC***'s! (soccer teams). There are two airports and a long navigable river to the Irish Sea. It's relatively wealthy, educated, and increasingly competes with London for various professionals working in offices. *Mancunians* live there.

manor -the land under the control of a rich man. He was probably a peer or maybe even a knight, but after the 18ᵗʰ century when the ***middle class*** got rich, they could have manors too.

market -regular open-air gatherings of farmers to sell their output to wholesalers and traders. These markets would come to include industrial output like cloth and manufactured goods. Later still, the towns where the markets convened would support permanent stalls and later still, shops. *Market towns* were given permission to hold a market which was an important thing for a growing town in the medieval era. Markets are the ancestors to ***fairs*** which were larger annual markets for a specific commodity.

Marques / Marchioness Number two in the peerage, below a Duke, but above Earl. These people were often used in England's colonies, particularly in Asia because there were similar positions there. The difference between Marques and other peers is a little vague, but it has to do with a vassalage on the border and therefore charged with a more defensive role than, for example, an earl who was safely inland.

Marquise of Queensbury Rules Rules of boxing, but may also refer to other sports. Not to be confused with ***According to Hoyle*** which applies to card games.

marriage Like a lot of English things, the American reader might best understand marriage in England with a little history. Not much is known about how the Celts did it. They left no written records. The Romans did it the way the Romans did it. This was a comparatively enlightened view of marriage by today's lights, and more so when compared to what would come later. After the Roman left, the Angles and Saxons held a view of women and marriage that would seem even more reasonable to modern folks. Women could own property, divorce was possible for various causes, they had a lot to say about whom they married, and most contrary to the way things would come to be under Christendom, they shared, for want of a better word, *ownership* of the kids.

 By the medieval, marriage was a transaction of property. The good news–such as it was–was that if neither party had any property, marriage wasn't really necessary. Marriage was also taxed and expensive at certain times and places so a lot of otherwise committed and loving couples didn't bother with it. Not being married makes divorce simple for the poor. None of this is to say people didn't love one another and look after their children tenderly, but things were different. Childbirth took a lot of women, war took away a lot of men, plagues came and went, and took everyone. This explains why we read about people who might have had three of four spouses. Add to this the fact that a 14 or 15-year-old was considered old enough to be out working and making his or her own way in the world. A stepmother, evil or otherwise, might be younger than her stepchildren. Such things that the modern reader might think of as part and parcel of fairy-tales, were everyday realities during the medieval.

On the other hand, if there was wealth involved it got terribly confusing. A daughter was not so much property as she was a liability and if dad wanted to be shed of a liability, he had to be to pay someone to take on that liability. This is why *dowry* shows up in English stories so often, but it was not paid to the groom, but rather the groom's family who assured that the girl would be able to continue to live in the fashion to which she had been accustomed even if the groom ran off with a more attractive woman. The church also weighed in with a long series of steps. First there was a contract between the parents. Next, the **banns** had to be read on three successive Sundays in the church were the bride and/or groom live. This would come to be the "let them speak now or forever hold their peace" part of a modern wedding. Then the couple had to exchange oral promises in front of witnesses. This was a minor part of the whole rigmarole that today we think of as the heart of the wedding ceremony. There was often a ceremony in the church but it was not necessary. It was followed by a feast if dad had any money left after the dowry was paid. Finally, there was the all-important consummation. Shakespeare's plays, or the romances anyway, often end with a marriage and often a secret one, but no priest shows up in the last act.

So it went for the merely rich. To some degree, all marriages were about making and rearing children and ideally a male heir, and thereby protecting & improving the families' wealth. For the royal families, it was so very much the case as to get even weirder. Charles II, (the guy whole father was executed by Cromwell and friends), married Catherine of Braganza, a Portuguese Princess. Her dowry was India. An entire sub-continent with millions of people was the price-tag to get a king to take on the liability that was a single woman.

Given the confusion of just who the next king might be, and who his father might *really* be, the bride and groom doing the consummation thing often had a witness or two—no less than there needed to be a witness when the bride and groom did their wedding vows. When the child was born, they all but sold tickets to the birthing room.

Despite **Henry VIII** having invented the Church of England largely so he could set aside some wives, divorce was not otherwise a possibility even among the rich. The Protestants and certainly the Catholics were against *divorce*, but when you consider the complexity of untangling property and negotiated inheritance, one wonders if this was not so much an ethical position as it was a decision just not to bother. Perhaps it was not all that important because being faithful to a spouse was not expected among the royalty. Take Chuck-2, the one with the Portuguese wife, as just one example. He had 6 mistresses for sure and seven more about whom historians are not sure. He admitted to fathering ten kids by the six for-sure mistresses. (Royal bastards are politely and euphemistically referred to as 'issue' by the historian crowd.)

In 1753 Parliament passed the *Marriage Act* that made the **Church of England** the point man in getting marriage standardized in England and Wales. The church also took on the responsibility of record keeping to the eternal gratitude of historic demographers. It also made very sure the parents gave their permission which in turn made for poignant stories of lovelorn young people, forbidding recalcitrant parents, elopement, disinheritance, and confusing melodramatic scenes like the one where Romeo thinks Juliet is dead, but she is only drugged, so he kills himself, and then Juliet wakes up and finds Romero dead and so she offs herself too. (Shakespeare used a lot more words to get it done though.) Finally, the church made getting a divorce even harder for everyone up and down the economic scale. In 1837 another Marriage Act finally legitimized Catholic weddings.

Thru much of English history, the average folks tended to postpone marriage till they were well established in careers etc. This was pretty much the same way in America but the Brits tended to wait a little longer. The average age for marriage thru the 1800's in England was 25 years of age. What is interesting is that during this time and despite the absence of reliable contraception etc., illegitimacy ran about only 4%. (In 2014 it was just a little over 40% in America.) It all made for some stories about long, indeed, very long courtships.

To bring it all to the 20th century, an 1870 law permitted women to keep their wages, and after 1882, they were allowed to keep the property they brought into the marriage, but because divorce was virtually impossible until 1937, it didn't do women as much good as might be hoped. see *women, dowry, divorce, servants*

A final note regarding the ring used as symbol of eternity and thereby marriage; it goes back to the ancient Egyptians. It was only about 800 that the church added it to the wedding ceremony. The double ring ceremony was an American invention beginning at the turn of the 20th century, and apparently, it was an idea dreamed up by the jewelry industry. During WWII in England, gold was in short supply so wedding rings were limited to *two pennyweights of 9 carat gold* rather than the usual 22 carat.

marow   -a winter squash with firm rind and is that is easily stored. It must be cooked before eating.

Martinmas   -St. Martin's Day. One of the quarter-days when rents were due during the medieval. It comes on November 11 when the crops are in, animals are slaughtered, and then, after harvest festivals and feasting, people settle in for winter, or at least they did until the industrial revolution and urbanization put them to work year around.

masons   More than brick-layers, masons were stone cutters, dressers, and setters. *Free masons* did extra fancy work in *freestone* or soft sandstone. The friend's society of this name has little to do with the mason's guild, other than to suggest that this was a high-status and well paid profession back in the day.

Meals   Breakfast has always been breakfast, but lunch, supper and dinner are terribly confusing. Before about 1850, the regular people ate their largest meal, dinner, at about 3:PM and variously called it *lunch.*. After 1850–well into the industrial revolution and factory work–*supper* was a light mid-day and the pubs served sandwiches and meat pies at all hours.

Rich people on the other hand, and ate a large *dinner* at noon. The 19th century Victorians had a light *lunch* at 1:PM and *dinner* had moved from mid-day to 5:PM and gradually moved still later in the evening during the 20th century. Children might be served a *tea* earlier. Supper was now a snack after the opera etc.

measurement   It's not quite as simple as metric system and the *other* one. There is also the Imperial and US measurements. Mercifully, it only involves volume. Yanks base their system on the English system of the 18th century, but then the English changed their system in 1824. Cubic inches, feet etc, are the same, but the measurements used in the kitchen work out with 1 US gallon equaling 0.8 Imperial gallons. Both gallons are still four quarts and eight pints, but the English P's & Q's are smaller especially when involving beer. Bushels and pecks and such are also different, but meaningful only to farmers.

Inches, feet, yards and miles are the same between the Yanks and Brits, but a nautical mile is 6076 feet or about 15% longer than a statute mile. Weights align, but there are three different systems, one for precious metals, one for medicine, and a third for everything else. Weighing big things like ships and barrels of grain involve pounds as a fundamental unit, but pounds gathered into tons, tuns, and tonnes. Other things were weighed in stones, (14 pounds), and hundredweights -which are not 100 pounds, but rather 112. It's not clear why this is.

This brings us to the metric vs. the English System which the English don't use. Only American use the English system. There are lots of measurements useful to scientists and engineers, but for the American reader, the following might serve:

1 liter = 1.06 quarts	100 grams = 3.6 ounces
100 millimeters = 4 inches	kilograms = 2.2 pounds
1 meters = 3.3 feet	kilometers = 0.6 miles
1 meters = 1.1 yards	sq. meters = 1.2 sq. yards
1 inch = 2.54 centimeter	1 kilowatt = 1.34 horse power
micro... μ millionth	kilo k thousand
milli... m thousandth	mega M million
centi... c hundredth	giga G billion / millard

Centigrade / Fahrenheit				
250° F				
200° F				
150° F	Water freezes at 32° F & 0° C			Water boils at 212°F or 100°C
100° F				
50° F	Room temp is 72° F & 22°C			
0° F				
	0° C	25° C	50° C	75° C	100° C

merchant   This was rather broad occupation. It ran from *merchant* in the language of the medieval era who was a businessman of any sort. Later it would come to mean an importer or exporter who likely owned or was part owner of ships like Shakespeare's *Merchant of Venice*. Stores as we might think of them today, were owned and operated in good size towns by *retailers*, and way out in the sticks, there were *peddlers or **chapmen*. see **mercantilism**

mercantilism   -the economic view that wealth derives from trade. This view holds that the correct role of government is to protect a nation's markets thru tariffs etc., and to protect its trade routes to foreign markets and sources of raw materials.
    Mercantilism is one of those word that get some folks all riled up, much like *capitalism* and *imperialism*. It worked by limiting imports other than raw materials. These raw materials were turned into more valuable finished products and exported. Importing finished goods was to be limited thru protective tariffs. It was all about what we would call a favorable balance of trade to bring gold and silver into the country. In England, we see the first materialistic policies arise as early as the 1500's. When history is viewed thru this lens, exploring the world to get things like pepper, spices, tea, and cotton begin to make more sense. Going to war to protect the merchant class also comes to make more–if sad–sense. It must be remembered that from the 16th century to about the 19th, the word *merchant* meant a guy with ships (like Shakespeare's chap from Venice) who was an importer / exporter and not the guy with a store. see ***colonies, work, Navy***

mess   -originally any group of people who ate together. The word has for some time now referred to military meals. As are many things English, mess is carefully divided up into class, one for officers, one for the middle manager like sergeants, and yet another for the private soldiers. This is not to make light of it; mess serves important social functions of communication and what would now be called *team building*. A *mess jacket* is an officer's formal dinner jacket and a *mess kit* is the less formal dress for dinner, but if you are or were an American Boy Scout, then a mess kit is a collection of dishes, pots, utensils etc for cooking & eating while camping.

meter   It's not just that measurement of length that is a little more than a yard, but rather what Yanks might thing of as a vending machine in the home or apartment. In England, if you were feeling chilly, you would drop some coin into the heater and enjoy a metered amount of heat from either electricity or natural gas. Since the late 20th century, the system has been changing to the American way with the meter outside and the meter-reader coming by periodically.

Methodism   -split off from the Church of England beginning in 1738. It was a fairly strict sect, but not quite Calvinism. To its credit, the Methodists missionaries reached out to the lowest levels of society in England. see *religion* and *baptists*

mews   -the alley behind the houses for horses and carriages. With the coming of the auto, little carriage-houses on the mews with the horse and servant's quarters upstairs, were converted to small homes. Because they were in wealthy old neighborhoods, an address on the *mews* suggested a trendy little home for literature's eccentric characters after the turn of the century.

MI-5   -Military Intelligence, Section 5. This is for domestic intelligence and security and a little like America's FBI
MI-6   -Military Intelligence, Section 6, aka *SIS or* the Secrete Intelligence Service. This office gathers foreign intelligence for Her Majesty's Government like America's CIA, It is also *James Bond*'s employer in various of his incarnations.

midden   -a garbage dump. Given that some middens were in use hundreds or even thousands of years ago, they are archeologist's favorite research libraries.

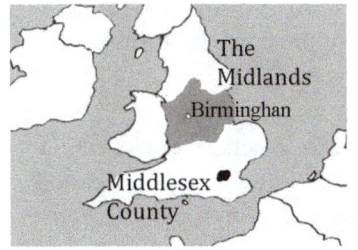

Middlesex   -literally, home of the Middle Saxons. To the east was Essex, to the south, Sussex, and to the west, Wessex. (Sometimes words make sense.) Middlesex has long been what an American would think of a suburb of London, which actually ate Middlesex in 1965.

Midlands   The east-west middle band of England. *Birmingham* is its largest city in this area, and the second largest in all of England. The Midlands were important to the Industrial Revolution, so literature about the Midlands in the 18th and 19th century might be thought of as like the big industrial cities in America's Midwest during the 19th and early 20th.

midshipman   -a boy or very young man who was being trained as an officer in the Royal Navy. He was usually the son of some variety of rich guy and acted as a servant. (George Washington wanted to be a midshipman when he was 15, but his mother forbade it. His older step-brother served under Admiral Vernon who was the inventor of *grog*.) Lots of cracking good sea-stories involve midshipmen.

Milk Tray -a box of chocolates made by Cadbury, and often a gift for a woman.

milliners -first a subset of haberdashers who dealt in fancy notions from Milan, Italy, and later became makers of ladies' hats.

millwrights -made and dressed the big stones used to grind things like corn, (what Yanks call *wheat*), barley, oats, beans etc. Each product needed a stone shaped and dressed in a particular manner.

mince -means almost the same thing in American as it does in British; to mince words is to chop them up small, chose them carefully, and perhaps not say much of anything as a consequence. *Minced meat* is chopped up extra fine like American hamburger, (note the D in the word.), BUT *mincemeat* is chopped fruit used to make puddings or the structural material knows as fruitcake.

minister -a **MP** from the **House of Commons** and in the **political party** that is the majority. He or she is the head of a ministry and may also be refereed to as a **secretary**. Some non-conformist churches are careful to call their clergymen ministers so no one confused them with Catholic priests.

ministry -like America's federal departments of this and that. While these departments in America are headed by secretaries, in England they have **ministers** or secretaries. Subtle point for the language freaks; in the English language, *ministry* and *minister* are the generic word applied to any government EXCEPT in the UK and the US, where the correct words are *department* and *secretary*. It hardly matters otherwise.

minor -like in America, someone under 18, but in schools, where they address students only by their last names, two related kids, or kids unrelated kids but with the same last name, are distinguished one from the other as, for example, Smith Major and Smith Minor.

Miss. A more discerning word in England than in American. For example, in the 18th century Smith family, the eldest daughter, Sally Smith, would be addressed as Miss. Smith, and her younger sisters, Linda and Betty, would be addressed as Miss Linda and Miss Betty. Furthermore, the American distinction between married *Misses* -Mrs.- and unmarried *Miss* blurs for a 20th century tradesman or shop assistant who was addressing a patron who might be young enough to be unmarried. A student would address his or her female teacher of any age, married or single, as Miss. Going way back, a mistress (Miss) was a concubine, courtesan, or kept woman.

mister   In medieval times, a mister was the *master of his craft*.

Mockney   -mock Cockney. Think of American high school drama nerds.

model   In the past, a model was the polite way to refer to a prostitute. At that time, a clothing model would be called a mannequin. Today in England to avoid any confusion or insult, a mannequin is now a fashion model.

moderns   -an old-fashioned word for those new-fangled classes at university that do not involve Greek and Latin. Medicine, engineering, and things that actually led to productive work were for students whose fathers probably also did productive things. Latin was for rich twits.

Monarchy   When viewed thru the lens of big history, our modern world without kings being in charge, is a brief experiment. Divine kings go back to the Porto-Indian that proceeded the Mesopotamian and Egyptian civilizations. To put it mathematically, and using the Yank's 1776 as a historic marker, for every 20 years with kings, mankind has had one year without.
    Today the world's only absolute monarchies are religious. There are 5 or 10 Islamic *absolute* or *semi-constitutional monarchies* on or around the Arabian Peninsula. The Pope technically is the king of the Vatican. There are some *sub-national monarchies* in Africa, Indonesia, and the South Pacific. A few *constitutional monarchies* are scattered about Europe in little tiny countries usually organized around casinos. Queen Elizabeth is also a constitutional monarch, but her realm is a ***commonwealth*** so outside of England, it doesn't count. It doesn't count for much inside of England either, except for ceremonial occasions, and besides that, they are all quite fond of the old girl. The following might help an American reader pin down who was in charge at a given time.

House / Dynasty	King / Queen	When	Literature	Events
Norman (French)	***William I*** (William the Conqueror)	1066 - 1087	King Arthur and Merlin were supposed to have fought against the Normans.	The 1st Crusade 1096
	Henry 1	1100 -1135	A complicated mess re. succession of French vs. English kings begins in 1101and lasts till 1154	
	Matilda	1141		
Plantagenet	Henry II	1154 - 1189		
	John	1199- 1216	Robin Hood[4]	

---

[4]   The legend of Robin Hood is scattered all thru the middle ages. The first recognizable writing about the archer outlaw shows up in 1377. It has been embellished and improved to this day in everything from

House / Dynasty	King / Queen	When	Literature	Events
Plantagenet, but neither Lancaster nor York	Richard I	1189 - 1199	Much confusion here. Robin Hood, Evil King John, and Richard the Lion Hearted are all tangled up together.	
	Henry III	1216- 1272	*Chaucer* 1343 – 1400 Canterbury Tales-1380	
	Edward I	1272 - 1307		The Last Crusade[5]
	Edward II	1307 - 1327		
	Edward III	1327 - 1377		Black Death 1348 - 1350
	Richard II	1377 - 1399	Another Robin Hood possibility, and a Shakespeare play. Richard's head cook writes England's 1st cookbook, <u>The</u> Forme of Cury, ('cury' derived from the French 'curie' -to cook).	
House of Lancaster	Henry IV	1399 - 1413	Shakespeare wrote plays about all three of the Henrys, skipped Edward, and did Richard III.	
	Henry V	1413 - 1422		Battle of Agincourt 1415
	Henry VI	1422 - 1461		Joan of Arc burned at the stake 1431
House of York	Edward IV	1471 - 1483		The War of the Roses 1455 - 1484
	Richard III	1483 - 1485		
	Edward V	1483 (never crowned)		
Tudors	Henry VII	1485 - 1509		Columbus doesn't find India in 1492
	Henry VIII	1509-1547	First *New Testament* written in English 1526	Martin Luther published his 95 Theses and Protestantism begins.
	Edward VI	1547 - 1553	William Shakespeare born 1564	
	Mary I	1553 - 1558	Reformation Lit.- mostly Catholic vs., Protestant writing.	Mary, aka 'Bloody Mary' executed lots of protestants.
	Elizabeth I	1558 - 1603	Shakespear: *Hamlet* 1600, *Romeo & Juliet* 1594	The plague kills 80,000 people in England in 1863.

The Tudors are a short-lived bunch, but did lots of interesting stuff and fought a lot of wars. Henry Seven's daughter was Lady Jane Grey and was thought to be the rightful queen.
Henry Eight -the guy with the turkey leg- married Catherine of Aragon, Anne Boleyn, Jane Seymour, and a few others. Things did not go well for these women and Henry died without a proper heir. Henry Seven's grandson, (Eight's nephew), James I would be the first of the Stuart kings

House / Dynasty	King / Queen	When	Literature	Events
Stuarts	James I	1603 - 1625	William Shakespeare died in 1616.	Shakespeare's MacBeth & King Lear -1605
	Charles I	1625 - 1649		Beheaded by Cromwell

Common Wealth 1649 - 1660
After beheading Charles I, *Oliver Cromwell* was appointed Lord Protector of the Commonwealth of England, Scotland, and Ireland. Very confusing, but very important. See the *English Civil War.*

| | Charles II | 1660 - 1685 | British take over New Amsterdam and it becomes New York. | |
| | James II | 1685-1688 | Newton published his book on real fancy | |

---

middle English ballads to Technicolor movies.
[5] The numbering of the Crusades is a complication beyond this Yank's understanding; there were eight or nine of them -unless there were seven.

			math in 1687.	
	William III Mary II	1689 - 1702 1689 -1694	*Pilgrim's Progress* 1678	Scotland + England = Great Britain in 1707
	Anne	1702 - 1714		
Hanover	George I	1714 - 1727	Enlighten-ment (political)	Jane Austen 1775 - 1818
	George II	1727 - 1760	writing, i.e.: Alexander Pope,	The magazine was inventer in 1731.
	George III	1760 - 1820	Johnathan Swift, & David Hume. Jane Austin *Pride & Prejudice* in 1813	The king who so annoyed the American Founding Fathers and was possibly mad.
	George IV	1820 - 1830		Napoleon dies in 1821.
	William IV	1830 - 1837	Dickens, *Oliver Twist* 1837	Slavery is prohibited throughout the British Empire
	Victoria	1837 - 1901	Darwin, *On the Origin of the Species* 1865	The source of all things "Victorian."
Windsor (Saxe-Coburg & Gotha)	Edward VII	1901 - 1910	H.G. Wells, *The First Men in the Moon* 1901	England launches the world's first Dreadnaught battleship 1906
	George V	1910 - 1936	Conrad, *The Secrete Agent* 1901	World War I 1914 - 1919
	Edward VIII abdicated his throne. in December of 1936.			
	George VI	1936 - 1952	Huxley, *Brave New World* 1937	World War II 1939 - 1945
	Elizabeth	1952 -	J. R. R. Tolkien, *The Lord of the Rings* 1954 - 1956	… and life goes o

Money   English money even confused the English, so in 1971 they 'decimalized' it. This means that now it's pounds and hundredths of pounds or pennies. Up until then you needed three numbers to put a price on things. Worked out roughly like this: the fist number (£) refers to pounds or something more than a dollar. The next one (s) is shillings and these are one-twentieth of a pound or a nickel. The third number (d) is for pennies –except that there are 240 pennies to a pound, so a shilling is actually twelve and a half pennies and an English penny is smaller than an American penny.

Slang

There are also various nicknames and slang terms Brits use to talk about their money, but in fairness, Yanks have their share too, i.e. buck, saw-buck, five spot, Hamilton, Franklin, etc. From smallest to largest, the English have…

farthing	¼ of a penny.
ha'penny	half a pence or half a penny.
tupence	two pence or two pennies.
thrupence	three pence or pennies.
tanner	six pence or pennies.
sixpence	half a shilling

shilling	12 pence or pennies or 1/20th of a pound.
bit	"
bob	"
two bob	2 shillings
two-bob bit	2 shillings + 6 pennies.
half-crown	" "
crown	5 shillings or 60 pence / pennies.
quid	a paper note for 1 pound sterling.
sovereign	a gold coin equaling a pound sterling.

Abbreviations, (and some Latin):

£ Pound sterling -from the Latin *libra*. Gives us *lb.* as our abbreviation for pound. It is not clear why it is necessary to put *sterling* behind *pound*, but it's always done and *Pound Sterling* sounds cool.

s Shilling -from the Latin *solidus*. Solid—as in solid metal coin.

d Penny -from the Latin *demaro*.
In the medieval, you would buy your nails 100 at a time. Big nails like the ones used to nail together your house might run you 16 pennies per 100 or 16d, while smaller ones used to hang a picture on the wall might be 6 pennies per 100 or 6d. Now we buy nails by the weight, (pounds in America), but their size is still described in pennies.

History of Money
To make things even more confusing, the English Pound has deflated as has the Dollar, and a single Pound back in the day of the three-number system was some serious money. Then there is the matter of translating it to dollars. Just a little historic perspective might be useful to sort things out. The Romans left in about 450, and the Germans came, actually the Angles and the Saxons. Then the French took over in 1066 but they called themselves 'Normans'. It was then that a Pound was an actual pound of actual silver and the divided up into twentieths, (1/20) and two-hundred-fortieths, (1/240). By the way, as of 2016, a pound of .999 silver would cost you $288 and not too long ago, would have set you back about $750. In 1864 a Pound, (the money –not the metal), would cost you just under ten American Dollars and has been drifting down ever since. Either the Dollar has gotten more expensive, or the Pound has gotten cheaper.

The following chart[6] will be useful if you are reading about some character who has just inherited a lot of money and it seems that inheritance from some long forgotten relative makes for lots of English literature. Basically, the **$'s per £** column tells you what you would have to pay for a Pound in Dollars. The **2015 $'s** column tells you what those dollars would buy today. Clearly, neither the Pound nor the Dollar have done well. Note that there are no values for Romeo and Juliet, Tom Jones, or Robinson Crusoe; at the time of these publications, there *were* no Americans or dollars. I include them just for interest. Furthermore, even the dollar was a pretty nebulous thing between one American state and its neighboring state until

---

[6]   Lawrence H. Officer, "Dollar-Pound Exchange Rate From 1791," MeasuringWorth, 2016 URL: http://www.measuringworth.com/exchangepound/

early in the 20th Century.

Year	Book	Author	Character	$ / L	2015 $'s[7]
1597	Romeo & Juliet	William Shakespeare	Romeo & Juliet		
1726	Robinson Crusoe	Daniel Defoe	Robinson Crusoe		
1749	Tom Jones	Henry Fielding	Tom Jones		
1791	Tam o' Shanter[8]	Robert Burns	Tam	$4.55	$119.00
1813	Pride & Prejudice	Jane Austen	Elizabeth Bennet	$3.75	$57.50
1837	Oliver Twist[9]	Charles Dickens	Charles Dickens	$5.10	$130.00
1859	On the Origin of Species	Charles Darwin	na	$4.90	$144.00
1915	Of Human Bondage	W. Somerset Maugham	Mildred & Philip	$4.76	$116.00
1920	The Mysterious Affair at Styles	Agatha Christie	Hercules Poirot[10]	$3.66	$35.50
1928	Lady Chatterley's Lover	D. H. Lawerence	Constance Lady. Chatterly	$4.87	$67.40
1949	1984	George Orwell	Winston Smith	$3.69	$35.30
1953	James Bond	Ian Fleming	James Bond	$2.81	$24.90
1979	The Hitchhiker's Guide to the Galaxy	Douglas Adams	Ford Prefect	$2.12	$6.92
2000	The Goblet of Fire	J. K. Rowling	Harry Potter	$1.52	$2.09
Year	Book	Author	Character	$ /£	2015 $'s[11]

monopoly   In the days of the powerful **guilds**, monopolies were granted by the monarch for a cut of the profits. They were thought to be good things that kept prices and employment stable for the monopolistic guilds. The

---

[7] (same source) This proves to be a complicated issue. It can be based on what it costs to buy commodities, what it costs to buy someone's labor, or a fraction of GDP, (or its historic equivalent). The number vary widely. I use the commodity value.

[8] This poem mentions an alluring naughty woman's night-dress -a "cutty sark," which gave its name to the famous Scottish tea-clipper the *Cutty Sark,* launched in 1864.

[9] Oliver Twist was published as a serial over about a 3 year period.

[10] Hercule was still at it as of the late '70's.

[11] (same source) This proves to be a complicated issue. It can be based on what it costs to buy commodities, what it costs to buy someone's labor, or a fraction of GDP, (or its historic equivalent). The number vary widely.

public on the other hand, had to pay what the guild said. The notion of free trade began to erode the monopolies and by the time Adam Smith published <u>The Wealth of Nations</u> in 1776. Monopolies were seen as bad things and so they remain today. see *mercantilism*

Sir Thomas More (1485 – 1540)   One of Henry's advisors who came to a bad end when he displeased Henry. He was a remarkably talented man. He was a lawyer, judge, social philosopher, author, and statesman He also served Henry VIII as Lord High Chancellor of England. He was also a Catholic and this wasn't necessarily a bad thing at the time -at least until Henry demanded everyone declare the King's Supremacy over the English Church. This was a step too far for More, so he was accused of treason, given a brief trial with all manner of court intrigues (No less the Thomas Cromwell played a part) and witnesses of doubtful honesty, and decapitated in 1540. His last words are well documented and telling. He said that he "died the king's good servant, and God's first."

morning coat / morning suit / morning dress   -variations on the old fashioned long formal men's coat with tails. It is worn with a *waistcoat* and high starched collar. It's not quite a tuxedo, which is for evenings, but to the American eye, they are similar. see *cutaway*

mote and bailey   -not to be confused with the picturesque water filled moat, a mote is a ditch surrounding a fortification of some sort with a wall (wood or stone) on top. The bailey is an open place or a court yard within the mote. Going way back before fairy-tale times, there was often a hill, usually artificial and often made with slave labor, with a *castle* on top.

MP's see *Member of Parliament*

muffins, English   -aren't English, they are American. The English have scones or Johnny cakes for breakfast. *Crumpets* are for tea.

mummers   In America, mummers are attached to either New Orleans' Mardi Graw, or New Year's celebrations, but in England back in the day, mummers were mimes or amateur actors doing small scale performances. They were often performed in inns and often on religious themes during Christmas or Easter. The clowns in Shakespeare's *A Mid-Summer's Night's Dream* were mummers.

mushy peas   -peas made mushy by cooking them in marrow fat and a little baking soda to make then extra mushy. They are a popular accompaniment to fish and chips and a lot of other English dishes.

In ancient Egyptian, the word for *snake* begins with a **n** sound, so the Semitic letter **n** is a squiggly drawing of a snake. Unless it's a fish as it is in Phoenician, Hebrew, and Arabic, but it's harder to see how a fish looks like an **n**. Make up your own mind on this. The experts don't agree.

Napoleonic War(s)   -a series of wars with France between 1803 and 1815. England fought many MANY wars, but given that their victory over Napoleon in 1815 was the beginning of the almost 100 year long ***Pax Britannica***, this war, or this series of wars, might have been the most important. Furthermore, and more important to readers, there is a lot of heroism, tradition, and literature arising from these twelve years.

Americans must be forgiven for thinking that the uprising in the western colonies might have been pretty important along about 1776, but to the English, it was a minor nuisance that took resources away from the more important war with France. It's a fairly straight line from the French and Indians on one side, fighting with the English and the American Colonists on the other side in 1750. Then, about 25 years later, the English crown tried to tax the Colonists to pay for it all. The Americans traded sides and revolted against the mother country. Yanks have to understand England's position–if only a little.

Once England got itself out of the American quagmire, (not unlike America's quagmire in Viet Nam about 200 years later), the English got serious once again fighting with the French.

Continuing our straight line from the colonies to the Napoleonic War, with a quick review of French history, Louis XVI and Marie Antoinette were killed in 1789, and the French Revolution went ***mad-hatter***-crazy with the guillotine. In 1803 Great Britain, Spain, and a few other countries formed the First Coalition to sort it out. Napoleon won, and would continue to for the next three Coalitions. The Peninsular War went badly for Napoleon when he lost to the Brits, Spanish, and Portuguese. But he went on to win the Fifth Coalition, and then made one of histories greatest blunders; he invaded

Russia in the fall of 1812. The French expected to be home again in time for All Saint's Day, (November 1), and they just packed sweaters and an extra pair of socks. By the middle of December, 400,000 men out of the 520,000 invaders died, most of them from cold and starvation.

Note the year -1812. The English were blockading France throughout, and needed sailors to do so. Being a sailor in the British Navy was the very definition of a miserable job and recruiting them got so hard that the Royal Navy simply took them off what ever ship their men-of-war happened across on the high seas, including American merchant ships. This lead to Act Two between America and England -the *War of 1812*. It was considered a draw. The American Navy raided all up and down the Atlantic and the Brits burnt down the American's brand-spanking-new Washington DC. In the end, everyone decided to more or less call it a draw and just go home.

Returning now to Europe, it went downhill for Napoleon from about then. The Sixth Coalition (England, Prussia, Austria, Sweden and a few others), was another loss for Napoleon. He was exiled to the Island of Elba off the coast of northwest Italy. The coalition restored the Bourbon Monarchy in the person of Louis XVIII and sat down to redraw the map of Europe.

But we weren't done with old Nappy quite yet. He escaped from Elba in 1815 and put together another army of about 280,000 men. The Brits assembled the Seventh Coalition made from the usual suspects -Britain, Russia, Prussia, Sweden, Austria, the Netherlands and a few wee German city-states. This was literally his Waterloo. He spent his last six years on another remote island, St. Elba, in the South Atlantic.
see *Nelson Column, Trafalgar Square*

Napoleon de Bonaparte (the man)   Born 1769, French military leader from 1799, emperor from 1804 to 1813, died at age 52 in 1821. Hard to say why he goes by his first name -Napoleon and not his last name, Bonaparte, but there it is. He was born on the Mediterranean Island of Corsica. He fought in the French Revolution at age 20 and was so good at military strategy and leadership that by 1799 he was France's top military guy and Emperor of France in 1804. To some degree, his success was a function of the mess that the French Revolution made where-in anybody who was anybody got their heads chopped off, and ultimately, anybody who knew anybody who knew anybody who was rich faced a similar fate.

His record as a military leader was impressive enough even if it made him England's greatest villain, but the guy did some impressive stuff quite aside from what the English call the Napoleonic Wars. He implemented liberal policies in France and much of the various countries he conquered. His legal code, the Napoleonic Code influenced legal systems all over the modern world. (It still makes up a lot of the way they do things in America's Louisiana today.)

According to the English historian Andrew Roberts, "The ideas that underpin our modern world–meritocracy, equality before the law, property rights, religious tolerance, modern secular education, sound finances, and so on– were championed, consolidated, codified and geologically extended by Napoleon. To them he added a rational and efficient local administration, and an end to rural banditry, the encouragement of science and the arts, the end of feudalism, and the greatest codification of laws since the fall of the Roman Empire." This from an English historian.

It is left to readers to compare his policies with those of–for example– England at the time, and decide for themselves just how evil he was. But one way or the other, he is responsible for a lot of rousing great stories wherein the Brits are heroes.

There are a couple of interesting "ya-buts" needing to be *ya-buted* about now. Contrary to popular tradition, Napoleon was not short, but of about average size for a Frenchman of the day. The French were just a little smaller that the English back then. (see *food*). There is also a lot of interesting, if speculative, writing as to how Napoleon died at a mere 52 years of age. Was he poisoned? By who? Why? And so it goes.

National Health   Health care in England has been paid for by a combination of health insurance deducted from employee's paychecks and general tax revenue from about 1948. Most healthcare workers are salaried government employees. People may seek out private care for better service, or for procedures not covered by insurance, but they have to pay for it privately. The plan worked well out of the box, but it has come under increasing criticism for delays and shortages.

Navies   -the people who first dug canals, then built railroad grades, tunnels and bridges etc. They were a huge army of rough laborers from all over England and Ireland. In 1850 there were more navvies, (from *navigation*), than personnel in the Army and Navy combined, but in building one particular tunnel, the odds of a navvie being killed on the job were greater than a soldier in the Battle of Waterloo being killed in action. They were well paid by the standards of the day, but hard drinkers, hard fighters and lived in appalling conditions. They were also viewed as barely human by most of the rest of society.

Navy / Royal Navy   As far back as the 11th century, English folks who owned ships could get out of paying taxes if they let the king borrow their cargo ships to move soldiers from place to place. (It's not clear what sort of shape the ships were when the got home again.) It was *Henry VIII* that really put together a functioning professional navy with real and designated fighting ships, cannons, officers, and a budget in the early 1500's. From then until at least WWII, the Royal Navy was all that. It would be hard to say if the Royal Navy was responsible for England's success in her colonies, or the other way around, but they certainly went together.

The navy had the added distinction of being far more professional than the army even if the navy had less status. This was because of a peculiarity of the English mindset. The navy needed skillful educated people running ships and navigating and occasionally doing math. Such people were selected based on their ability rather than who their fathers were. On the other hand, the army was where the rich people sent their younger sons or those too dumb for the clergy. They were often inbred nitwits who were more interested in riding horses, pretty uniforms, and drinking gin. Furthermore, sailors also were often away for years at a time and couldn't come to the requisite parties. James Bond, for example, is/was a Commander in Her Majesty's Navy!

needle-makers   Yes, they made needles, but there is more to it. Needles, pins, nails, screws and all manner of small metal fiddly-bits were made in the **putting-out system**, or as one writer described it -*white slavery*. If you come across a needle maker in your reading, he or she was probably very poor.

neeps & tatties   -chopped baked rutabaga and potatoes and the traditional side dish with haggis.

Nelson, Lord Horatio   -England's greatest naval hero was born to an upper-middle class family in 1758 and died at sea in 1805. Nelson perfectly demonstrates the Navy's odd practice of promoting talent rather then social rank the way they did it in the army. He entered the navy as a

common seaman at the age of 13, shortly began training as a mid-shipman, and had his own command at age 20. He rose thru the ranks, but was left unemployed at the end of the American Revolution. The French Revolution and Napoleonic Wars put him back to work in the Mediterranean and Atlantic. His greatest victory was the **Battle Trafalgar** against the French & Spanish off the coast of Spain in 1805, but he was killed by a sniper during the mopping up operation. The English people were so grateful, that they built **Nelson's Column** in **Trafalgar Square**.

Nelson's Column   -a 170 foot tall column erected in 1843 in Trafalgar Square as a memorial to Nelson's victory at Trafalgar. There are four large bronze bas-relief plaques at the base made from French cannons that the Brits captured and melted down. Kind of a huge *F___ You* to Napoleon.

Newton, Isaac (1642 – 1726)   Newton had a tough life as a boy. He was born prematurely and his dad died before he was born. He didn't get along with his step-dad, but nonetheless, discovered lots of stuff important to physicist, (optics and his famous laws of motion), astronomy, (gravity, the planets & their orbits), and math (calculus). He also dabbled in theology, biblical chronology, and even helped the Royal Mint track down counterfeiters after he did his scientific work. He actually disguised himself as a drunken wastrel and went undercover.

Newgate   -originally a gate to the old city of London. It was a prison for London's worst criminals from 1188 to 1902 and held then in deplorable conditions. From 1783 till 1867 it held public executions for the enjoyment and edification of the citizenry.

the N word   Horrible word by today's light, but not always so and, more to the point, not as insulting in England as it is/was in America. As late as the middle of the 20th century, a n_____ or *wog* shows up in English literature and meant someone from India, or anyone of dark complexion for that matter.

Nonconformist   Shortly after Henry split the *Church of England* off from the Catholic pope, Protestantism split itself off from the *Church of England.* Then some varieties Protestants like the Presbyterians, Quakers, Methodists, Puritans, and Baptist- did not conform and also split. They were suppressed like the Catholics, but for slightly different reasons.

Norman Conquest   In 1066, the Norwegians invaded the north of England and the Normans, Brentons, and French, (but they were all French), invaded the south. This all had to do with an Anglo-Saxon king dying without an heir. Much war and upheaval happened and William the Conqueror came out on top and ran England. He did this by kicking out all the rich landed Anglo Saxons (see The *Doomsday Book*) All of 8000 Normans settled in England, but they replaced the exiled landowners. The French language got to be fashionable among the hoity-toity. This is where fancy hard-to-spell words in the English language that are a vexation to this day came from. Historians are conflicted as to whether the Normans were better or worse than the ruling Saxons. Slavery went away, but was replaced with serfdom, which was not much better.   see *women, history,* and *language*

Norfolk   A rural county with lots of farming to the north-east of London. Historically, it was only a moderately successful Roman settlement because this was where *Boudica* lived. The Romans, the Angels, the Danes, Vikings, and the Normans all tromped through at one time or another. Today Norfolk, (the *northern folk*), is among the most conservative crowd in England, and is considered a tad provincial by English writers–sometimes going so far as drawing them to be what Yanks might consider *country pumpkins*. Lately, the Green Party has made significant headway there.

North Sea oil

-largely a modern thing, but oil was mined on Scotland's coastline as early as 1850. *Mined* is the appropriate word here. Drilling for deep oil would have to wait for the 20th century and doing it off shore, particularly in deep water, would have to wait till the 1960's. Today England shares the North Sea oil with Norway, Germany, Denmark and Netherlands but declining production has lead to England once again becoming a net importer of oil.

Northern Ireland

-part of the United Kingdom and home to about 1.8 million people who are mostly, but not entirely Protestants. Works out to about 30% of the population of Ireland and 3% of the population of the UK. It split from what would

become the (independent) Republic of Ireland in 1922. Friction between the Catholics and Protestants grew to the *Troubles* by 1990. Historically, it was the more industrialized and wealthy part of the island, but declined during Troubles. It has been recovering slowly but today 20% of the economy is subsidized. see *Belfast*, & *Ireland.*

Northumberland

Just south of Scotland, Northumberland is England's most sparsely populated county. Its history involves mostly warfare with Scotland and usually border skirmishes. There are lots of Roman ruins there, the most significant of which is Hadrian's Wall which was made to keep the Scots out. Now Northumberland is a good place to raise sheep.

Norsemen

-the vikings. Yes, they pestered the English from roughly 790 to 1150 -the 'Viking Age,' bit it must be said that the French were also a problem -at least to the mind's of a couple of kings who wanted to own parts of France. What about the poor Irish, you ask ;yes, they were also pestered, but Ireland made convenient bases of operations d pod for the Norse / Vikings convenient to raiding England.

Number 10 Downing Street, or simply *Number 10*

-England's executive residence, their White House. Historically, it was the official residence of First Lord of the Treasury, but in 1905, the *Prime Minister* and Treasury roles were combined. Today it is the *PM*'s home and headquarters of Her Majesty's *Government*, given that in England, one party

IS the government and the other party is the **Loyal Opposition**. The building is 300 years old and has over 100 rooms. The Prime Minister lives on the third floor, and it's close to **Buckingham Palace** (the queen), and **Palace of Westminster** (**Parliament**).

numpy -being both nagging and grumpy. Often an elderly women.

nurse -the servant who cared for the **middle class**'s very youngest children. A wet-nurse nursed babies. She may have slept in the nursery in the house, or the child may have been sent to live with the wet-nurse until the child was weened. This happened at no later than at eighteen months and often sooner. From the nurse, the child would be passed off to a **nanny** and later still, a **governess.** A *nursemaid* was neither a nurse nor nanny, but rather a maid who tended to the nursery. see **servants, governess**

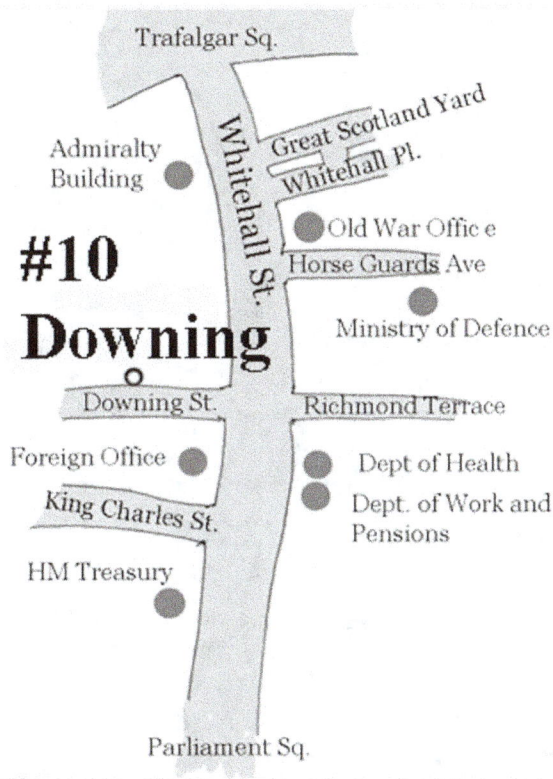

nursery The Victorians used this part of the house to keep children politely invisible. While the children were only occasionally let out of the nursery on special occasions, it was rare. The nursery was a combination bedroom, living / playroom, dining room, and classroom with an attached bedroom for the nurse, nanny, or governess.

nursery school -like America's pre-school, it was prior to infant school or America's elementary school.

It's been a circle just about forever. The Phoenicians thought of it as an eye and drew-wrote it accordingly, but it was probably a consonant back then. The Greeks made it a vowel–Omega. Non-Semitic languages like English, write the letter like a little mouth making the *oh* sound. Or so say the language weenies.

oak   Yes, it's a tree, but the British Navy made some whacking great ships out of the stuff, so oak is a symbol of the toughest, bravest, and altogether the best of all things British.

oakum picking   Oakum is the individual fibers of worn out rope that are unraveled and used in the seams of oak ships as caulking. Tedious, but not very challenging work performed while sitting down and often done in prisons.

OAP   -old age pensioner

oat(s)   -grown in the north and a pretty staple food for the Scots. In England, it was usually fed to horses, except in porridge or watery gruel. see *food*

OBE   -Order of the British Empire. Sort of a catch-all for the non-noble people who needed or deserved a little appreciation and recognition. Everyone from civil servants to rock-stars might get this order, and be called sir or dame. Comes in five levels. From highest to lowest, they run...

GBE	Knight / Dame of the Grand Cross
KBE	Knight / Dame Commander
CBE	Commander of the British Empire
OBE	Officer of the British Empire
MBE	Member of the British Empire

The swells actually get a little snippy about the lower levels of the list. Members of the KBE, for example, sometimes snicker at the OBE as *Other Bastards of the Empire*. Such are the English.

Observer   -the world's oldest, (first published in 1791), Sunday paper. It's well respected for its liberal view. (Conservative Brits read the *Sunday Times* which sells slightly better.)

OC   -officer Commanding like the American CO or Commanding Officer.

Official Secrets Act   -goes back to 1911 and criminalizes revealing anything the government doesn't want revealed. It has been amended regularly, most recently in 1989.

Odds and sods -American *odds and ends* or English *bits and bobs.*

old boy, old thing, old man, old son, old girl, old chap etc. -are all expressions of affection or respect.

O-Levels   -exams given to students of about age 16 from 1950 to 1988. The ***forms*** vary from school to school and have varied thru the years, but what has not changed is that these exams indicate whether a student was going to university or into the trades.

OM   Order of Merit These are handed out by the monarch for distinguished service in military, science, art, literature. There are only 24 members of this club at any one time.

113-B Baker St.   -Sherlock Holmes's fictional home he shared with Doctor John Watson.

opportunity shop   -a second hand store. It is often a charitable operation like Goodwill or the Salvation Army in America.

opposition / Loyal Opposition   -members of the minority party in Parliament. Given that the majority party grows it own Prime Minister and all the cabinet members (Ministers of this and that), the opposition, loyal or otherwise, doesn't do much.

Orange, the House of   -William III's home in Northern Ireland along with his buddies before he became king in 1795. It's more important meaning was about the Protestants. Orange was the opposite of Green (Southern Ireland), Protestantism is the opposite of Catholicism, and Northern Island is the opposite of Southern Ireland. The *Orangemen* were a political society supporting the Protestants and unity with England. It was relatively benign until the 1880's when the idea of Irish independence took hold in the south. Things went down hill from then and reached a head between the early 1960's and 1998 with all but full-out guerrilla warfare between the Orange and the *IRA,* the Irish Republic Army.

orangery   -a greenhouse used to protect ornamental orange trees that were fashionable in the 19th century.

Ordnance   -a detailed and accurate map or set of maps of the whole country. Think USGS topos in America. (US Geological Survey Topographic Maps)

osteopath   -chiropractor

OTC   -Officer Training Corps -like America's ROTC

outhouse   -either what Yanks would call an outbuilding on a farm, or what they think it means. Once sanitation, (sewer systems), came to a town, the pipes often went down the alley (the *muse*)and no further than the back wall of the garden, so the British outhouse was not a merely hole in the ground under a seat, but rather almost-a-bathroom. But it was still a separate little building in the back yard.

outsize -XL, XXL, etc, -clothes

Oxford   A nice town in central England about 60 miles NW of London on the River Thames. Its history, aside from the university, is Saxon and in fact, Oxford means *ox ford* or a place where ox could ford the river. It was variously invaded by the Viking Danes and Normans. After one too many such bothersome conquests, they built a castle with a chapel and living-quarters for monks and this brings us to its origin as an university town. Back then, a university was more like a think-tank than it was a place where teaching got done to any great degree. The thinking that was done, was done entirely about religious things, and moreover, was done in Greek or Latin. Teaching happened, but it was done to replenish the ranks. (Oxford Fellows were not allowed to marry until 1880.)

Oxford University[*] is probably the oldest in England, (*Cambridge* is a close second), but exactly what is meant by *university* is historically fluid and fuzzy. Something vaguely like a university in Morocco goes back to 859 and another one in Bologna, Italy got its start in 1088, but Oxford's birth in the 1100's is impressive. In 1225 we see the first *hall* emerge, but a few years later, *colleges* phased out mere halls. Both were originally where monks copied books and translated from Latin and Greek. Things went poorly for religious people on both Catholic and Protestant side during the back-and-forth of the Civil War and Oxford suffered more than most places in England, not to mention the assorted plagues and poxes before and after.

Between then and the early 1800's, education in Oxford and all of England for that matter, served mostly to train clergy. As the industrial revolution got going, there was a need for more educated people, both in the trades, as well as in the head-office, not to mention the need for people to go off and attend to matters in India. Nonetheless, it was only in 1960 that Oxford set aside the requirement for students to study Latin.

So many Oxford grads have entered high levels of government that the simple expression *Oxford* implies the British Establishment. It is necessary to mention Cambridge in a discussion of Oxford. Between the two, many of England's best and brightest have gone on to enter government, as well as the arts and the sciences. Cambridge leans more to science, and Oxford is the more liberal of the two.

The town is not a large one, but growing fast and has the distinction of being the most demographically diverse in the kingdom, but this is a function of its student body. Its industry is similarly influenced by the university, with publishing, information technology, and scientific & business research.

* Oxford is not a single university, but rather a collection of colleges each with their own rules and classes that often duplicate one another, but it seems to work out for them.

The letter p -π- is a handy thing when dealing with circles, circumferences, and diameters and all, but for the Germanic Angle Saxons, the letter *f* was the way to go. Words beginning with *p* are foreign and almost entirely French, Latin, Greek, or maybe a little Slavic. *P* also used to abbreviate pence, (a penny), back when a penny was real money. When a Yank would say *50 cents*, a Brit would say *50 Pee.*

PA   -personal assistant. What yanks used to call a secretary is now an administrative aid / assistant, or simply an *admin.*

packet -a ship traveling a regular route and originally carrying the mail.

pack drill   -punishment in the army. The guy had to do regular drill wearing a full pack or one filled with rocks.

packed-up -broken down as in a packed-up machine.

Paddington / Paddington Station   A neighborhood in northern London and a railroad & canal hub back in the day. Now it is a lower middle class neighborhood, but is undergoing gentrification with artists and hip young computer nerds.

Paddy   -mildly derisive nickname for the Irish -from the name *Padraic.*

padre   There is no such clergy in England, but it has come to be a military term for any sort of chaplain.

page   -originally a knight's servant and maybe a young knight in training. He was often the son of a noble or some other rich guy who sent him off to the castle at the age of seven to learn what passed for manners of the day. He would act as a minor but elevated servant while doing so. The next step up at age fourteen was to become a full-time knight's servant, a **squire.** After the middle ages, a page or page-boy became what would be to modern mind, a messenger or go-for.

page three   In the 1970's the tabloid paper *The Sun*, used page three for pictures of healthy young women who had somehow misplaced their tops. These women had much in common with Hugh Hefner's centerfold girls regarding their endowments and were called the *page-three-girls*.

paint makers   -made paint. Not surprising perhaps, but it was only in 1866 that two chaps by the names of Sherwin and Williams hit on the crazy idea of premixing paint and selling it in cans. Up until then, if you hired someone to paint your house, he would show up in a horse-cart with bags of colorful powder, (dirt), some turpentine, and linseed oil. He then mixed whatever color you wanted provided you wanted an earth-tone.

pajamas/ pyjamas   -American pajamas, but more. They have always been a loose comfortable garment from India no less, but worn by Muslims rather than Hindus. During the Blitz, men and women wore pajamas not only for slouching around on weekends, but also to bed because they might be rousted out of bed in the middle of the night if the Germans were bombing the area.

Paki   -an old-fashioned word for someone from Pakistan. In general, words like *Paki, Wog,* and the n-word for African American, would horrify an American, but they are not as fraught in England, but this is changing.

pale   -a wall of sharpened stakes quickly erected around English colonies during the various invasions of Ireland. *Beyond the Pale* means out there where things are uncivilized.

pancake   There is no such thing as what an American thinks of as a pancake in England. What they call a pancake, a Yank would call a crepe and their flapjacks are robust things made from sugar, butter, and oats.

pants   -not what you think, pants in Britain are underpants. They wear trousers. When they say *pants,* it is mildly naughty.

paper makers   Go back to about 1490 and paper was an expensive commodity, but no one could read anyway, so the cost was no big deal. In the 17th century, rag pickers would sort all manner of trash into big vats and whale the tar out of it till it could be made into paper. It was not until the 19th century that they hit on the idea of making it from wood waste and by then it became capitol intensive and no longer a craft. Before paper, if it was important enough to be written down, you would get yourself a...

parchment maker   -part of the paper-making industry, but parchment was made by carefully slicing off the top layer of sheep-skin. (The bottom layer became chamois, the stuff they used for gloves. Today, car freaks use chamois to dry their cars.) Much after the 17th century, parchment was used only for certificates and deeds.

parade -both the street show with marching bands & floats, as well as what Americans would call a pedestrian mall.

paraffin -kerosene. Liquid paraffin is mineral oil and is used as a laxative

parish Originally the community surrounding a single Catholic church and its priest was a parish. (A cathedral was the hang-out of a bishop.) As the Catholic church came to share things with the Protestants, the Church of England followed these divisions and after the *Civil War* the civil or non-secular government worked within these boundaries, but with the comings and goings of the Catholics and Protestants, the borders were drawn and redrawn to a fair-thee-well. In 1888, they tidied things up and did *counties*. Until then, parishes were more than a town, but less than an American county. After that, the *administrative* parish became the lowest level of civil authority that mostly just looked after the poor. see *divisions* of England.

parish school During the 1700s and 1800's the parish schools were usually (but not always) taught by the church. They taught the local kids a little math as well as reading and writing, but the reading was to be done in the bible. They were limited to the local kids and hence were called *private schools*. *Public schools* on the other hand were open to anyone whose father could afford the tuition.

parish pump -gossip gathered while getting water from the parish well.

park -both what Americans would think a park ought to be, but also a wild area where the noble's deer were available for hunting and where only the nobleman could hunt them. see *poach / poacher*

Park Lane -terribly toney road along *Hyde Park*. The authors who have set scenes on Park Lane include Arthur Conan Doyle, (Sherlock Holmes) Agatha Christy (Hercule Poirot), John Galsworthy (various Forsytes), and many more, not to neglect the game of *Monopoly.*

parlor -originally a monk's visiting room, then a small room off to the side of the medieval great hall, then a private room for the family, then it turned into a formal place to receive guests. In this last iteration, the family, or the children anyway, did not otherwise enter. In the modern American home, the parlor would be the *front room* and *familyroom* would be where the family hung out and watched television. the It's all very complicated with respect to class and history. see *homes*

parson -originally a (Catholic) parish priest, and later a rather generic and sometimes snotty term for any clergyman. A more formal address would also be more specific like *vicar* or *rector*. A parson's home is a *parsonage.*

party-piece From the time before TV, people entertained themselves at parties. Someone's party-piece in England would be their *shtick,* or their *thing* in America.

pastie / pasty / Cornish pastie -a meat pie made with game. In time past, they were made with partridge, pheasant, venison and / or hare. Now they are usually beef, but the fancy ones may have rabbit, venison, or pigeon.

Cornish Pastie:

Pastry:
2+	cups flour
¼	teaspoon salt
1	teaspoon baking powder
½	cup butter, chilled and diced*
½	cup ice water

Filling:
1+	pound roast
1	onion
2	potatoes
2	carrots
½	teaspoon salt
½	teaspoon black pepper (more spices for the American palate might be good)

1. Cut the butter &/or lard into the flour, salt, and baking powder. Add the water and bring it all together till it just makes big crumbs. Add the extra flour as necessary.
2. Wrap the dough tightly in plastic wrap and refrigerate.
3. Dice & boil the carrots and potatoes for 5 or 10 minutes -depending on how tender you want them. Rinse, drain, and set aside.
4. Dice the meat and season it. (If you have an American palate -or like Mexican food- you will probably want more spices than just pepper.) Set aside.
5. Roll the pastry out to about ¼" thick. Cut it into 6 circles about 6" in diameter. Do not stretch the dough.
6. Combine the vegetables with the meat. Cover half of each circle -leaving an edge for gluing it all together. Fold it over, wet the edges, and press them together with the tines of a fork.
7. Put them on a baking dish, cut a steam slit in the top, brush with milk.
8. Bake at 350° for 45 - 50 minutes.
9. If you find yourself down in a mine, reheat your pastie on your shovel over the flame from your miner's lantern.

* For real authentic Cornish pasties, use all lard. Or split the difference and go 50 / 50 butter and lard.

patience -America's solitaire. English *solitaire* is played with marbles.

paviours   -were pavers, but not just of roads, but floors as well. Roadways might be cobbled with stones, (having nothing to do with the shoe repairing cobbler), but when folks could afford something nicer than hard-packed earth bound with ox-blood, there were floors covered with flagstone, tiles, and even marble.

Pax Britannia   From the end of the Napoleonic Wars in 1815 until the beginning of WWI in 1914, the world was relatively calm and it was all the fault of the British, hence the Pax Britannica or the *Peace of the British*.

PAYE   -pay as you earn. It's withholding for income tax and national health insurance.

pay packet   -a little envelope with cash and a slip noting deductions etc. Many English workers do not have checking accounts and so receive their pay in cash. As late as 1989, unions have fought any move toward pay checks. This practice is slowly changing, particularly among the salaried workers, but the English *Post Office* is still the common way for bills to be paid and paid with cash. see *banks*

PC   -*Privy Council* of the United Kingdom

pea   THE most important vegetable in England. Eaten all the time despite the availability of various other vegetables frozen, canned, or fresh. *Mushy peas* are boiled with baking soda and then pureed and to make extra sure they have no texture whatsoever *Peas porridge hot* from the nursery rhyme is just this, but it is likely only a Brit could enjoy peas porridge cold.

pea soup   A mixture of very dense fog and pollution that is/was actually yellow colored. The first reference to pea soup fog shows up in 1820. People actually died of various lung diseases.

peat   -partially decayed vegetable matter. Bury it deep, give it a few million years to think about it, and it becomes coal. Bury it even deeper, give it even more time, and it becomes oil. But just as it is, it can be dug up and put in your garden to make the turnips grow nicely, or dried and used as fuel. It was used as fuel in Ireland, and is still burned to dry malted grains for scotch whiskey in Scotland.

pecker   -as in *keep your pecker up.* Not as dirty as it would be in America. In England, a pecker is a bird's beak. Best to keep it up when one hits a bad patch.
peckish -a little hungry

peeler -a policeman, bobby, or constable.

peer (as an individual)   Given the Brit's preoccupation with keeping people in their places or at least knowing who is better than who (whom?), a Peer of the Realm is an equal or a peer to the entire kingdom. This is to say that the proper order of the peerage is–and will ever be–first king, duke, then marques, earls, viscounts, and finally, mere barons. Knights do NOT make the cut.

Peerage, English (as a group)   Basically, rich people. The Peerage of England was replaced by the Peerage of Great Britain in 1707 with the Act of Union with Scotland. (Ireland and Whales were still out in the cold.) Up until 1899 and the House of Lords Act, all peers could sit in the ***House of Lords***. (Women peers were admitted to this club only in 1963.)

These positions are hereditary; the oldest kid got the title. Baronets are hereditary, but not peers. Knights, Dames, Ladies etc. don't rate. These peerages come from long ago and have confusing histories that are made all the more so by different rules between England, Scotland, and Wales.

peg -either a clothespin or coat hook on the wall

Pembrokeshire   -a vacation spot on the south coast of Wales. This county is surrounded on three sides by the Irish Sea and has among the most beautiful coastlines in the UK. There are lots of birds, marshes, and environmental considerations and conservation. Its very oldest history was actually more Irish that English–until the Romans came.

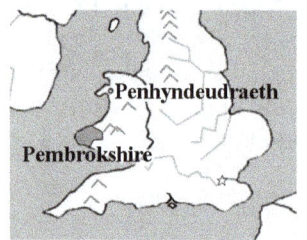

Today there is a little agriculture and fishing to round out tourism. It's not quite the same thing as Penrhyndeudraeth*, but similar. The latter is a beautiful Welsh seaside resort to the north just dripping Victorian / Italianate Architecture and is where they filmed the 60's classic spy television drama *The Prisoner.*

* Yes -that's a real word. See ***Wales*** for more on the Welsh fondness for impossibly long strings of letters.

Penal Colonies   America was a fine penal colony for the English for a long time. Some 50,000 convicts went to the Chesapeake Colonies. Georgia, for example, was settled by a 17th century entrepreneurs who bought wholesale lots of people out of debtor's prison and shipped them off to Georgia. These were not so much father stabbers and mother rapists, just shmoes who couldn't pay off the 17th century equivalent of 20th century credit cards. But not just debtors, also Scots and Irish or pretty much anyone undesirable in the eyes of the English at various times in history.

When America became a unsuitable for English exports after 1776, they turned to Australia and added advocates of Irish Home Rule and Labor Unionists to the list of folks to be gotten get rid of. Other English vacation spots for the undesirables include Bermuda, Singapore, a little island in Indonesia, and another one off the coast of India.

pence   -2 1/2 p or the plural of penny. see ***money***

Pennines / Pennine Hills   The
mountains running up the center of northern
England are also considered another one of the
single most scenic part of England. The highest
one is Cross Fell at 2930 feet above sea level.
Only seven other mountains make it over 2000
feet in elevation in England.

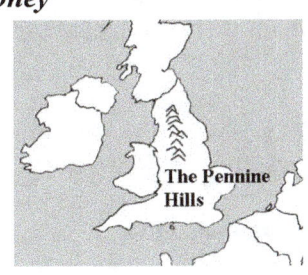

penny-farthing   The high wheel bicycle
popular in England from about 1869 till 1880 when
the *safety bicycle* was introduced. (If, for some
unfortunate reason, the big front wheel stopped
turning, inertia and physics tossed the rider over the
handlebars and onto his head rather violently. This
gives the expression *header* for a bad forward fall.)

The penny-farthing had a short life but is very iconic of the Victorian era.
Also, something done in a *penny farthing* manner was something done in a
sloppy way.

pension   -much like America's social security but with some funding
differences. It is arguably more soundly financed than FICA.
pensioner -either a retiree or a student who pays his own way

pepper-pot   -pepper shaker
pepper rent   -rent so low that it could be paid with a single pepper corn.

Pepys, Samuel *(*1633–1702)   Pepys was a ***MP*** and administrator in the
Royal Navy, but he is best known for an extensive diary he kept from 1690 to
1699. His work has been a valuable primary source for ***Restoration*** history
when it was first published about a hundred years after he died. He covered
the ***Great Fire***, the plague, a couple of wars, and some gossip including vivid
details of his own extra-marital dalliances.

perambulator -a baby carriage or stroller

perishing   -general purpose modifier for very or complete, i.e., it's
perishing hot, or someone is *a perishing wanker.*

periwinkle   a tiny blue flower, or small sea snails / whelks that are not
eaten much anymore. As a verb, to *winkle out* something would be to pull it
out as if pulling a periwinkle out of its shell.

Permanent Secretary / Undersecretary
Because the ministers / secretaries of the English government come and go
with elections, the actual experts in matters of state, foreign relations,

economics etc., are the under-secretaries. They are presumed to be apolitical and advise their elected boss who sets broad policy. They also tend to the annoying day-to-day details of government.

perry -cider made from pears rather than apples. One variety is made with honey and is said to lead to epic hangovers when enjoyed too much.

petrol -gasoline

Petticoat Lane   -the nick-name for a market in Middlesex Street in east London that dealt in used clothes going back to Shakespeare's time. It is held only on Sundays because it was in a largely Jewish neighborhood. After about 1880 Jewish immigrants from Eastern Europe settled in the area and were active in the garment industry.   The Christians tried to shut it down from time to time up until 1936. Today it's a tourist place.

phaeton   -light four wheeled carriage with an open top pulled by one or more often two horses. All carriages were owned by rich people during the Regency era and Jane Austen's crowd favored this sort of carriage for purposes of seeing and more importantly, being seen. It is indeed as ridiculously high as it is shown because it lifted the passengers high above the hoi-polloi and protected their pretty frocks form mud. A woman needed a step ladder and footman to get in and out.

Piccadilly Circus   No clowns or elephants, a *circus* is a circle, or an American round-about or traffic circle. Piccadilly Circus sits in London's West End and is the middle of shopping, theater, and nightlife. It is also lit up even more than New York's Times Square, and is perhaps even more tasteless. Even so, the Brits are terribly fond of it as the symbol of all things exciting and trendy. Its name comes from a successful tailor who made *piccadills* or fancy collars in 1692.

Picts   -a subset of the Celts living in Northern Scotland from well before the Romans came. They survived on to the early medieval era. Much of what is known about them comes from Roman writing and their beautiful and intricate stone carvings.

pie   -a pastry usually filled with meat. Such a pastry eaten for desert is called either a *flan* which is filled with custard-like goo, or a *tart* which is filled with fruit.

piece -a vulgar but shorter equivalent to the American *piece of a__*.

pilchard -sardines but a little bit larger than what Americans eat out of cans.

Pilgrims Way   -a road running from Winchester to Canterbury. While it shows up in Chaucer's writing, it is not clear exactly where it was. ***The Pilgrims*** in question were on their way to get some miracles from ***Thomas Becket's*** tomb.

pillar box   -a red five foot tall mail box that goes back to about 1850.

pinafore / pinny   -a 19th century smock-like garment pinned over a little girl's dress to keep it from getting dirty. Later a pinafore came to refer to what an American might call an apron. Its use in the Gilbert & Sullivan's comic opera *The HMS Pinafore* is for comedy and satire.

pinchbeck   -fake gold showing up on the uniforms of poor naval officers needing to look the part. It's also synonymous with cheap.

pint   -a measure, usually of beer, of 20 ounces rather than the American 16-ounce pint.

pip   -fruit seeds. Consider Sherlock Holmes's case involving *Five Orange Pips*. A pip may also be the little metal do-dads worn on the epaulettes of British officers higher than a Lieutenant Colonel. The more pips, the higher the rank. The spots on dice are also called pips.
pip emma -military-speak for PM. *Ack emma* is AM.

Pipemakers   -not for plumbing, but smoking. Pipes and   *churchwardens* (long thin pipes)*,* were made of fired clay and somewhat disposable, or as disposable as anything was back in the day. ***James I*** hated smoking and taxed tobacco heavily. Smuggling sought to fill demand until about 1750 when the tax was lifted.   Pipe smoking took off about then, but started downhill in the 18th century when snuff became popular, and in the middle of the 19th century cigarettes and briar pipes killed off the whole ceramic pipe thing. Given that pipe makers put their names and dates on these pipes, and given further that they were more or less disposable, and given finally that fired ceramic survives being buried for a long <u>long</u> time, pipes are very useful to the anthropological / historical crowd given to digging about in old ***tips***,

pirate stations   When rock and roll arrived in England from America (and before going back the other direction with the ***British Invasion***) the BBC didn't respond to the demand from young people for this sort of music, so a number of unlicensed radio broadcasters set up shop on ships anchored close off shore.

pish   -nonsense. *Pish-posh* or *pish and toss* are more of the same and often dismissive. The expression is used by those of a lower class trying not to sound vulgar.

piss   Yes, what Yanks think it means, but going back to Shakespeare's day when it wasn't vulgar. It's a very useful if only mildly vulgar word today in England. *Pissed* is drunk and a *piss-up* is an occasion of heavy drinking. *Piss off* means to leave quickly and a *pissing-while* is brief time. *Pissed on from a great height* variously means either someone who is despicable and should be pissed on, or being reprimanded from a very high rank, or trying to fight city hall, (per American parlance), and utterly loosing. *Piss-a-beds* are dandelions.

plaid   -does not refer to the pattern, technically, that's a tartan. A plaid is a large bit of wool cloth worn over the shoulder and wrapped around the waist. See **kilt**

plaster / sticking plaster -an adhesive band-aid.

platoon   -an army unit consisting of three **sections**. Four platoons make a **company**. Platoons are usually commanded by a lieutenant. see **army**

plimsoll(s)   -a shoe with a rubber bottom and a canvas top. It's a tennis shoe. They are so named because they are thought to look a little like a...
Plimsoll line   In 1872, British MP Samuel Plimsoll devised a law requiring ships to have a mark on their hulls that indicated the greatest depth to which they could be safely loaded. Good ideal for shipping, but it is a little vague as to how the symbol resembles a tennis shoe.

Plough / Plow   The constellation that is so clearly the *Big Dipper* to Americans is equally clearly a plow to the English. The Greeks thought it was a bear–a big bear–*Ursa Major.*

plowman's lunch -bread, cheese, and often beer.

plugs / points / power points   The English were slow to adopt and standardize that new-fangled electricity stuff and so they use a variety of different plugs or what Yanks would think of as outlets. Appliances are therefor usually sold with bare wires to be attached into whatever plug fits. Of greater importance to Americans who might plan to visit England with their own electrical toys, is the fact the electricity coming out of the walls is 240 volts vs. America's 110 to 120 volts.

plus-fours   What Americans would call knickers, but

having another four inches below the knees.

Plymouth   Literally the mouth of the River Plym, and a very historically important harbor. It was the embarkation point for many ships going off to the colonies, the Mayflower being the first and perhaps the most important, at least to the Yanks. Much of its shipping activity was commercial but it also has a Royal Naval shipbuilding facility. (The Royal Navy did most of its non-building thing in Portsmouth to the east.) It was heavily bombed during WWII but nonetheless, it served as an embarkation for the D-Day invasion.

Today, Plymouth is home to about a quarter million *Plymothians* (!?!), and remains an important harbor with the usual blended economy of administration, health, education, engineering, and military, but military jobs in Plymouth have been decreasing of late. They also make gin, rnd have been doing so since 1793.

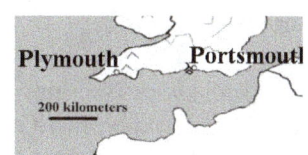

poach / poacher   After the ***Enclosure Acts***, it got a little harder for everyman to feed his family after Lord Whomever claimed all the land and all the game for himself. Snaring a rabbit for the stew pot would get a man ***transported***. Rather a nasty thing all around and the sadistic game-keepers you find in some writing from the 18th and 19th century are not exaggerations.

police   It depended on how large the community was, but what we might think of as policing activities were done by the ***beadles*** in the earliest times. Up until the Civil War and Protestant Reformation, the church took it upon itself to put people in the ***stocks***, pillory, or lock-up if the church felt

they needed it. The Parish Constables was appointed a year at a time and did the dirty work in these cases. Again, it depended on the size of the community, but a Petty Constable would enforce manorial law. These were laws that derived from the rich guy who was Lord of the Manor. Justices of the Peace and / or the Chief Constable might have larger duties including what we might think of as being much like today's police duties. These were things like keeping things calm down at the taverns and ale houses, as well as running off vagrants, dragging in unwilling jurors, drunks, & prostitutes, chasing down the fathers of bastards, and so forth. Certain civil matters fell to them as well, like collecting taxes, organizing elections, raising the local militia, finding places to sleep for any soldiers who happened to be marching thru, keeping track of weights and measures, raising the local militia, and occasionally even sorting out commercial conflicts.

In 1749, a Justice of the Peace and *MP* Robert Peel set up a small detective force to combat the general lawlessness of London. In 1812 the Luddite uprising got so out of hand that it prompted the crown to send out the army. This seemed a little bit of an overkill so there began to develope the idea of something more intimidating than a one-man Justice of the Peace and but less so than a Division of His Majesty's Calvary. After 1829, an act of Parliament created what we might think of as the beginnings of a modern police force with constables who carried a truncheon, (club), and whistle. They had to be at least 5'7" tall, under 35 years of age, literate, and of good reputation. But they worked only in London. They were initially resented by the commoners as traitors to their class. (The high collars on their uniforms were protection against garroting.)   Within a few years, they were thought of as friendly but firm disciplinarians and were nick-named *Bobbi*es after Robert (Bobby) Peel.

Between 1835 and 1856 various laws were passed to duplicate London's Bobbies outside of London. There were also some specialized police forces like the Marine Police who protected property on the River Thames, Railway Police who covered all England's railways as well as the London Underground, and dockyard light-rails. There was also a separate Royal Military Police. Women joined the Bobbies in 1919, but could not arrest anyone till 1923.

American readers, particularly those that read crime stories and most particularly Sherlock Holmes, will bump into various of England's constabulary. They are a little different from the American police force and rank as follows:

Constable PC, (Police Constable) or briefly WPC, (Woman Police Constable) after women entered the police force but in the 70's it was decided that the W was not PC (i.e., America's *Politically Correct*), so both genders are now just PCs.

Sergeant

Inspector The following are what Americans would call plain clothes.

Chief Inspector

Superintendent

Chief Superintendent

Commander From here on, these positions are more political than as otherwise.

Deputy Assistant Commissioner

Assistant Commissioner

Deputy Commissioner

Commissioner Reports to the mayor.

A final matter of trivia -the checkerboard design on their hats is called a *Sillitoe Tartan* from Scotland. A couple of cities in America use the same design to distinguish the police from security guards who had tried to duplicate the police uniforms. see **Scotland Yard**

Political Parties   England's political parties are another subject of surpassing importance to English writers and American readers, but also a subject of equally vast confusion. America has had a couple hundred years to argue about which side of the aisle was right in its thinking and which side was made entirely out of self-serving dunderheads. England has had considerably longer to sort it out and it seems they are still at it. A consideration of history might help the Yank get a grip on it, if only a little.

The ***English Civil War*** might be as good a place to start as any, but the two sides were by no means political parties. They were opposite sides of a war that killed almost 200,000 people. It was between the Catholics who supported the pope & the monarchy, and the Protestants who felt the Parliament was the way to go & felt the pope had to go. This is of course an oversimplification, but let's say the Catholics (nick named 'Cavaliers' because they dressed flamboyantly), were in favor of things staying the way they were on the conservative side of the aisle. The Protestants were called *Round-heads* because they cut their hair short and dressed in somber black. They wanted things to change in a progressive direction.

With this as a starting point, the following will help the American reader have a better idea of whom the author was suggesting was right thinking and who was an utter dunder-head.

Dates	Left Leaning "Liberal"	Right Leaning "Conservative"
Roman Occupation AD 43 - 410	Nope. No political parties then. The Romans on top and the locals on the bottom. Julius Caesar topped off his Gallic Wars with a swing thru Britannia between 55 and 54 BC.	
Between the Romans and the Franks	Because politics–such as it was back then–was essentially about issues only the aristocracy cared about, alliances were formed and dissolved to serve the various goals of individual rich people.	
Norman Conquest / Occupa-tion 1055 - 1204	It was only slightly more complicated now. We have about 8000 the Normans (French) displacing the Anglo-Saxon rich guys. Various revolts, wars, and such, but for the little guy, not much changed. Nor was there much of what we would think of as political polarity.	
1215	The English nobility force King John to sign the ***Magna Carta***	
1265	England has the world's first Parliament meeting. Still had to do with matters only the rich guys cared about.	
1642 - 1651	English Civil War: Now we see some real division of opinion -still rich people having the opinions and the little guy playing the role of canon fodder, but it's a start.	
	Protestants Parliamentarians	Catholics Royalists
1680 - 1850	1678 - 1681 The Exclusion Crisis leads to ***Whigs*** and ***Tories.*** Very confusing and religious. Charles II was restored to his executed father's throne, (see ***Charles I, & Cromwell***), but his uncle James, Duke of York who was a Catholic and could'a should'a might'a been the king. This did not sit well	

	with the Protestants who weren't too enthused with ANY sort of a king to being with, so they exclude him. This gives us the...

	Whigs: Protestants -supported constitutional monarchy	**Tories**: Catholic -supported the Stuart kings and absolute monarchy

	American Revolution 1776 - 1781: Americans tend to forget that some good people were not enthused about splitting from England. The first 'American' political divisions might be said to be the Loyalists (loyal to the king and to England) and the Patriots in favor of revolution.
	The Whigs and Tories were still not so much political parties as we might think of them today, but rather loose alliance of interest.

1850 - 1900	**Liberals** (evolved from the Whigs)		Conservatives -evolved from the Tories -haven't change or evolved as much as the liberals - the majority in His / Her Majesty's Government for 57 years of the 20th century.
At long last, we see some concern for the little guy. At least the little guys in a labor union.			
1900 - 1920	(regular) Liberals	Liberal Unionists -closer to the conservat- ives	
1920 - 1939's	Labor Party -the Anti-Tories -labor movement, labor unions, and socialism		
1929 - 2010 (?)	From somewhat before WW II and on to 2010, things sloshed back and forth between Labor and Conservative Parties. (see *Churchill, Winston*)		
2010 - ???	No single party could claim a majority, so this becomes the age of *Coalitions*. Some of the various parties that hooked together to form these coalitions, include: Liberal Democrats: -third largest party until 2015. Scottish National Party -third largest party in terms of seats. United Kingdom Independent Party (UKIP) -third largest in terms of votes		

poll tax   According to Parliament, it wasn't really a poll tax, but a local per-head community tax to augment the *rating system* or what Americans would think of as property tax. It got its start started in 1990, was immediately wildly unpopular, and was replaced by the Council Tax in 1993 which adjusted (upward) property tax. see ***inland revenue***

pommy   Australian slang for a Brit, perhaps one just a little bit on the feminine side. (Aussies call Americans 'Yanks' and by all accounts, quite like Yanks.)

poof / poofter -homosexual. The thoroughly offensive American expression 'faggot' in England refers to either a bundle of wood or a cigarette in England, but poof or poofter is at least as offensive in England as *fag* is in America.

pool -an informal lottery where the bettors pool their money in anticipation of the outcome of usually some sporting event. The idea of deliberately splashing around in a big pool of water for fun has never caught on in England.

Poor Laws To the credit of the Brits, the notion that government ought to do something about the poor arose sooner there than in most of the rest of Europe. It goes back to 1536 under Elizabeth. In 1834, they tightened things up in order not to encourage indolence and laziness. They did this so well, that the workhouses that were a part of relief were so miserable and prison-like that some of the poor preferred the gutter and starvation. The modern system of welfare started after WWII and set aside the Poor Laws.

pop -as in *pop in*
in pop -in hock
poppers -party favors / crackers, or clothing snaps
poppet -doll or a cute small child
pop-socks Nylon stocking worn under slacks. The modern implication being that that a woman would never wear pop-socks if she expected to be in a romantic situation before she could remove them in favor of something less old-lady-like.

porridge -hot cereal and usually a breakfast food. In the old days, it might have been all there was to eat. Oatmeal is one example of porridge, but any grain can be boiled into porridge, for example cream-of-wheat, grits, rice, or even peas. During comparatively good times in the otherwise bad times of the dark ages, porridge might have a bite or two of meat.

Today 'porridge' is what is given to babies when they start eating solid (mushy) food and in this use of the word, it might be made from things other than grain.

porters -show up in a lot of English stories, but not all were simple carriers of any old stuff. As far back as 1604, it was a matter of guilds that defined who got to carry what. Alien porters dealt with imports and collected duties on these goods. Billingsgate porters had a monopoly on schlepping corn, (wheat), coal, salt and a few other commodities. Wine porters carried only wine, and street porters carried goods to and from the waterfront. Tackle House porters were the first crowd licensed to haul almost whatever they wanted and only in the 19th and 20th century. Today a porter carries luggage around train stations, airports, or in the better hotels.

portion   The eldest son was given the bulk of the estate, but younger son might inherit a much smaller ***portion***. Daughters were also given a portion but in the form of a dowry and probably before dad died.

Portsmouth   The port where ***Henry VIII***
built his navy; perhaps his greatest contribution
to the kingdom and England's first
'professional' navy. Today, Portsmouth IS the

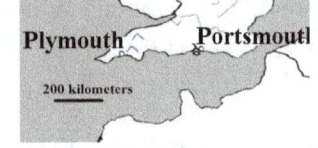

British Navy. Here we find Nelson's flagship the HMS Victory and the *Mary Rose*, hauled off the bottom in 1982 and restores from where she sank in 1543.

Henry built the worlds first dry-dock in Portsmouth. It was the world's most fortified city from the 1700's onward. It had the world's first mass production line and was the world's most industrialized city for most of the 1800's. It was both heavily bombed during WWII and an important embarkation point for the D-Day Invasion. It has greater population density than London today, and is actually an island. The University of Portsmouth is among the best modern universities in the world.

Shipping and the Royal Navy are unquestionably the cornerstones of the city's economy, but it is also the home to several multinational corporation. As far as literature goes, any Napoleonic War story involving the navy inevitably has one or more scenes in Portsmouth, as do various crime stories. Charles Dickens was born here in 1812,

POS   Permanent Under Secretary

Posh, posh-boy   -elegant, refined, and a little derisive description of the swells. There is the explanation, particularly in ***CANOE***, that POSH stands for *Portside Out, Starboard Home* because in the days of Empire when people going to and from India by ship. The left (port) side of the ship was cooler than the right (starboard), and vice versa on the way back to England. It's a lovely story. It's also untrue; there's not a shred of real evidence.

post -the mail
to post -to mail
post code -zip code
postman -mail man
postal order -money order

Post Office   While the post is more efficient in England than mail is in America, (England is much smaller after all), this business of getting mail twice in one day is largely past, but packages come via a separate delivery so it might seem that way. Still, the English Post Office is considerably more than a place to stand in line for inordinate stretches of time like it is in America. The English Post Office goes back to 1635 and has taken on various tasks including:

1780	-established regular carriage routes that carried both mail and passengers.
1840	-built the first 'modern' postal system with the help of the rail roads and a fixed rate of an 1d self-adhesive stamp for all letters.
1861	-opened the Post Office Savings Bank.
1868	-acquired private telegraph companies and was responsible for all telegraphy by 1870.
1878	-began telephone services.
1880	-sold government bonds.
1904	-controlled radio broadcasting until 1922 when the BBC was formed and took over.
1960's	-offered general banking services thru the National *Giro* for the working man.

Potato   -arrived in England from South America sometime between 1588 and 1593. It was more popular in Ireland for reasons having to do more with being able to get enough to eat than taste, but they were big in England too. Potatoes have long been served almost every day either fried as chips or mashed. The popular notion that the were brought to England by either Sir Francis Drake, or Sir Walter Raleigh doesn't hold up. It is more likely they got to England from Spain or even Amsterdam. see *food*

potato famine   While it is called the Irish potato famine, it actually hit Germany with similar, but less dramatic results. The Irish were almost entirely dependent on the potato for food. Between 1845 & 1852 about a million people died and another million left Ireland, usually to America. see *food*

potted -in a can, (food), or a growing in a container, (a plant).
potter   -as in *pottering about*. Like American *puttering around* is doing nothing of compelling importance.
potty   -a little nuts, but if you are rich you are just eccentric.

pound   -a *Pound Sterling* was never an actual pound of silver, but rather 240 old silver coins. A transaction large enough to need pounds of silver was usually done in gold *sovereigns*. see *money*

prang -a crash -usually in a car.

pram / perambulator -a baby carriage

prat   -originally the bottom -hence *pratfall*. Later a prat came to mean someone who was an annoying ass.

prefect -someone, usually an older student, in charge of maintaining discipline in a public school.

Prefect was a popular low-priced family car made by Ford from 1946 till 1961. It's also the name of a wonderful character from the science fiction trilogy <u>The Hitchhikers Guide to the Galaxy</u> who came to earth and mistook the car name "Ford Prefect" for a common name for people.

prefects / prefectures   This sort of geographic division occurs in many part of the world particularly in Roman Colonies and Asia. Fortunately, for the American reader, its use in England is probably related to church matters. In general, a religion's *territory* may be divided into districts, smaller parishes, and the smallest division, prefects.

prelate   a bishop or other high-ranking clergy. It may refer to a person, or an office, (the prelature) or the territory which a given prelate has jurisdiction. Keep in mind that as the English were sorting out the whole Catholic / Protestant kafuffle, Parliament had a whole compliment of prelates, bishops, and arch-bishops. The ***House of Lords*** still does.

prep school   -a public school charging a fee for boys from the age of about eight to twelve to prepare them for admission to a public boarding school so beloved by the British aristocracy and writers, and so hated by students.

Presbyterian   -originally a non-conformist and somewhat Calvinistic splinter of the Church of England. It tended to be more popular among the wealthy and Scottish. It has been humorously called 'Catholicism Lite' and not without good reason.

press gang   The Royal Navy needed men and because there was no draft, they simply sent out gangs of thugs to go out and kidnap whatever men they could find. They would then be dragged back to the ship where they were virtual prisoners until the ship sailed off to war. The poor guy had no choice but to learn to be a sailor, and if he were slow in learning, the cat-of-nine tails, (the lash), would hurry him along. It was a brutal practice that lead to the mutiny of 1797. A similar practice that involved taking American sailors off American merchantmen lead to the War of 1812 which was sort of the American Revolution, Mark II.

pretender / pretender to the throne   -someone claiming a throne or other powerful position occupied by another. Given the confusing laws of succession regarding the throne and given further the confusion surrounding, for example, ***Henry VIII*** and his various wives and children, there have been many instances of pretenders in English history. see ***Bonnie Prince Charles***

primary school   -basic tax supported schools for students from about age five to eleven. These are roughly equivalent to American elementary schools.

Primate   -the most senior bishop or archbishop in one of England's Anglican Church Provinces. A Catholic Primate is entirely honorific.

Prime Minster   -like America's president, but with some exceptions. He, (or she, Margaret Thatcher was the PM from 1979 to 1991), is selected by the members of Parliament's majority party.   Up until about 1700, the king's ministers ran the tedious parts of government leaving the king free to start wars and get venereal diseases. Parliament was increasingly important and had a hand in whom the king could appoint to the various ministries. The First Lord of the Treasuries evolved into the Prime Minister about 1800. see ***Parliament, government*** and ***Ministry***

prince   -the son or sons of the monarch, but only the immediate sons. The title is not inheritable. This means that while Prince Charles is prince, his sons will only be princes once he becomes king. The same applies rule applies to princesses.

Prince Consort   -the spouse of the ruling queen, but only ***Victoria***'s Albert was consort. ***Elizabeth II***'s husband is the Duke of Edinburgh.

Prince of Wales   -he was Prince Charles till the Queen died; now he's the King. Prince William is the new heir apparent to the throne. NOTE: There are very confusing rules surrounding princes and princesses, but technically only the immediate heir apparent is the real 'prince' -popular press to the contrary None but the Brits understand them and even then, only the older ones.

prison   The brutality of the old days is well illustrated by the English prisons. Bad people–or those whom the elite viewed as bad–were quickly tried and hanged so a stay in prison was apt to be pretty brief. People who were somewhat less undesirable, were transported. They were shipped off the various colonies. Debtor prisoners, however, kept people locked-up for as long as it took to get the debts paid off. Throughout, they were private businesses wherein guards were largely paid by bribes or tips. There was some reform in the early 1800's with fewer hangings and less transporting, but prisons were still private or run by the local council. In 1877 the crown got involved and things slowly came to look a little like they do today.

private   -much the same meanings as in America, particularly in the army, but with a few extra meanings. A *private gentleman* has no titles (and the Brits are pretty keen on handing out titles, orders, and honorifics), *private member* is a member of the ***House of Commons*** who is not a part of any ***ministry*** and is likely a ***back-bencher***. A *private trader* would be a closely held corporation or sole-practitioner in America, and a ***private school*** is more like an American public school.

private school   Schools that limited enrollment to local, (and often working class), students. see *schools*

privatization   After being frightened by the General Strike in 1926, the Brits began carefully nationalizing important industries, and kicked it into high gear after WW II by taking over the Bank of England, electricity, coal, the rails, iron & steel, in short, all the heavy industries. During Margaret Thatcher's term in the 80's, many of these industries were returned to private ownership but with publicly held shares.

privy   -from the French *prive* -meaning private. The monarch's *Privy Council* was his inner circle of advisers who would advise him or her in the *Privy Chamber.* As the monarchy became increasingly ceremonial, and the role of the ***Prime Minister*** increased, the role of advising fell to the Cabinet.

It was only about the 19th century that the privy came to mean the outhouse in the back yard. Later when plumbing moved inside, the name stuck but *privy* is now a little old fashioned. The American word *bathroom* in England refers to a room with a bathtub or shower, that may or may not have a toilet, so if there is a degree of urgency, it is best to ask for the biffy, the loo, the head, or simply, the toilet.

Privy Council   Originally, they advised the monarch, but with the ascendency of ***Parliament*** and its use of ***Cabinet*** for advice and administrative chores, the Privy Council has become largely ceremonial. The Privy Purse is the monarch's allowance from Parliament, and the Privy / Great Seal the final and ceremonial step in making laws or writing big checks.

Protestant Restoration / Reformation   see ***Restoration, Protestant*** and ***Reformation, Protestant***

provinces   -the sticks or anywhere outside of London, or outside of any city wherein the speaker lives and thinks is pretty posh or certainly more posh than *the provinces.*

Pub   -short for Public House. A pub is a neighborhood bar, but with considerably more history. It depended on how strong the drink they served, how may lodgers they were prepared to have, and in no small part, the crown's need for license and tax money. For example, when gin became popular in the late 1700's, pubs that served the stuff were required to be licensed. Therefore, pubs that served only beer became more popular until they too were required to be licensed. They were primarily working-class, but after WWII such distinctions broke down and all classes enjoyed the sense of community that typifies pubs. Most pubs serve simple food like fish and chips and some very few still rent rooms to travelers. All in all, an English, Irish, Scot's, or Welsh pub would seem familiar to an American who spends time in a neighborhood bar. see ***inn***

public convenience -public restroom.

public oven -a communal bake-house common in the medieval.

Public Records Office -the national archive.

public schools -schools that anyone, (but usually boys) may attend, provided their daddy is rich. see *school*

pudding   For the Brits, *pudding* is one of those useful words that covers a lot of territory. Consider plum, figgy, Christmas, bread, and Yorkshire pudding. *Pudding* may mean desert or a specific type of desert. The Brits are very keen on pudding or *pud*, and make a dozen or more varieties. Neither savory *pudding*-pudding, nor *desert*-pudding are anything like the chocolate, banana, coconut, butterscotch, or vanilla goo that Americans make out of the little box. Such would be called **custard** in England. (Being a member of the *pudding club* is to be preggers.)

Like the fruitcake your Aunty Fanny gives you every year? There you go–English *pudding*. These puddings are essentially fruit cakes in different shapes and with different assortments of dried fruit. Some of them are flammable with copious amounts of rum or brandy, but both rum and brandy are perfectly nice with out all the other stuff cluttering up matters. Fewer calories too. Here is a more or less authentic English pudding that is well worth the effort to assemble.

pukka   -solid and reliable. The word is usually applied to a military person. The word comes from India and in the modern use, it is not only solid and reliable, but a tad dull.

Punch   -a weekly humorous magazine published until 2002. It was noted for its cartoons and satire. It's a little like America's *Mad Magazine*, but for a far more sophisticated readership. The name *Punch* comes from the rather nasty little Punch and Judy Puppets popular in the Victorian era. Lower case **punch** is wine or liquor and fruit juice. The non-alcoholic beverage served from a big bowl at bridge parties is called a *fruit cup* in England.

punch-up -a fist fight

punt   -a small flat bottom boat useful for summer romance among students, particularly in Cambridge or Oxford.

punter -a loosing bettor or otherwise a sucker.

push-bike   -an old-fashioned word for bicycle and distinct from a *motorbike*.

push-chair   -baby stroller.

puss / pussy   -usually a cat. Its vulgar use was common in Shakespeare's era and beyond, but later came to be an affectionate term for a woman. The vulgar, (American), use is coming back and is used when the speaker, often an older woman, is unaware of what her use of the expression 'my pussy' might mean.

putting-out system   As the industrial revolution got going, and before factories became huge coal-burning soul-sucking behemoths, manufacturing was often done in specialized home shops. An *undertaker* would gather up the raw materials and take it to one worker's shop–often in someone's' the home–for a single process to be performed. He would pick up the finished work he had dropped off previously, and pay a piece-rate price for that work. Then he would take it to another shop for the next part of the process and so on till the product was ready for market. One example of this process might begin with a bunch of dirty hair sheered off of a sheep, and turning it into clothing. It turns out there are a lot of steps.

Moving from agriculture, or sheep anyway, and turning to manufacturing things made from metal and such, the same system worked. The pay for this work depended on the skills and tooling necessary to do the work. From the undertaker's point of view, costs could be pushed down as far as possible if the steps were broken down to the smallest degree that needed the least skill and the fewest and cheapest tools. Because of this business reality, the putting-out system was sometimes called 'white slavery' with the entire family laboring dawn to dusk at tedious dirty work in the living room and earning a bare substance. The system, however, might have been better than what was to come, the factory system.

Q is a ridiculous letter. There is some use for it in Semitic languages like Arabic and Hebrew, but the English could have gotten along without if it perfectly well if it were not for French. There is also the issue of Q needing always to be helped out by a following U. Zee is the only letter less popular than Q.

Quakers　　Most correctly, they are *The Society of Friends* and theologically not much different from American Quakers. (The name *Quaker*, comes from a Quaker preacher being tried for religious blasphemy in 1650. During the trial, he "bade them to tremble at the word of the Lord.") What is not often understood by Yanks is that the Pilgrims and Quakers came to America not only because the thought they were being persecuted, but also because as the crown increased its authority over assorted miscreants, and the church was not able to slap people in the stocks as often as they liked. They wanted room to persecute others as *they* saw fit.

BTW -the cereal maker Quaker Oak Company has nothing to do with the Quakers other than the two guys that started the company heard that the Quakers were all about good quality, honesty, and integrity

quarriers　　-hauled several things up out of big pits in England, the most important being granite and lime. The former was a building material and the other was the source of cement and mortar, whitewash, bleach, hide tanning solutions, as a disinfectant for graves & garbage tips, and even as a soil treatment. Cotswold stone came from around **Cotswold**. Kaolin (porcelain) came from Cornwall, and coprolite (phosphate fertilizer) was dug up around Cambridgeshire. Flint was very important to prehistoric English cavemen for their arrow & spear heads, later as a building material, and still later in flint-lock firearms.

quarter days   -goes back to the Medieval practice of paying rent quarterly, but when few people understood calendars, the four days every year was based on church festivals etc. For example, and depending on the part of the British Isles in question, Christmas, Lady Day, Michaelmas, and Mid-summer. Labor contracts were also based on quarters for working people who didn't pay to rent land and grow crops.

que / queinging   -a line or taking one's place in a line. The English are so polite if they happen across a que, will stand in that line even when they have no interest in whatever is at the head of the que. Not really, but compared to their European neighbors to the south for whom such things are more of an athletic contest than a way to maintain order, the Brits vividly demonstrate their legendary politeness.

Queen   A male monarch is simply the king, but the word *queen* is far more complicated. There have been only five or six monarch queens: Elizabeths I and II, Victoria, and (Bloody) Mary being the most important ones. The queen may also be the wife of the current king and technically the *Queen Consort.* The widow of the king is the *Queen Dowager.* The *Queen Mother* is the most complicated. She is the mother of the queen, but there are no king mothers. Or queen fathers for that matter. Elizabeth II is queen, but even as the mother of Charles, grand mother of Harry, and great grandmother of two more, she is not the queen mother. Her mother, on the other hand, was the widow of George V and she was the queen-mother throughout the reign of her son *Edward VIII*, who hung it up and then of George VI. All this brings up a fun game the English play. For example, what would happen if the king and queen were also cousins and childless, and the king had no other siblings, and his cousin was also heir presumptive. And it was a month with an R in it. Only the English can play this game enjoyably. Or at all.

Queen's Bench   -it's now the Queen's Bench, but in due time, it will be the *King's Bench* again.

Queen's / Queens' College   There are three of them and one is just for girls and one Queen's University is for the Irish. All of them are expensive.

Queen's Council   An old and presumably accomplished barrister available to advise the Queen, but they never do. *QC* is just another little squirt of alphabet the Brits like to hang off the back of their names.

Queen's Guard   -the infantry and cavalry who guard the royal residence. (When the monarch is king, they are the King's Guard.) They wear tall bearskin hats. They are not to be confused with the

Yeoman of the Guard who wear flattened top hats. By the way, the guns the Guards carry? They are real guns with real bullets and an equally real bayonet..

Queen Scout -   like an American Eagle Boy Scout.

queer   -feeling poorly -as in *come over queer*. To be living on *Queer Street* is to be on the verge of bankruptcy, and *queer the pitch* is to interfere with business. Only recently has it come to take on the American meaning of homosexuality.

quilting   -an important home industry to bring in a little extra cash during the 1600's and 1700's.

quince   -a hard pear-like fruit. It needs boiling before it can be eaten and even then it is used sparingly in pies or jelly. BTW -the Portuguese word for quince is *marmalo* and the original quince jam was called *marmalade*.

quing   -transgender or neuter queen-king. There was an old joke that ***Elizabeth I*** was the king, and ***James I*** was queen. Otherwise it's very modern slang.

Quisling   a traitor -a person who collaborates with the enemy occupying forces. From Vidkum Quisling of Norway who cooperated with the Nazis during WWII.

Scapa Flow

North Sea

North Atlantic

Scotland

Edinburgh

Northern
Ireland

Glasgow

Belfast

Pennine Hills

Isle of
Man

L:iverpool

Dublin

Birmingham

Ireland

England

Cambridge

Wales

London

Cardiff

Thames River   Dover

Southhampton   Brighton

Portsmouth

Calais

Cornwall

Isle of
Wight

English Channel

Gernsey
Jersey

France

R is a controversial letter. It's closely related to *P* in ancient Greek, but related to *D* in the older Semitic languages. It fell to the Romans to add the tail to rho to get our *R*. (Note that the Greek π already has a tail and a rather fancy one at that.) In English-English spelling, the *r* in words like *centre* precedes the *e*, but in American-English spelling, it's *center*.

RAF   see ***Royal Air Force*** and ***military***

railway   To understand he English rail road system, it's important for Yanks to remember that England is much smaller that America. Getting from one end of the Sceptered Isle to the other end is child's play compared to–for example–getting across the desert from Denver to Los Angeles. Automobiles also came much later to England than they did to America. European trains are better than American's and England's trains are better and busier yet.

They were originally a conglomeration of privately owned railways but have been being glued together in various ways during most of the 20th century. Today there are a little more than 10,000 miles of railroad track in England.* This includes hooking up with Europe thru the ***Channel Tunnel***, the ***London Underground***, other municipal transit systems and finally, various narrow-gauge tourist junketing lines. The Brits simply do a much better job of organizing railroads than the Yanks over and above the issue of the sheer size of America. Moving trains also make great settings for murder mysteries and the whole crime-solving crowd so popular in English literature and movies.

* US has 140,000 miles, but depending on how passenger miles are measured, the US trains carry less then one tenth as many passengers.

ranks, military   The subject of military ranks is hugely complicated; so much so that the following addresses—with much oversimplification—the way it is today, and this will have to serve the casual reader. The serious student of military history is on his (or her) own. This compares the English

Army with the American Army and adds the English Navy for good measure. Both the USAF and the RAF ranks sort of straddle line between the Army / Navy ranks. This is because the USAF split off from the US Army only after WWII, whereas the RAF more or less invented itself at a time when the English Army was recovering from WWI.

English Army	American Army	English Navy	Notes:
Officers:			
Field Marshal	General of the Army	Admiral of the Fleet	All of these ranks attain only in times of war.
GENERAL STAFF: The way the English and Americas rank their officers is almost identical. There are three further breeds of General; (regular) General, Lieutenant General, and Major General		There are 3 types of admirals; (regular) Admiral, Vice-Admiral, and Rear-Admiral,	In the army, a division (10,000 – 50,000 soldiers) is commanded by a Major General.
Brigadier	Brigadier General	Commodore	Commands a brigade of 5,000 to 10,000. A Naval Commodore commands a flotailla of ships as part of a larger naval force.
Colonel		Captain	
Lieutenant Colonel		Commander (James Bond is / was a Commander.)	In the army, a Lt. Colonel would command a battle group of 700 to 1000. A Comander in the Roayl Navy might run a frigate, destroyer, sub, aviation squadron, or shore installation.
Major		Lieutenant Commander	Lieutenant derives from the French lieu as in lieu of the tenant
Captain		Lieutenant	-the real boss who is out of town.
1st Lieutenant The Brits pronounce it *lef-tenant*. This is probably because it's a French word and they didn't get along for a good long time with the French.		Sub-Lieutenant	An Army lieutenant may command 30 men, as might a Naval Sub-Lieutenant or Midshipman.
2nd Lieutenants		Midshipman	
Between the officers and enlisted men, there is a confusing grey area of highly specialized—and often highly educated—warrant officers and Petty Officers in the Navy. These people serve important functions that may fall outside of regular military purposes.			
Enlisted Men:			
Army Sergeant Major		Warrant Officer of the Naval Services	These ranks are cerimonial, and in some ways, these men may tell a much higher ranking officer where to get off—and do so none too politely if he is so inclined.
In both the English and American Army's, most of the important work is done by sergeants or in the Navy, it's done by Chiefs. There is a very complicated variety of these people and they don't line up one-to-one very easily. None-the-less, they run as follows:			
• Warrant Officer			

English Army	American Army	English Navy	Notes:
Class 1 (Regimental Sergeant) • Warrant Officer Class 1 (appointed) • Warrant Officer Class 2 (Company Sergeant) • Color / Staff Sergeant • Sergeant	• Command Sergeant Major • Sergeant Major • First Sergeant • Master Sergeant • Sergeant First Class • Staff Sergeant • Sergeant	• Warrant Officer Class 1 • Chief Petty Officer (equivalent to an Army Sergeant First Class)	Most sergeants have been in the enlisted ranks eight to ten years before they make sergeant. A sergeant will normally advise a lieutenant in charge of a platoon of 30 to 50 men and may directly command an 8 to 12 men Section on his own. BTW, the word derives from Latin *servient*, meaning serving or servile
Corporal	Corporal	Petty Officer	Most of these service men are trained to be specialists in various tasks or functions.
Lance Corporal	Specialist	Leading Hand	
Private Class 1 to 3	Private 1st Class	Able Seaman 1 & 2	
Private Class 1 (Junior)	Private 1 & 2	New Entry	

rasher   -a slice of bacon that is thicker that an American slice.

Rat Catchers   -actually earned more than common laborers. Rat and vermin infestations were a real problem in warehouses, barns, and homes, but there was a market for live rats for blood sports involving dogs or ferrets. There was not a lot else to do evenings in the 16th century. Rat pie was a delicacy among the commoners and moles were valuable for their skins.

rates   -property tax, and among the highest in the world.

rationing   America rationed gasoline and a few other food commodities from 1942 till 1946 as part of the war effort, but it was only polite patriotism compared to what the poor Brits went thru. England rationed from 1940 until 1954 when the last ration on meat was lifted. (It was rationing in America that left the Yanks with an enduring love of macaroni and cheese as a substitute for meat. One stamp was good for two boxes of the stuff !)

Reader, University   -about the same thing as an Associate Professor in America. A university reader is typically a lecturer who has presumably done some serious original research. The hierarchy of English academic big-wigs is not much different from that of America, but with slightly different vocabulary. It works out as follows:

Chaired Professor or even   Professor (un-chaired)
    Prof. Extroridnarius !   Reader

reading   In Parliament, a bill must be read three times before the vote. It seems to work better then the American system of committees and amendments etc.

Ready, steady, go   -equivalent to America's *On your marks, get set, go.*

receipt   -a sales receipt as well as recipe, but when it's a recipe for medicine, it's Rx. Both words come from the Latin *accipere* meaning *receive.*

rector   In the Church of England, the parish priest is either a vicar, a curate, or a rector, but the rector is paid better. It's a little different in the Episcopal Church where the rector is in charge. The same thing as a **vicar** in the Church of England. An academic rector is a *chancellor.*

Recusant   -someone who didn't go to church as often as the Church of England thought they should. It was largely a means of suppressing Catholicism, but as Protestantism and the nonconformist movement unfolded, it was used to suppress anyone who took a different religious view. The word now applies to anyone who disagrees with any currant authority.

Reform Bill (of 1832)   As the industrial revolution unfolded, people moved from the countryside to big cities which until then had been little more than places with markets and occasional fairs. All well and good, but the Parliamentary representation remained in the countryside where it was further dominated by the rich land-owners. The Reform Act then was the culmination of a long legislative battle toward what Yanks would call redistricting. One member of Parliament might represent 12,000 electors and another represent as few as a dozen in what were called the 'rotten boroughs,' and they may have been little more than his family and his servants. The Reform was an important milestone in England's march to democracy. It was also the end of the **Tory Party.**

Reform Club   A gentlemen's club contemporaneous with the **Reform Act** and as progressive as the **Whigs** of the era. It was so *modern* that it actually admitted women in 1981!

Reformation, Protestant   This all started when Martin Luther nailed his 95 thesis–complaints actually–against a Catholic church door in Germany in 1517. It's hard to say if it was a cause or effect. One of Luther's biggest objections was the church selling indulgences. You could buy a get-out-of-jail-free cards for sin. Unquestionably a doubtful practice and most of Europe was increasingly tired of Rome and the Catholic Church. Luther lit the fuse, but it was probably going to happening with or without him in short order.

England was sort of on the sidelines till Henry VIII wanted to set aside his first wife, Catherine of Aragon, and the Catholic Pope wouldn't let him. In 1533 he said to hell with the pope and gave himself a divorce anyway. He started his own ***Church of England*** a year later. So began the ***Reformation*** in England. Things between the Catholics and Church of England–the Almost-Protestants–bumped along but came to a deadly pass during the ***English Civil War*** between 1642 and 1649.

regent -a substitute for the king usually until he reached the age of eighteen. For example, Henry VIII's dad Henry VII shuffled off in 1509 when VIII was only 17. His 23 year old fiance, Catherine of Aragon, would act as his nominal regent for a short time. Then, about 30 years later, his only son, Edward VI, would be king form age 9 to the boy's death at age 16. During these seven years, a Regency Council tended to matters. The most important regency, however, was during the...

Regency Era From the time George III went mad in about 1811, until his death in 1820, his son George IV's served as his regent. There is some argument as to just when it started; there are those who suggest the Regency actually went back to 1795 when III started loosing it.

The Napoleonic Wars ran thru much of the Regency, and this caused a good bit of social, political, and economic change, but despite this, the era was notable for fashion, romance, and elegance as well as significant achievements in art, literature, and perhaps most importantly, ***architecture***. It ended with the death of William IV, George III's youngest son and William's little brother. Queen Victoria was next and so began the ***Victorian Era.***

regiment To understand the importance and ubiquity of the regiment in English writing, it is important to understand that in England, the word 'army' was a loose abstraction that referred to a collection of independent

regiments. From the very earliest medieval, military matters were somewhat economic affairs. The people who had land paid the crown 'rent' in the form of knights and /or soldiers. This gave them the right in turn to collect rent from farmers. This arrangement would evolve into a for-profit industry. As late as the 1600's, a regiment could be assembled by a self-appointed Colonel who paid to equip it out of his own pocket. Then he collected money from Parliament or what ever monarch had need of soldiers. He usually did so at a tidy profit.

Up until 1871, military officers bought their ***commissions*** from the officers who owned the various regiments much like someone today might buy a going and profitable business. It was only after the embarrassment of the Crimean War that this practice was discontinued and the crown 'bought back its army.' Up until then, officers and private soldiers joined a given regiment, He did not join 'the army.' Even after that point, a soldier's membership in a given regiment was very telling of his status if only among other military people.

Today a regiment is still the organizational unit of the Army. In theory, it is more or less self-contained and is responsible for logistics, deployment, and training its own personnel. It depends on the regiment's purpose as to its size and chain of command. In America, the various divisions of the Army -armies, divisions, battalions, and regiments and such, were numbered or lettered. Not so in England. A cursory reading of the fiddly-bits that make up the English Army today will reveal the *Royal This*, and the *Guards of There*, and *Queens Own That*. The very highest organizational authority was an ad-hock General Staff that gathered only in times of war, otherwise it was, and still is, all about the Regiments.

The Regiments were then divided into three main flavors, the Household Cavalry, Royal Armored Corps, and the Infantry. There are three lesser or supportive regiments, the Combat Services, Combat Support Arms, and Other Combat Arms. Consider just the Household Cavalry as an example:

Household Calvary & Royal Armored Corps
   Household Cavalry
      Life Guards
      The Blues and Royal Horse Guards
      1st Dragoons
   Heavy Cavalry
      Queen's Dragoon Guards
      Royal Scotts Dragoon Guards
      Royal Dragoon Guards
   Light Cavalry
      Queen's Royal Hussars
      The Queen's Own Royal Irish
      King's Royal Hussars
      Light Dragoons
   Royal Tank Regiment
   Yeomanry
      Royal Yeomanry
      Royal Wessex Yeomanry
      Scottish and North Irish Yeomanry
      Queen's Own Yeomanry

These regiments still exist, each with its own uniform, insignia, and even its own marching music. An officer of a given regiment is a member for life even if he has retired. It's somewhat less so for the enlisted men, but all of them take pride in their regiment. In times of war, the General Staff might reshuffle personnel as needed, but people are not transferred as in the American Army; they are seconded (lent) to other groups. This sometimes leads to a situation wherein a given officer might have one rank in his regiment, and quite another rank when he reports to work for another officer.

It is unlikely that an American reader will be able to extract as much meaning from the whole. There is a story told of two officers arguing about which of them was the more important and impressive. One officer, a

Lieutenant Colonel in the Royal Regiment of Artillery expected respect from a mere Major. The Major pointed out that while he was indeed only a major, he was a major in The Blues and Royal Horse Guards, he had two weeks of seniority, and furthermore, he attended Eaton while the Colonel attended Wigglesworth. Therefore he actually outranked the Colonel. Only the English–and probably only those English who serve in the military–can ever hope to understand all of this.

registrars -originally were in charge of collecting birth, marriage, and death records. After 1867 the also kept track of vaccinations.

religion   Today religion in England is much like it is America; people practice whatever religion they like and are pretty much left alone. It wasn't always so. Hang on tight here, it's a confusing subject and we are going thru it pretty fast.

From about 500 BC to 500 AD the pagan Celts worshiped the forces of nature, occasionally sacrificed people, and did what their priest class, the Druids told them to do. There are no written records from the Celts and what little is know about them comes from the Romans who got there shortly before the time of Christ. By the time the Romans left in 450, Christianity was well on its way and what little was left of the Celtic religion had changed to resemble the Roman polytheistic deities -Jupiter, Venus, Mars etc. with a little of the Norse stirred in, i.e., Thor, Weden. Odin etc.

But Christianity and subsequent Catholicism were the big thing, at least until Martin Luther pulled the rug out from under the pope in 1517. By 1521 his 94 Thesis really messed up the pope's wholesale market for indulgences to such an extent that the Diet of Worms in ex-communicated Luther that year.

In 1533 *Henry VIII* wanted a divorce and the pope wouldn't give him one, so he declared himself the head of the Church, not the Catholic Church, the *Church of England*. It wasn't Lutheran nor Protestant quite yet, and other than replacing the Pope with the king, relaxing ideas on contraception, and thinking that holy communion was more symbolic than real, the Church of England was pretty much the same as Catholicism.

Henry VIII died in 1547 and his daughter Mary ("Bloody Mary") by his first wife *Catherine of Aragon,* was crowned. Sort of. There were a lot of people who felt she was not the rightful monarch. Mary was a devout Catholic (like her mom) and a lot of non-Catholics died, as did those who thought she was not the rightful heir but that was pretty much the same thing as not being a Catholic.

By the time Mary died and Henry's second daughter, *Elizabeth I* became queen in 1558, the Church of England has become thoroughly Protestant. Elizabeth was a Protestant so things turned back the other way. This puts us somewhere in the *Protestant Reformation*, but various flavors of Protestants (Lutherans, Calvinists, and Episcopalians etc.) were growing all over Europe. The Reformation might be said to have ended in 1555 with the Peace of Augsburg with allowed both Catholicism and Lutheranism to coexist, if only in Germany. It ended some more in 1648 with the Treaty of Westphalia that ended the 30 Years War. This was a long hot mess of a war, but didn't settle things between the Protestants and Catholics in England. Nor were they sorted out until the end of the **English Civil War** in 1651, and even then...

In 1791 the policy of excluding, pestering, fining, and otherwise suppressing *recusants*, (people who didn't go to the Church of England) were set aside. Today and for the last long while, the Catholics and Protestants have gotten along. But not in **Northern Ireland.**

Remembrance Day -November 11 -aka Armistice Day and the end of WWI. After WWII it is to memorialize all the British war dead.

remittance man -originally an emigre to one of the colonies who received money from back home. In literature and in the days of **Empire**, a remittance man was an embarrassment to his family and the colonies were a convenient place to be rid of him.

Renaissance England had a renaissance, but it's a lower-case renaissance compared to the Renaissance starting in Italy quite a bit earlier. Picture Queen Elizabeth and William Shakespeare as the English renaissance. In fact, think theater and literature and you are pretty well done. The painting and visual arts that Italy did so beautifully well were stomped out by the Protestant Reformation, (beginning about 1530), which set aside anything and everything religious. For the following hundred years, English art was pretty much limited to landscapes and portraits of... you may have guessed, rich people.

rep / repertory / repertoire In general, it's someone's bag of tricks, but in the performing arts, it is a company's set of plays, operas, or ballets to be performed in a given season. A rep company would hire talent for a season to perform the entire repertoire in a cycle of days or weeks. This was the norm in Shakespeare's day and out in the countryside, it continued much later. Typically, only a theater in London or on Manhattan's Broadway, and only comparatively recently, would a company hire their players and do a single performance night after night.

resident -the top representative of the crown living in one of the colonies, particularly India. see *viceroy*

Restoration, Protestant -either the restoration of the monarchy to Charles II, or less commonly, the restoration of (Catholic) church properties to the bishops.

Historians go either way. It amounted to much the same thing. Eleven years after chopping off **Charles I's** head which he needed rather badly, they brought his son, Charles II back from exile in France and made him king in 1660, but with the firm understanding that Parliament would have a greater say in the way things were to be done. As to the bishops getting back their estates, it had more to do with giving some rich guys back their stuff, than it had to do with giving it back to the Holy and Apostolic Catholic Church.

Riot Act / Read the Riot Act In a curios, yet very British combination of brutality and courtesy, the Riot Act of 1714 gave local authorities permission to open fire on any gathering of 12 or more people who would not disperse when told to do so, but only after the Riot Act had been read aloud to them.

road / roadway -any street, or highway in the city or country. The *roads* on the other hand, are a sheltered part of the coastline where ships can anchor.

road making -didn't much change in England from the time of the Romans until the Scotsman John McAdam invented the modern way to make roads in about 1816. It was much like the way Romans did it, but with tar mixed into the topmost layer to make *tarmac*. It worked so well, we still do it that way.

rocket -what Yanks might colorfully refer to as *an ass chewing*. It used to be a military expression, but is now common throughout.

rod -a very old measure of length (5 ½ yards) used in measuring land.

roger -have sex with. It's vulgar, but used across all social classes.

rollmop -pickled herring curlicues on a toothpick.
roll neck -a turtleneck shirt.
roll-on -get on with something enjoyable -like America's *let the good times roll,* or the New Orleans equivalent *Laissez les bon temps rouler !*

rook / rookery A rook is England's crow -large, smart, black, noisy, and prone to stealing. They live in rookeries. When the word refers to where people live, it's a slum which is also full of noise and theft.

rooms -an apartment. A *flat* is an entire floor and a *house* is a house that probably needed servants. The meaning of the word has changed over time. Sherlock Holmes and Dr. Watson had rooms, two bedrooms connected to a sitting room, but no kitchen. (Mrs. Hudson fetched up tea and occasional meals.) see ***architecture*** & ***houses / homes***

ropemakers   -made the miles and miles of rope necessary for ships and they did so in sheds that were literally as much as a mile long.

Rovers   -boy scouts

rowing   -the preeminent college sport. Rowing those long skinny boats up and down rivers is hugely popular among college students, but it is not as hideously commercial as American college athletics, but rather more like intramural sports run by the students. Even so, it was not all that democratic. The whole thing got organized back in 1886 and excluded both professional rowers and anyone "who is or has been by trade or employment for wages a mechanic, artisan, or laborer."

royal / royalty   The word shows up so often in England that is has lost all meaning other than having some often tenuous connection to the monarch and his or her family. This being said, there are some royal things that want a little discussion.

Royal Academy (of Arts) A conservative and exclusive club of mostly old artists who get to put RA behind their name.

Royal Academy of Music -a very old association of professional musicians and a conservatory that actually teaches music.

Royal Arsenal -goes back to Henry VIII who set it up as the headquarters for his navy's cannons. It still is an arsenal.

Royal Assent -ceremonial approval by the monarch to any law passed by Parliament. No king or queen has refused to sign-off since 1708 when Queen Anne decided against setting up a Scottish Militia. (The Scots were mostly Protestant then and Anne was a devout Catholic.)

Royal College of Art Unlike the **Royal Acadamey**, this is an actual school, but it tends not so much toward the fine arts as toward design and fashion.

Royal College of Music -attached to the **Royal Academy of Music**, it teaches music.

Royal Court -a theater in London going back to 1870. It tends toward the avant-garde.

Royal Geographic Society -an independent collection of geographers going back to 1870 and bent on mapping the world. Consider the famous "Dr. Livingtome I presume" asked by Henry Morton Stanley when he happened on the good doctor in deepest Africa. Both men were members of the Royal Geographic Society.

Royal Highlanders -the Black Watch regiment of Scotland.

Royal Historic Society -a club of historians and writers going back to 1868.

Royal Horse Guards -one of the army's highest status regiment. When they are not parading around on horse-back and presumably protecting the monarch, they drive tanks.

Royal Hospital -one of England's two veteran's hospitals; one is for soldiers and one for sailors.

Royal Household -as Parliament and the Cabinet took over more and more of the issues of government, the royal household came to concern itself with the monarch's safety and comfort–often lots of comfort. see ***servants***

Royal Observatory

The observatory was established in 1673 to sort out celestial navigation for sailors and the Royal Navy. It did this so well that the town where it was originally located, Greenwich, is now the prime meridian where both longitude and time start; it is 0°longitude and Greenwich Mean Time (GMT) is where / when the day starts.

Royal Shakespeare Company

-a comparatively recent national and nationally funded theater based in Stratford, but with a touring company.

Royal Society -an important club of scientists going back, depending on whom you ask, to sometime between 1657 and 1667. At one point it was called the "College for the Promoting of Physico-Mathmerical Experimental Learning." Fellows and members included Issac Newton, Charles Babbage, Charles Darwin, Albert Einstein, Steven Hawking, and even the woman biochemist Kathleen Lonsdale in 1945. Benjamin Franklin was not a member but demonstrated his lighting rod there in 1751. Their motto is worth noting: "Nullius in verba." -*Take no one's word for it*. see ***college***

Royal Air Force / RAF   England's air force got its start late in WWI and is the world's oldest independent air force. (The USAF separated from the US Army Air Corps only in 1947.) At the end of WWI, the RAF was also the world's largest air force. Its finest hour was undoubtedly the ***Battle of Britain*** during the Blitz of WWII. It was when Winston Churchill said of the RAF that, "Never in the field of human conflict was so much owed to so few."

   An important difference between the USAF and the RAF–and this is controversial–is that the RAF acts to support the army and navy while the USAF can't be bothered. The American Army has helicopters for ground support, and the navy has its own pilots who are so good they can land on a wee ships in the middle of the big ocean. see ***military***

royal residences   -the queen's homes are grand locations of state, but usually non-political functions. All of the residences are open to the public to various degrees and at various times. If this list seems long, remember that Elizabeth II had 60 residences. In general order of importance they are...

Windsor Castle

Buckingham Palace

Kensington Palace: -built in 1769 and where Queen Victoria was born and grew up. It is also the official residence of all manner of dukes and duchesses including the queen's kids, grand kids, and now great grand-kids. If Kensington was an American university, it would be considered a party school with lots of pretty media people, pop stars, and athletes.

Balmora Manor: Near Aberdeen Scotland, it's the summer place to go for shooting.

Sandringham Estate: Built in 1862, it's one of the newest. It's near Norfolk and a country estate with woodlands, heath, and beautiful gardens.

Hampton Court Palace: Not used much by the queen, but it is very popular with the tourists because of its Tudor architecture and its garden with a huge hedge maze.

rubbish tip   -a dump. The old word is *midden*.

Rugby   If English football is American soccer, than rugby is really English football and it's called Rugby Football to distinguish it from regular football or soccer. It's not played with pads or helmets. It should be, but it's not. This is because English rugby players are so tough they eat their own dead. Like American football, the object is to carry the ball over the goal line and touch it down. It doesn't count until the ball carrier literally touches it to the ground. So they call it a goal. In American football, they call it a touch-down, but the ball carrier only needs to put a foot into the end zone. I don't know why. Instead of downs, rugby sorts out who really gets the ball with *scrums*. Scrums look like lines of scrimmage, but there is no cute little buffer zone between the opposing linemen; they stick their heads into the other team's shoulders and push as something of a tug-of-war in reverse. Once the ball comes out they follow various rules that look much like soccer, but they use their hands. *RU* is the Rugby Union.

rum   -spirits distilled from the by-products of making sugar, particularly molasses. Something like rum has been made all over the world from earliest recorded history usually in tropical places that grow sugar cane. In England, rum had to wait for the sugarcane to grow in the Caribbean during the 17th century. One document from Barbados sent back home to England said, "The chief fuddling they make in the island is Rumbullion, alias Kill-Devil, and this is made of sugar canes distilled, a hot, hellish, and terrible liqour." It would improve. It came to be very popular in the American colonies where they first started turning molasses into rum in Boston in 1664. Supposedly, every American colonist man, woman, and child drank about three gallons of the stuff every year.

Rum and the Royal Navy go back to 1655 when they captured Jamaica. Sailors were given a *tot* or 2 ounces every day up until 1970. It may not have been rum, but rum or brandy depending on what was available. Availability was often a function of what ships the navy might have captured recently, or with whom the were they were trading at the time. The word *proof* also involved the navy. The Royal Navy bought rum only after testing it for strength. They would mix it with gun-powder and if it burned, it was said to be proof. (BTW -100% alcohol is equal to 200 proof.) At roughly the same time the Royal Navy was active in the Caribbean, pirates were as well. The connection between pirates and rum is more that apocryphal. Rum was a valuable commodity and as such, pirates were at least as interested in acquiring it as a trade-good, as they were in drinking it.

There is a final story involving rum and the Royal Navy. Sailors were not given a tot of pure rum. If they were to save up their tots over a period of some days, a mild buzz from the tot could grow into a more serious and debilitating bender. The English Admiral Edward Vernon hit on the solution of diluting the two ounces as it was taken out of the barrel at full proof. This diluted run would spoil before the men could collect up enough to really tie one on. Vernon was a pretty decent guy among the mixed bag of often dictatorial and sadistic British navy officers. He had the habit of wearing a grogram coat and was fondly nicknamed *Old Grog* among the sailors. The product of diluted rum came to be named *grog* after Vernon. Vernon had a young cabin boy -the son of a rich English family living in the colonies. This young man remembered Vernon so fondly that when he would go on to achieve a great measure of success, Lawrence Washington would name his estate Mt. Vernon after his old boss. George Washington, his step brother, would later inherit the place.

Rushes   -a useful grass-like plant with long hollow stems. During the medieval and beyond, they were used in weaving, as a crude candle, and spread on the medieval packed-earth floors for insulation and cushioning.

RWV   -robbery with violence -a mugging.

Scapa Flow

North Sea

North Atlantic

Scotland

Northern
Ireland

Edinburgh

Glasgow

Belfast

Pennine Hills

Isle of
Man

L:iverpool

Dublin

Birmingham

Ireland

England

Cambridge

Wales

London

Cardiff

Thames River

Dover

Southhampton

Brighton

Calais

Portsmouth

Cornwall

Isle of
Wight

English Channel

Gernsey

France

Jersey

S was a mild and useful letter from its first appearance in the Semitic alphabet (Šîn *teeth*). It bumped along thru Greek and Latin with some minor confusion as to how to handle *s* vs. *ss*. About the middle of the 18th century newspapers got into it. No less an American than Benjamin Franklin wrote to a friend in 1786 that "the Round s .... begins to be the Mode, and in nice printing the Long 'ſ' is rejected entirely." Remember, Ben was a printer and publisher. See *f*.

SAE   either the English equivalent of the American SASE -a *self addressed stamped envelope* or the *Society of Automotive Engineers*. This system of measuring nuts and bolts in fractions of an inch is sometimes called the English system, but it not used anywhere but in America. England went metric in 1965. see **measurement**

sahib   -an address of respect used in India for an European -a memsahib is a European lady.

Saint   The word S*aint* prefaces even more expressions in England than the word *Royal*. Some of them have churches, towns, or other locations named after them. Some have feast days celebrated by the Catholics or the Protestants or both.

    St. Andrew -patron saint of Scotland and the white and red diagonal cross on the flag of the UK. His feast day was originally November 11, but was moved to November 30 and is now a bank holiday.

    St. Bartholomew / St. Barts -two churches in London, a hospital, and a fair for cloth makers up until about 1850.

    St. Blaise -February 3 -important to wool growers

    St. George -two churches in London -one is in Mayfair -the most exclusive expensive neighborhood in London and THE place to be married. St. George is the patron saint of England and his cross is the red one in the flag of the UK. He was supposed to be a Greek soldier working for the Romans until he found Christianity and was summarily tortured to death. The bit about the dragon was a myth from the mid-east that the crusaders brought back to England.

St. James -A toney neighborhood in London known for Restoration **architecture** and clubs. St. James' Place is Henry VIII's country home, and now the Court of St. James is where England keeps ambassadors. St. James's Park on the edge of London was a deer hunting park until the 19th century when it was landscaped to a fair-thee-well.

St. John -a couple of colleges -one at Cambridge and one at Oxford, an ambulance Brigade, and a woods.

St. Martin in the Fields -originally a church sitting out in a field. The *Academy of St. Martin in the Fields* is now an orchestra that plays there.

St. Michael and St. George, the Order of -a ceremonial order for diplomats and civil servants. It's given to anyone who stays in the civil service long enough and its memebrship has gotten a little large. This rather defeats the whole notion of an exclusive club.

St. Paul's -a huge popular cathedral that was used as a prison, burned down at various times going back to Shakespeare's time, and ultimately escaped bombing by the Germans in WW II, and became an icon of England's defiance. There are several other churches named after St. Paul, but none have the fame or architectural gravitas of this cathedral.

Saint Patrick -the apostle of Ireland and a real person. He was the son of a Roman official in England born sometime in the 5th century. He kidnapped by Irish pirates, (sort of local Vikings), at about age 16. He was sold into slavery in Ireland but escaped as a young man and made it back either to England or to Rome, but there is some confusion here. Somewhere he became a Christian and returned to Ireland. The Irish were then a literate crowd -unlike nearly all of Europe at the time- and even then were given to telling stories. Stories surrounding St. Patrick became beloved Irish legends. For example the one about his banishing snakes is doubtful because Ireland has had no snakes from the last ice-age. His demonstrating the holy trinity with a shamrock is perhaps a little more believable. At one point he was said to have stuck his walking stick into the ground and it became a living tree. This is all fine and well, but there are three locations in Ireland claiming the tree in question.

St. Stephans -a chapel in Westminster used for meetings by the House of Commons between the time of Henry VIII and 1834 when it burned down. It was rebuilt.

St. Swithin's Day -something like America's Groundhog Day predicts winter, the weather on July 15 predicts 40 days of fog and rain.

St. Thomas Hospital -where Florence Nightingale founded the first nursing school.

salad   -any cold dish eaten with a fork that may or may not have lettuce and tomatoes. It likely involves *salad-cream* -a thinner and blander form of mayonnaise. *Salad Days* referred to youth from Shakespeare's time, and later came to refer to fluffy theater about nostalgia and innocence.

Salisbury   -a little town in southern part of the country and has
nothing to do with steak of the same name. It sits in the middle of the
Salisbury Plain which is about 300 square miles of chalk plateau. It's a
rather desolate and forbidding place but it's where the Druids built
S*tonhenge*.

salters   -made salt -usually by evaporating sea water, but sometimes
from inland salt springs. (Towns ending in *wich* like Nantwich and
Middlewich etc. probably were sources of salt.) In the 17th century rock-
salt was mined in Cheshire.

salt beef   -corned beef
salt pot   -salt shaker
salts   -Epsom salts
saltings   -a tidal or salt marsh.

samosa `   -a triangular deep-fried pastry from India stuffed with meat
and vegetables. It is similar to, but much spicier than a **pastie**.

sanctuary   During the medieval, sanctuary in a church was limited to
40 days. It was good against civil authorities at a time when the church was
arguably stricter than the civil authorities and perfectly willing to hang,
burn, impale, press, dunk and otherwise utterly ruin people's days. The
practice was banned for criminals in 1623, and in 1723 it was set aside
altogether.

sand bag   -a *cosh* or American black-jack. To be *sand bagged* is to be
mugged or, (metaphorically), betrayed by someone you previously trusted.

Sandhurst   -a town a little southwest of London where the Royalty
Military College was located. The college goes back to 1799 and was used
to train those lads whose ancestry was not aristocratic and rich enough for
the lad to buy a **commission**. By the 20th century, the army decided that
perhaps looking good on a horse was not all that made a good officer and a
little training might be in order. Now, a reference to Sandhurst -or its Royal
Military Academy- carries about the same weight as America's West Point.

sandwich   The story of the 4th Earl of Sandwich -John Montague, 1718
– 1792, having a good run at the poker table and asking for a slab of meat
between slices, or 'rounds', of bread is evidently true -or true-ish.
Nonetheless, the English sandwich is a much simpler affair than the
American Dagwood. It is rarely more than a slice of cheese or some
cucumber on a single round of white bread. The English have come to
enjoy the American hamburger, but they are not proud of it.

sardines   Yes, the canned fish, but also a game similar to hide-and-seek but when the seeker found the hider, the seeker would squeeze into the hiding place until it was crammed full of –typically– teenagers who would then enjoying the opportunity for a little *slap-and-tickle*.

Saturday   In 1850 textile mills were required by law to shut down at 2:PM Saturday Gradually other industries and businesses followed suit and the weekend was almost invented for the working class. A modern Friday night's cutting loose, and Saturday's chores, errands, shopping and the occasional sports game all had to be done between Saturday afternoon and Sunday morning when church happened. see *weekends*

Savile   -a London club associated with writers and actors. *Savile Row* is a street in London where the best men's tailors do business

Savoy   -a neighborhood in London where you will find the Savoy Chapel, Savoy Theater, Savoy Hotel, and the Savoy Hill. The last is was where the BBC first set up shop.

sawyers   - sawed wood. Mark Twain's Tom Sawyer? Evidently the descendant of a man who made his living in a saw pit. This had to be the very definition of miserable work -particularly for the guy down in the hole looking up at the boss and getting a face full of sawdust. One contemporary source insists that all sawyers were 'drunkards and wastrels.'

Saxons   -not to be confused with *sextons*, the Saxons were half of the famous Anglo Saxon team. Both were tribes from Northern Germany that raided England and then settled there after the Romans left.

SAYE   -*Save As You Earn*. An automatic savings plan -like *PAYE*, but with money coming in rather than going out. It has tax advantages somewhat more generous than America's IRA's

Scapa Flow   The channel between the far north end of Scotland and the Orkney Islands. This is where England kept it Grand Fleet during WW I and where the Germany's High Seas Fleet was scuttled after the war's end. Being almost out of the range of German bombers during WW II, they kept

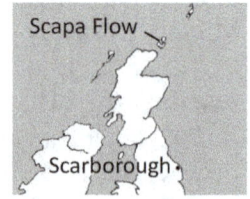

part of their navy there again. It didn't quite work as planned. In 1939 a German U-Boat sank two ships with torpedoes, and a few days later, a Luftwaffe bomber did minor damage to an old decommissioned battleship before it was shot down. Recently, it has been very important in fetching *north-sea oil* to market and an important location for recreational divers who enjoy diving on wrecks and being cold.

Scarborough   -a wee fishing village on the North Sea that used to be a fashionable resort. Simon and Garfunkel's lovely ballad *Scarborough Fair* derives form an old, (at least as early as 1650), English folksong about a man who asks a traveler to ask an (ex?)-girlfriend to perform a series of impossible tasks. One of which it make him a *sark* or a shirt (the same *sark* after which the tea-clipper **Cutty Sark** is named.) The melody goes back to middle English, and the lyrics originally were about impossible tasks going both ways between a man and a woman. An evil elf, a market fair, the plague, and finally, **Robbie Burns** get all tangled up in it the various versions of the lyrics. One 17th century duet runs as follows:
Man:
> *For thou must shape a sark to me. Without any cut or heme, qouth he.*

Woman:
> *I have an aiker of good lay-land, Which lyeth low by yon sea- strand.*

The Simon and Garfunkel version asks for a *cambric shirt without no seams nor needlework* and then adds a 19th century reference to *parsley, sage, rosemary and thyme* just for good measure.

scheme   -a plan or procedure -no sneaky skulduggery involved

schilling   -an obsolete British coin equal to twelve pence or one twentieth of a pound. see *money*

schiltron   This is a late medieval battle formation involving a bunch of guys with long lances all gathered into a very prickly square. It's sort of a Roman invention, but the Scots used it to great effect against English guys wearing metal clothes and riding horses.

Schools   Public and private schools are exactly opposite of what the American reader might guess. In theory, public schools are open to anyone, or anyone whose daddy is important and rich. Private schools, on the other hand, limited their enrollment to the kids of working man who lives in a given neighborhood or parish. Pretty thin gruel but that's the way it is. More than one writer has suggested that English schools confuse even the English. As is so often the case, a little history might help sort it out.

Charlemagne, (747 - 814) was big on culture and learning. He was an indifferent scholar himself, but was responsible for the survival of most of the classic Latin by having it gathered up and copied. The 'Carolingian Renaissance' saw the flowering of art, architecture, literature, and even mathematics. But this subject properly belongs in French history. In England and the rest of Europe, books were copied by hand, usually by monks and often monks who were themselves illiterate; at least until after Gutenberg invented the printing press in about 1440.

Until then, literacy meant being the king, a bishop, cardinal, or high ranking priest. It also meant reading and writing Latin. Literacy among kings goes back as far as Alfred the Great before the Normans. All the kings, (and the few queens), could read and write. Many could do so in several languages beside English.

Literacy and the ability to write business letters gave the Catholic Church tremendous power, over and above its purported ability to get stable-muckers and onion-harvesters into heaven. To the credit of the church, it made some progress teaching the aristocracy Latin. In addition to the rich kids, some few lads from the countryside might also get an education, but only if they seemed very bright and inclined to enter the clergy. The oldest such school in England was Oxford which probably got started in 1096. In 1167 Henry II forbade English scholars going off to school in Paris and Oxford grew apace. In 1209 some of these scholars got in a twist with the townspeople and decamped to Cambridge.

On the continent, things weren't much different. It all well and good to point to Gutenberg and his printing press of 1439. The Renaissance was picking up steam, but it had more to do with art that literacy, and furthermore, if no one could read, no one would buy books and Gutenberg was a businessman. It was the Protestant *Reformation* that was really the big thing that put reading over the top. (The Reformation started in 1517 in Germany with Martin Luther, and finished up in England about 1537). Up until then, the Catholic Church appointed itself as the authority on what was necessary to get into heaven. It worked out as follows; people needed to know precious little except what the church told them, what they were supposed to do was give money to the church, and as to what they were not supposed to do was mostly anything enjoyable. If someone slipped up and did have some fun, that was OK, but then they had to give money to the church for an indulgence. This last thing was the thing that got Martin Luther in such a twist. After the Reformation, people took to reading the Bible on their own without the help of a priest, or at least the Protestants who were literate did.

So from roughly the time of Queen Elizabeth (who spoke several languages herself and was something of a Latin scholar) what little education that was available to the masses was reading the bible and while they were about it, maybe doing just a little business math.

But before we step off to the Enlightenment when the world became enlightened enough to have something to teach, we need to review the pragmatic *apprenticeship* system. This concerned itself with entirely unenlightened matters like making and building things. An apprentice –or his parents actually–would indenture the lad to a master craftsman for seven years to learn a craft. Of course it depended on the craft, but a little extraneous education had to happen; printers probably had to be able to read and builders might need a little math. This system certainly served a quality control function, buildings ought not fall down and apothecaries ought not hand out poison more that was absolutely necessary, but the most compelling reason for apprenticeships were to protect the guild. This kept competition down and wages up if there were only so many workers in any a given field. Apprenticeships were by no means unique to England, it's the way things were done in Europe and America too for that matter. In defense of apprenticeships, it must be said that they did provide job-skills to people who went on to build and make and just generally increase the *Wealth of the Nations*[*].

Along about 1810, the English noticed that there were lots of things that needed dong in the economy that the medieval guilds just couldn't handle, so they repealed the *Statute of Artificers*. This old law defined both who should be doing things, and how things should be done. Scarcely surprising. With the coming of railroads for example, the need for the guild of long-haul oxen driving teamsters diminished, and contrary wise, the question of what guild was be in charge of those new-fangeled steam engines arose. But we are ahead of ourselves. We will come back to the educational consequences of mercantilism and the industrial revolution after we revisit religion and education.

The notion of what we might think of as charity is a function of the enlightenment that suggested that life just maybe was about more than suffering and getting into heaven. The parish church took up the role of looking more carefully after the health and welfare of the poor, rather then just their souls. While about it, they came to concern themselves with their minds as well.

Early in the 1800's, non-conformist and / or non-denominational schools began to take students from the purely Protestant churches. These "British Schools"[†] were still charitable and still had a religious connection, but they teaching as many as 25% of the school-age children. In 1833 (4 years before Victoria's coronation) Parliament voted sums of money to build schools. Various acts and state funded programs unfolded thereafter, In 1880, for example, education was compulsory for children between five and ten years of age. The *leaving age* was raised to 11 in 1893 and 12 years of age in 1899. It wasn't all fun and games for children however; any child working full time who was under the age of 13 had to produce a certificate of *education standard* or the employer was fined, but it was apparently not a very steep fine. By the end of the 1800's, there were fee charging schools for the rich, parochial schools which charged fees on a charitable or sliding scale for the particularly devout, and state funded schools for everyone else. Curriculum was standardized and modernized, but Latin was still taught throughout.

As all this was going on, England was the center of the world, She imported raw products from all over the world, making fancy expensive things out of the stuff, and shipped products back out to the rest of the world at great profit. Lots of engineering, administering, and merchandizing created the need for technical educations and technical colleges which were initially funded by a whiskey tax! There was even a Department of Science and Art which approved the curricula. In 1900 the leaving age was moved up to 15.

A few comparisons with education in America are appropriate about now.   School in America have more intensely local affairs than in England, if only up thru secondary school. In 1862‡ the Morrell Land Grant Act provided for agricultural and engineering education. In 1916 the federal government began to provide for vocational education in somewhat the same way England began technical education, but quite unlike England, America got itself all tangled up in race and segregation issues from as far back as 1890.

The 20th century begins a very confusing series of reforms and acts in England that were the consequence of two world wars and the machinations of the conservative and liberal governments. Perhaps the most important one, the Butler Act came along in 1944. This was a three part system consisting of grammar schools, secondary modern schools, and secondary technical schools. It hinged on a test students were given at age eleven that determined if the would go on to what to the American mind would be vocational / technical schools. Better students would go on to grammar school, or what American would think of as high-school or preparatory schools.

* The Wealth of Nations by the English philosopher Adam Smith, was published in 1776 and is considered the first and perhaps most important book on what would come to be the science of economics. Adam Smith suggested that his famous 'invisible hand' (an internal market-driven control) was the best way for economies to regulate themselves rather than external controls like government caveats or the even guild / apprentice system.

† The Scots were funding schools for everyone as early as 1660.

‡ At about this time, America was one if the most literate countries in the world.

scones   -a little round biscuit made with suga, egg wash, and sometimes with fruit, raisins, or sultanas (yellow raisins), but without yeast like **crumpets**, These are very important accompaniment for tea and clotted cream. American scones are made in little triangles. No one knows why. In the southern part of England, scones are pronounced to rhyme with *tone*, but to the north, it rhymes with *gone*. These various pronunciations also differentiate between the classes, but only a Brit can sort it out. The capitalized *Scoon* is a palace in Scotland with the *Stone of Scoon* -an actual rock- where the Scottish kings sat. (Some tough and unpretentious buggers these Scot kings.)

schooner   -either a glass a little larger than Americans might expect for sherry, or smaller if for beer.
-or- -a smallish ship fore-and aft rigged with two masts, the taller one being at the back, or a larger ship with a similar rig of three or more masts all the same height.

scotch eggs   a hard-boiled egg rolled first in sausage meat, then rolled in egg yolk & breadcrumbs, and deep fried. Classic picnic food. Think of American deviled eggs, but meatier and greasier.

Scot   -someone from Scotland. Scott is either the first name, or the proper name for the *Clan Scott*. **Scottish** is the modifier, NOT to be confused with...

scotch -whisky made form malted grain usually dried over a peat fire that gives a characteristic smokey flavor. The word *whisky* is tricky. Scotch whisky is not to be confuse with Irish whisk*E*y.

Scotland   -to the north of England. It was the second kingdom which, when Wales is stirred in, gives you Great Britain. To understand the English and the Scots, begin with the English view that Scotland is at least less troublesome than Ireland. It goes back to the Romans who built Hadrian's Wall to keep out the Scots –the Picts actually, who were a particularly tough variety of Celts and the Celts weren't any too sissy to begin with.   Things did not improve and there was pretty constant warfare until the English finally subdued them in 1707 when the two kingdoms were unified, at least to the minds of the English. The Scots did not see it that way and kept fighting till 1745 when **Bonnie Prince Charles** lost the battle of Culloden. More of Scotland was Catholic than was England and this did not help matters.

To put it in terms of American History, the Scots were a little like the South after the Civil War; exploited, impoverished, and increasingly patriotic to Scotland as a consequence. Today Scotland has its own Parliament, church, breakfast sausage, and whisky. They are better engineers and the North Sea Oil is in their back-yard. Every so often, the Scots get together to vote on the possibility of dropping out of the Great Britain / United Kingdom thing. They haven't yet, but stand by. BTW -*scotch* is a type of whisky.

Scotland Yard   -a street in London where the Metropolitan Police built their headquarters in 1829. The nick-name has stuck so well that when they moved their headquarters across town to Victoria Embankment in 1891, it was still called Scotland Yard, but sometimes referred to as the New Scotland Yard. Whatever its name, it is NOT England's equivalent to America's FBI. It is a big city police force with enough personnel to have specialists that many from time to time be called on to help out the local constabulary. For the big cross-boundary crimes, the **Special Branch** might be called upon to do the sort of things the FBI does in America.

Scottish Highlands   Yes, they are high, both in terms of elevation and latitude, but the word comes from Scots Gaelic word *Ghaidhealtachd*, shortened to Heilands, meaning the *place of the Gaels*.

Lots of history, poverty, rebellion, and horrible exploitation by the English. This led to forced mass emigration, first to Ireland and later to the colonies. In literature, someone from the Highlands is to be taken very seriously indeed. It is also beautiful in a wild and rugged way. Today it is a vacation spot for the wilderness camping crowd.

scratch meal -made from left-overs

screw   -a twist or *spill* of paper to hold a small quantity of something, or a prison guard.

scullery   -a room behind the kitchen for cleaning pots and pans. A scullery maid was at the very bottom of the household servants hierarchy.

Scunthorpe   -England's equivalent to America's *Podunk*. Both towns are verbal shorthand for hopelessly dull, insignificant, and provincial. Scunthorp is an industrial town, (steel making), of about 65,000 souls in north-east England.   While it doesn't show up in English literature other than in comedy, its name contains the a horrible word which triggers a number of internet obscenity filters. It has been variously listed as *Scoonthorp*, and *Scumthorpe* etc. and is at the center of what is now called the *Scunthorpe Problem* which is an example of robotics and censoring run amok. BTW, it's pronounced *skun' thorp*.

Sea Lords   -four members of the Royal Navy's Admiralty who did large scale planning along with two civilian members who did not do the strategic command and control thing.
After 1964 the Admiralty was absorbed in to the Ministry of Defense and five more civilians were added. At the time of the sinking of the Lusitania and America's entry into WWI, **Winston Churchill** was a senior Sea Lord, while across the pond, FDR was the Secretary of the Navy.

Seymour, Jane   Henry's third wife. She was born about 1504 to an old but obscure Norman family. She was considered a beauty and of somewhat loose morals so she became a pawn in Henry's court. The intrigues were successful and at about age 32, she married Henry shortly after Anne Boleyn's execution. To Jane's credit, she learned from her predecessor that it was best to be seen and not heard and not seen to too much either. In 1537, she gave birth to Edward VI and died shortly after. Her son would be king from age ten to age fifteen when he also died.

Season, the   From about May to early August, the trendy swells needed to be in London for all the fashionable parties and to turn out their daughters.

secondary school   -before about 1960, these schools were for students up to about eleven years of age to prepared them for vocations. They were replaced with the **comprehensives** and now are roughly the equivalent of American high-schools. see **schools**

secretary   He or she may be a stenographer or executive assistant, but more commonly it refers to a position in the Cabinet. The term is largely interchangeable with **Minister**, but the later is more current. Originally a nobleman's secretary handled correspondence and the administrative details of running the holdings and may be thought of as a consultant more than a servant. The secretary of a clubs and societies, particularly charitable ones, not only keeps the minutes, but is the administrator and is probably beholding to an elected board of directors.

Secretary of State   A little like America's Secretary of State -but more complicated. Today this position is one of the four Principal Secretaries of State, (The other principal offices are the Prime Minister, Exchequer, and Defense.)
    Historically, the king had a clerk and later a secretary who wrote letters for his signature or seal. As time went on, this position morphed into Secretaries of State of the Northern and Southern Departments. Both dealt with Home Affairs but divided Foreign Affairs -the northern district dealing with northern Protestant counties and the southern department dealing with the Catholic southern counties.
    After the union with Scotland in 1708, a Secretary of Scotland was added and later two more, the Home Secretary and the Foreign Secretary. The third secretary, the Scottish one, was discarded, but two more were added, one for the War Department and one for India. All this is probably unimportant to an American unless you bump into one of them in some romantic novel.

Secretary of the Treasury   The minister just under the **Chancellor of the Exchequer**. Between the two of them, they sort out how much money the other ministers get, how much public employees will be paid, what and how much the government buys, and where the money comes from.

see   -a bishop's territory.
see off   -escorting someone out -without their necessarily wanting to
        go.
see out   -politely seeing someone to the door for friendly good-byes.
see over   -to inspect.

see right   -to settle up what might otherwise be a fraught situation.

Selfridge   -a department store second only to Harrods in size and prestige.

sergeant   -like an American military sergeant, but coming in only two flavors in England, the Sergeant and Sergeant Major. (America slices and dices them up into several different levels.) The English Sergeant Major is the oldest sergeant in a company and the Regiment Sergeant Major is the top enlisted man. An English police sergeant is much the same as an American one, a level up from the constable. Finally, a sergeant is not to be confused with a serjeant -an old and obscure term for a high-status and expensive barrister.

semi-detached   -a duplex. These are much more common in England than in America and as in America, the owner lives in one and rents the other.

seminary   Historically, this was a school for a specific profession perhaps educating the clergy but not necessarily. They acquired a bad reputation among Protestants in the 1860's because the Catholics trained guerrilla priests to infiltrate and spread popery. The Church of England actually stopped using the word all together. In the early 1800's, *ladies' seminaries* came about and acted as what we might think of as finishing schools today.

sennight   -seven nights -a very old word for week.

servants, domestic   There is much to be said about servants in England. First thing is to say it was a much less enjoyable life than TV and movies would have us believe. Second thing to remember is that it started way WAY back with slavery during the Roman occupation, improved only slightly under Norman feudalism, became the backbone of the monarchy and government during the Renaissance, and bumped along for hundreds more years and finally reached its starched-uniform-wearing, stuffy, formalized, rigidly hierarchical, sexist, and oppressive pinnacle toward the end of the 19th century. Good stuff if you are writing Gothic Romance. Sucked for the people involved, but, by WW I, it was mercifully pretty well on its way out.

Begin with the second thing first and consider the Roman Governor of Britannia. He had to report back to his boss in Rome. Even **William the Conqueror** had to go back to France now and then on business and when there, he 'owed fealty' to the French (Frankish actually) king. To some degree even the English kings owed something to the pope, at least until

Henry VIII set aside Catholicism and started his own church. Perhaps not the king, but from there on down and throughout history, everyone worked for someone higher up the food chain. The *peerage* -the mystifying order of who was the coolest richest bossiest guy or gal really came down to who their daddy was and thereby, who had to kiss the fewest butts. It is perhaps to the credit of the American mind that this sort of thing is a little incomprehensible.

Getting enough to eat was one of the big concerns back then and land was where food came from, so land was the source of power and wealth. Feudalism was the system of land ownership mixed together with the ownership of labor. The modern notion that a worker owned his own labor hadn't occurred to the various land-owning nobility, nor–it must be said, had it occurred to the peasants who were pretty preoccupied with staying alive till they got to heaven, so the church was another big concern. (The church had its own land and its own rigid hierarchy of bosses too.)

The final big thing back in the day was war. It was often among varieties of Englishmen over this religion or that. It was often with the French, but Spain and Denmark as well as a few other kingdoms show up in history. The middle managers in all these big things were the *knights* who were useful and owed *fealty* to the nobility and / or the church. Between hostilities, this meant extracting food and taxes from the locals. Occasionally they would go off to war with their own servants -*squires*, and recruits etc. They did so with abundant awareness of who kissed whose what. As a part of this business of service and ranks and hierarchy, we have the military. This was not a small thing, but military rank was pretty well nailed down by the Roman and the English took it up where the Romans left off.

England and most of Europe set aside war for the plague between 1348 -1349. The plague killed off one third to one half of the population so war would have been a little redundant. Bad news if you died, but if you survived, it was a good thing because a labor shortage down on the farm led to rising wages. Things got so bad in the eyes of the aristocracy that in 1351 Parliament passed the Statute of Laborers which was sort of a 14th century wage and price control measure, but it only controlled wages. Prices –particularly for food– went up, and it all fell apart.

After various rebellions and revolts, serfdom was eliminated. Up until then, the surfs were not *technically* owned by the local lord, but rather owned by the land which in turn WAS owned the lord. Pretty thin gruel of a legal fiction to my mind but it wasn't 'slavery.' The big news for onion diggers and stable-muckers was that they now could go down the road if the employment grass looked greener over yonder. By 1450, English workers had the highest wages in all of Europe and would continue to do so well until the 19th century. We begin to see just a hint of a middle-class about now, but for the greatest number of people, they still had to put in time on the squire's farm or in his household. And heaven help Joe Onion-Digger if he had a pretty daughter who caught the Lord's eye, but more on this later.

At the very top of the heap (in London rather then being down on the farm and out in the sticks) was court. ***Queen Elizabeth***, (1533-1603), had a grand court that provides an illustrative intersection of servants (ceremonial and the actually productive ones) the peerage, and the operation of the government at the time. At the bottom, were the servants who made beds, did laundry, scrubbed pots, and cleaned out the stables. This crowd numbering in the hundreds was invisible at the time, other than showing up in the occasional rags-to-riches story written much later. There were also dozens of career servants who were well paid by the standards of the day, but the queen had the best and most experienced people in the roles of...

- almoners who gave alms to the poor.
- kitchens -various kitchens with various capabilities and specialties, and many of the best cooks in the Realm.
- cellars for wine, as well as butter and cheese.
- acataries who bought and processed meat, fish, and salt.
- poultry for not only poultry, but other white meats.
- laundry for table and bed linen as well as towels (Clothes were done elsewhere.)
- scullery men and maids.
- woodyard for cooking & heat, as well as rushes that soaked up what we now put in the toilet.
- spicery for spice, fruit, and wax to seal the bottles of spice.
- stables

Each of these departments were so large and busy that the various department heads fulfilled their roles more as accountants and managers than actual cooks and stewards etc. A large part of everyone's job was to impress visiting royalty and diplomats as well as to look after the queen and all her hangers-on. It was good work if you could bet it and it was a lucky peasant boy who got a job shoveling out the queen's stables. He could go far.

A little higher up were the monarch's guards. (Not to be confused with Queen's Guard -the guys in the big black hats standing outside her

residence. These guys carry loaded guns and are very serious about their job even though they look a little silly to the tourists.) The guards were hired based on their height and looks. The regular queen's guards who guarded the queen had wore pretty uniforms, but were presumably skillful in matters of defense and arms. (The desirability of tall impressive guards would survive until well into the 19th century when the most desirable footmen servants, the ceremonial body-guards were the tallest.)

Still higher were the government professionals. Usually put into position, once again because of daddy. But not always. Some number of these councilors were actually talented and skillful at things like diplomacy, economics, foreign trade, and what we might today call executive management.

From here on up the ladder, Elizabeth's servants were entirely ceremonial and always the kids of some important personage. These include six Maids of Honor, two or three Ladies of the Bed Chamber, some Grooms of the Privy Chamber, and one Gentleman Usher. All of them looked after the queen. Even at this level, there is a hierarchy. At the bottom were the servants of the Presence Chamber which was pretty much the whole court.

Next up, was the Privy Chamber with its compliment of servants, both ceremonial and productive. This is where she met with her councilors and did most of the business of being queen. 'Privy' means *private*. It came to mean the toilet / biffy only much later -for obvious reasons.

Finally, there was her Bed Chamber with her most trusted crew. Even here, she was hardly ever alone. Elizabeth acted the role of a virgin her whole life, and historians are doubtful about her virginity, but given the number of people were around her 24-7, it seems they are justified in debating the real state of her chastity.

The ceremonial servants were her bare-bones traveling staff and each of them had their own staff of servants who did some actual work. Each of her 60 (sixty- -yes -that's a big six-zero) royal residences had another layer of local full-time professional servants. The Queen and her court would typically only stay at a given palace for a few weeks at a time, before it needed 'airing and sweetening.' This is to say they needed to gather up all the used rushes and air the place out.

So it went thru the Englightment, Regnecy and other eras till we come to the Industrial Revolution. Several things to remember about this revolution; first, there was something to buy besides turnips. Second, land was no longer the only source of wealth. Some people got rich my making things and other people got rich by selling those things to well-paid farm workers. (This is of course a gross oversimplification. People got rich lots of ways that often involved the colonies.) The final thing to remember is another of those things very confusing to Americans; actually doing something productive for your money was not nearly as cool as having a rich daddy *give* it to you.

But first a few words about 'class' that will also baffle Americans. Yanks view class a function of money or of some combination of education and talent which often leads to money. Stir in pluck, and you have the whole Horatio Alger thing. Brits, or old-time Brits, take a different view. You are what your daddy was and will only ever be only what your daddy was. Period. Full stop. At least until after WW I and for the blue-blood-blue-hair crowd, only after WW II.

You can take some small pity on the English. Until after the *Restoration* (1660 - 1685) there were only two classes, the nobility and everyone else. Actually, this is another over simplification; to over-simplify slightly less, there were the nobility who both owned land and could pass it on to their kids, and then there was the gentry. Useful word *gentry*. Its meaning has changed over the years. Back then it meant the knights who could not pass heir land on to their kids. Then there was everyone else. Briefly, lawyers. doctors, professors and a few other professionals were allowed into the gentry, but this would change.

London was the biggest urban area in the western world from the time of Elizabeth. (New York would surpass it in population only about 1925.)

As industrialization and urbanization continued, things changed. Manufacturers and merchants got rich and tried to become a middle class, by being what Americans would call snooty; they put on airs. They became so intensely interested in being all social and proper that they kicked the merchant class (who were often their fathers who got rich in the first place) out of middle class and into what is called the 'working class,' along with doctors and lawyers. They also got themselves servants just to prove that they had made it. The more servants they had, the closer to the gentry they felt themselves to be.

 There were some splinter classes no one knew quite what to do with and whom American readers may trip over from time to time. For example, there were independent farmers who owned a lot of land and were rich and important, but they did actual work and occasionally got muddy, so they couldn't be allowed into the middle class. So the middle class simply ignored them, but they ignored everyone who they felt was beneath them anyway. Sometimes these rich muddy farmers make it into English literature.

Then there were educated young women who for whatever reason weren't married. They became governesses and are the very center of a whole lot of literature. Then there were the younger sons of the nobility went into the clergy, or if they were too stupid for preaching, they went into the military. These hapless chaps also show up as useful characters in certain literature staged before WW I and a bit later.

David Grote* defines the hierarchy vividly and completely as follows:
1. Nobility
2. Genrty (non-inheritable titles, landowners, leisured)
3. Professional gentry (civil servants, clergy, officers -from gentry families)
4. Middle-class professionals (doctors, lawyers, officers, dons)
5. Modern professionals (engineers, architects, headmasters)
6. Middle-class businessmen (industrialists, brokers, bankers, foreign traders)
7. Middle-class merchants (wholesalers, operators of chain stores)
8. Servants of the gentry
9. Office workers (clerks, bank tellers, bookkeepers, schoolteachers)
10. Farmers
11. Shopkeepers
12. Servants of the middle-class
13. Artisans (including actors and musicians)
14. Shop assistants
15, Skilled industrial workers
16. Semiskilled industrial workers
17. Manual laborers (urban or rural)

But by far the biggest and most important splinter class was the servant class. Notice where they fall in Grote's hierarchy. We began this essay with the observation that everyone was a servant to someone else, and this was no less true in the 19th century. A great part of the population, as many as two million in London alone, were servants by the end of the century. The curious thing was that not many stayed servants. There were certainly career servants, but because a married servant was utterly unacceptable to the middle class (I don't know why) men and women both passed out of service and on to other work and started families. But if they didn't get married and go on to make other servants, where did the middle class replenish the supply? In a word -the sticks. Young girls fresh off the farm were in big demand. Once she had a little experience under her belt, women servants were the highest paid women in England at the time.

So let's review things as they were when Queen Victoria (1819 - 1901) was nominally in charge. We have the tiny nobility with titles like Baron and Viscount and all. Next we have the gentry who own land, but so do the middle class by now -if only a summer place and if only to impress the other middle class. Then there is the working class or the poor people 'in the trades' & professionals, and finally, the servant class. Depends on how you count, but this was probably the biggest class anyway you count it. At the time, England's *middle-class* was a whole lot richer than what Americans think of as their middle-class. They differ from Yanks in another important way. While American struggled to move up the ladder and are admired for doing so, the English were pretty content to know their place and stay in their place. The rich middle-class were content to stay rich-middle-class, but very interested indeed in showing the world just how classy and rich they were.

Now gentle reader, we have at long last laid the ground work to understand butlers, maids, governesses, and the whole bodice-ripping, loin-burning, bosom-heaving genre of Gothic English Literature.

The poorest <u>urban</u> household aspiring to be middle-class, and even many a working class household would have a maid-of-all-work. She was apt be as young as 14. When she learned she was expected to work ten to twelve hours six days a week and only half a day on Sunday, she was delighted to have it so much easier that she had it down on the farm. Better prospects of marriage in the big city too.

A step up and the family would add either a cook or, if children were in the house, a nurse-maid, and / or perhaps a chamber maid or parlor maid. The chamber maid tended to the family's needs in their chambers, (bedrooms), and was therefore more intimately involved with the family and was necessarily more trusted and of higher status than the downstairs parlor mail who tended to things downstairs and was therefore of lower status in the chain of command. (The maid between floors, the *tweeny* was an apprentice and was sent to wherever she was needed.) These four or five women were the minimum of aspiring gentility.

There is some flexibility as to what servants got added next, but a butler was considered a very good thing to have. He would supervise all the other servants including the cook who might have been a super-star cook who earned more than the butler. The butler in addition to being management, acted as waiter, valet, may have looked after the family horse and carriage, and finally dealt with vendors and tradesmen.

A lady's maid or an assistant cook might be added next. If the family was wealthy enough, they might add some combination of a coachman & groom, laundry maid, scullery-maid, upper parlor-maid, another nursemaid etc. Footman were added at the very top end of the urban household's domestic acquisitiveness. If the staff grew large enough, (and the lady of the house wasn't inclined to do so), there would also be a house-keeper who managed the female staff while the butler managed the male staff, but he was superior to the house-keeper.

This is for an <u>urban</u> household. A county estate involved an entirely different and larger staff, much like a combination of Elizabeth's traveling and non-traveling local servants. Some of the urban servants would travel with the family when they left for the country and cared for the family, but the locals looked after the estate. It might take only a handful of family servants but twenty or thirty estate servants.

At the top of this particular heap was the land or estate steward. He was an expert in farming if the estate grew things, and he collected the rents. Just under this position was the house steward who managed things beyond the butler's purvey. Both of these positions were not so much a servant as a professional and respected much like an accountant or lawyer would be today..

The gardener was as important for impressing the guests as was the cook, and he might manage a staff, but he did not live in the *house* but rather had a cottage on the grounds. There was a head groom or stable master to tend to the horses and perhaps master's dogs, and he might have managed a staff as well. Add a game keeper or two and a grounds keeper and the estate stood ready to impress guests. (But not weekend guests. People who worked during the week were of necessity of the working class and therefore were never invited.

This leaves us with the most literary character of all, the governess of heaving bosom variety, who is drawn initially to the younger fair-haired brother but, against her better judgment, falling in love with the dark, brooding, and vaguely threatening elder brother as we learn the charming younger brother is deficient and broken in some way. Only it rarely ever happened this way. The governess was hired to educate and look after the family's daughters. The boys were sent off to boarding schools as soon as they left the care of the family nurse-maid, but girls were more problematic. The Gothic romances got at least one part right, the governess was typically the well educated but unmarried daughter of a fallen or impoverished ex-genteel family. As such, it would be unthinkable to be a servant, but a girl has got to eat. She was hardly part of the family as having come from a failed family. The servants viewed her as no better than they were, despite her education. It was typically a sad & lonely existence for governesses.

It must be remembered that there was no social security in the 19th century. Furthermore, industrializing and urbanization were changing things in England faster than society could easily adjust. A servant was happy to have food and a warm, (warm-ish) & reasonably dry place to sleep. There is also the English fondness for propriety and knowing one's place. Only the most professional and highest paid servants stayed servants much past the times in their lives when they would marry and start families. Finally, there wasn't much to spend money on. They didn't need cars, or computers. Health care was minimal for everyone, even the rich. Fashion was limited to a nice bonnet to wear to church. The following lists the earning of a servant in pounds with a base year of 1860 and 2016 buying power in dollars.

Position and Pay -in historic pounds and in 2016 dollars.					
grounds keeper	Ł10	$1440	cook (basic)	30	$4320
stable boy	10	1440	first footman	30	4320
scullery / kitchen	13	1870	gamekeeper	40	5760
& laundry maids			housekeeper	40	5760
head groom	15	2160	butler	50	7200
nurse	15	2160	house steward	74	1080

chamber maid	20	2880	head gardener	120	17280
governess	25	3600	land steward	200	28800
head nurse	25	3600	cook (super-star)	300	43200
lady's maid	25	3600			

So what happened to the servants? The very rich still have them, but they are more apt to be authors and rock stars than *middle-class* land-owners. For starters, both wars took a lot of people out of the workforce. Some didn't return for very unpleasant reasons, but many didn't go back into service because they found better jobs after the war. Next there came various labor saving devices like washing-machines, vacuum cleaners, and such that made it faster & easier for people (women) to do their work. Certainly social fashions played a part. It simply came to be seen as tacky to have a house full of servants. With more women working, other women could earn good livings, (without the master providing room and board), working as a char-woman or *dailies*. But the biggest reasons were economic. Various tax reforms beginning in 1909 and continuing on to pretty much on to this day made owning large estates increasingly expensive. Adding to this problem was a depression in the cost of food during the 20's, followed by a long general depression during the 30's, and then finally a long downward trend in the cost of food starting in the 50's and continuing on to this day. This also made owning land less profitable, if not actually an expensive money pit.

   * British English for American Readers, A Dictionary of the Language, Customs, and Places of British Life, Life, and Literature, Grote, David, Greenwood Press, Westport Connecticut London. An excellent resource for serious study.

Severn, River   At a whole 220 miles, the Severn is England's longest river. (The Mississippi River is 2320 miles long) The Severn empties into the Bristol Channel on the southern border of Wales.

service lift   -what American call a dumb waiter, This is the elevator thing that appears in English mysteries for hiding dead bodies and other nefarious purposes. The British *dumbwaiter* is what Yanks would call a *Lazy Susan*.

serviette   -a napkin, usually a paper one.

set up   -the opposite of America's setting up someone for a downfall or to be a target, in England to *set up* someone is to give them a good start.

sexton   -an officer of a church, congregation, or synagogue charged with the maintenance of its buildings and/or the surrounding graveyard. In smaller places of worship, this office is often combined with that of **verger**. The sexton is the head usher in The Church of England

shag -not necessarily to make love, it also means friend or mate -as in "Thank you mate. You're a good shag."

Shakespeare, William   -born -
1564, died 1616, wrote a lot of stuff in between, and knew **Queen Elizabeth I**. What can be said about Shakespeare that your high-school literature teacher hasn't nattered on and on about to distraction? Well, for starters, much of the way both the Brits and the Yanks speak and write can be laid at the Bard's feet.   Your teacher might have mentioned he wrote 38 plays, 154 sonnets, two long narrative

poem and a few other things for which he apparently didn't take credit. What your teacher may have missed is that when he was 18 he married a 26 year old woman who had a baby six months later. Some people who insist they can understand a writer as a person by studying their writing insist that he had a long term affair with a married woman, but another crowd of the same ilk say he was in love with another man.   No one knows for sure, and for that matter, no one knows what he looked like. He never sat for a portrait. The image we have of him today with what is called the *Shakespearean brow* comes from an engraving on the cover of a book published seven years after his death, but people who knew him said it was a pretty good likeness. BTW, *bardolatry* is excessive idolatry of the Bard of Avon.

shandy   -a mix of beer and ginger beer or lemonade. A polite and not-quite-serious drink for women and children. Just for the novelty of it, an American might mix ginger ale and beer in about equal portions. Or zest a lemon, muddle a mint leaf, squeeze & sweeten some lemon juice, and mix it all with some beer. Or just squeeze a large slice of lemon into a cold one, or a lukewarm one if you really want English authenticity.

Sheffield   A stone-age village that became a medieval market town, and then in the 1740's, became the source of the best steel to be found anywhere. Sheffield knives and silver tableware are still the best to be found anywhere. Sheffield knives and silver tableware are still the best to be found. All the steel making and silver plating also made it one of the most polluted places in England as far back as the end of the 1700's. That has all changed. Now Sheffield is home to a little over a million and a half people whose income averages just a little below that of London.

sheep   Today England's sheep industry ranks behind Nigeria, but ahead of New Zealand. Nonetheless, sheep play an important role in England's economic history. In 1265 the crown enacted an export tax on wool and a century later it was so important that the boss of the **House of Lords** had to sit on sat on a ceremonial sack of
sheep's hair -the *Wool Sack*. He still does given how keen on tradition the Brits are.   The American colonists were forbidden to trade wool anywhere but with the mother country in 1699. (Things did not improve till 1776, but this is another story.) It was the industrial revolution and the perfection of power looms in England that really kicked wool into high gear using a lot of wool imported from another English colony–Australia.

sheriff   Not unlike American sheriffs, or American sheriffs of the 18th century anyway. They were local police but in England they were far more involved in protecting the king's deer from poachers and making sure everyone paid their taxes than they were involved in protecting the local peasants from the bad guys. 'Sheriff' is the contraction of *shire reeve* or local royal representative. In the Robin Hood legends, the Sheriff of Nottingham was a corrupt thug who raped and pillaged in the good king's absence. By the 18th century, the sheriff's job came to be more of an expert in farm and estate management. In Scotland, sheriffs are judges.

Sherlock Holmes   -a consulting detective who was the product of the imagination of Sir Arthur Conan Doyle. Doyle's character was the very embodiment of cold logical reasoning, but Doyle himself was a bit out there. Besides writing detective stories, he researched and wrote The History of Spiritualism and tried to contact his dead wife thru séances. To his credit, however, he was also a fervent advocate for justice and his efforts lead to two innocent men being exonerated.

    His first success was in 1887 -*A Study in Scarlet*- and he wrapped up his career in 1927. The total was four novels, and 56 short stories. As for Sherlock himself, he holds the world record for being in more movies than any other character in all of the world's literature. BTW -he never said "Elementary my dear Watson," but *was* fond of saying "Come Watson, the game's afoot!"

Sherwood Forrest   Yes, it's a real place where the probably fictional character Robin Hood hung out. Sadly the forest part has largely been chopped down to make ships for the Royal Navy back when.

shillings   -a coin worth twelve pence -12p- or one twentieth of a pound. 20s = £1. The first shilling was issued by Henry VIII and up until 1971 the shilling was a basic coin in the country, but when England went metric with their money, it was discontinued.

shingle -small round pebbles usually along the shore. In a few million years, shingle might erode enough to become sand and the English sea-shore will be a proper beach, but it's probably not going to have surfers and young women in bikinis unless global warming gets real serious.

shinglers   -were roofers in oak, elm, and later, red cedar from America. see *tylers* and ***thatchers***

Ship Masters   -the technology superstars of the day who were rated in various competencies like inland or offshore waters, oceans, types of ships, navigation, sail / steam etc. (*Supercargoes* either owned the cargo, or represented the cargo's owner. He was more of a merchant or business agent than a sailor.)

ship of the line
   The largest battle ships of the Royal Navy from the 17th thru 19th century. They were all about fire-power; whichever side could get the most and biggest cannons in the right place usually won. Three decks and 60 to 90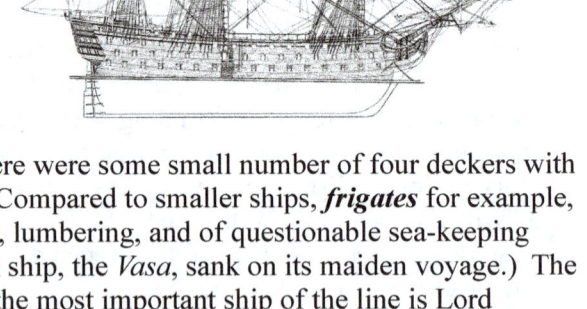
guns were common, but here were some small number of four deckers with upwards of 100 cannons. Compared to smaller ships, ***frigates*** for example, ships of the line were slow, lumbering, and of questionable sea-keeping ability. (One such Swedish ship, the *Vasa*, sank on its maiden voyage.) The most famous and perhaps the most important ship of the line is Lord Admiral Nelson's flag ship the ***HMS Victory***. It still exists as a museum ship in ***Portsmouth***.

shipshape and Bristol fashion   The expression 'shipshape' means the right way to do things. It goes back to about the 1600's. 'Bristol fashion' (first appeared in 1840) is more than merely *shipshape*. The harbor of Bristol has some huge tides -as much as 40 feet. So ships at anchor there regularly were completely out of water laying on their sides because of their keel. Things needed to be tied down much more carefully in Bristol than they did in other harbors.

shire   A handy word that means what ever the author wants it to mean but it is pastoral and probably either has sheep or hobbits wandering about. It used to mean a *county*, but this is also a nebulous thing in England.

shooting   -obviously hunting with a shotgun, but the *hunt* is riding a horse after a fox and does not involve a gun. (Only the Scots hunt deer now and they use rifles. *Henry III* used a lance to hunt boar. One nearly killed him.) To throw a *shooting* meant you owned enough land to be out hunting your own private birds and would invite your friends. A *shooting box* is the comfortable little house out in the county where the shooter lived while hunting and a *shooting brake* was the carriage used to carry the hunting party and all their equipment out there.

Shooting in England comes it two varieties. The sort American hunter would recognize comes in two sub-categories. The first is called *rough shooting* -a single hunter and his dog tromping around the countryside on the lookout for the right sort of bird. The related *wild fowling* is hiding and often laying down next to a cold body of water before first light and waiting for the ducks or geese to come flying over.

The second variety is iconic of Victorian English rich people having weird fun. This is where a line of peasantry (the people -not the bird) go out and beat the bushes to drive the grouse, ptarmigan, or pheasants (the bird, not the people) toward a line of people with shotguns who blast away with varying degrees of skill as fast as their loaders could load their several guns. After all the excitement and noise, they pile back into the hunting brake and head back to the manor house where they would change their hunting togs to luncheon togs for a big meal and nice nap before dressing for dinner. As this was happening, the servants–including the beaters who had the good fortune not to get shot by their betters–went around and picked up all the dead birds.

The English are generally not as keen on guns as are Yanks, and so hunting and shooting is a very expensive status thing. Today there are shooting clubs where for astonishing amounts of money, people can participate in a proper (Victorian) shoot.

shop   An English shop may be either a small neighborhood convenience store, or a store specializing in a certain line of merchandise. In this case, the store was referred to by what it sold, i.e. the grocers, the stationers etc. Shopkeepers still sometimes live above the shop, but England is slowly coming to follow America's example with mega or *big-box* stores. S*hop assistants* are American sales clerks, and s*hop-gazing* is window shopping.

Americans must remember that refrigeration and cars came to England much later than they did in America, so readers will find English women seem to spend an inordinate amount of time shopping for small purchases. A final historic note, Napoleon is said to have insulted England as "a nation of shop-keepers" but there is no record of his ever having done so.

Shrove Tuesday   -the day before Ash Wednesday and the first day of lent. It has also been called *Pancake Tuesday* because people wanted to get rid of all the good perishable stuff they were giving up for lent. To s*hrive, (or shrove),* is to go to confession which is /was a requirement at the beginning of lent.

silly season   -August & September. Parliament in in recess and people are on vacation resulting in so little real news that the media is reduced to telling silly stories.

singing hinnies   -currants, (raisins), fried in (pan-)cakes. The singing refers to the sizzling sound they make and the *hinny* is a term of endearment.

singlet   –a man's wool undershirt or -more currently, a vest-like athletic top. A *doublet is* a man's padded jacket from about 1300 to 1600 and a jerkin is about the same thing, but made of leather.

Sir   -the proper way to address a knight or for that matter, any other armored chap carrying a sword.

sitting room   In a lower middle class home, the sitting room is just for sitting. This is to say a room where the family might just sort of slouch around, sometimes with a friend of the family, but a real guest was be entrained in the parlor. In modern American terms, the drawing room was the family room and the parlor was the front room. Living room is a fairly recent term. see **house, the English**

six, hit for	-in cricket, a hit out of bounds is good for six runs, so like hitting for six is like hitting a home run, a very good thing indeed.
Six Counties	-the six counties the make up Northern Ireland.
six of the best	-six strokes with a cane administered to a miss-behaving boy -synonyms with punishment in general.
six over six	-perfect vision or what the Americans call *20-20*.
sixpence	*s*-half a shilling see *money*
sixth form	-in school it is the optional grade level for college preparation. see school

skinners   -processed the skins of ermine, lambs and rabbits. Their work differed from tanners in that skinners preserved the hide with the hair still on. Now they would be called furriers.

skinheads   -like the American white supremacists subculture, but going back to the 1960's in England. see **chavs**

skittles   -a lawn bowling game in Europe, but a miniaturized version is played in English pubs. It's a little like American shuffleboard, but harder.

slate miners / slaters   -dig up slate in various places place in England from Roman times. Wales had the biggest and best slate quarry in the world and still has. Because slate can be cleaved into thin pieces, it is an excellent roofing material, but it also has many uses such as chalk boards, kitchen sinks, mantles, millstones, and even tombstones.

sleeping partner   -in business, a silent partner.

sleeping policeman   -a speed bump.

slimming / slimming cure -a diet

slipper   -both a bedroom slipper, and a man's slip-on or loafer. It may also be a formal leather shoe suitable for dancing.

Sloan Rangers / Sloanies   Sloan Square is a very expensive corner in south-east London. Young women who live and shop there have been called Sloanies. From the 70's, they are seen as old monied, entitled, arrogant, rude, and clueless.

slot machine -a vending machine

small beer   -low alcohol beer or anything week.

small holding   -a farm that is not profitable but is operated for fun. It's likley to be bigger than an American vegetable garden.

smalls, the   -personal adds.

small   / small clothes
-men or women's underwear.

Smalls   -a first year placement test given at Oxford on Latin and Ancient Greek. It was set aside in 1960.

smelters   -melted and cast various kinds of metal for various purposes like cannons, (bronze), cannonballs (iron), and very high tech things for the day (steel). The Celts were an iron age crowd, but it would have to wait for the industrial revolution for smelting and iron or steel to be more that a rare and exotic material in England.

Smiles, Samuel   -an author of the very popular book Self Help published in 1859. He was roughly a contemporary of America's Horatio Alger (1832 – 1899) and a predecessor to Dale Carnegie (1888-1955).

smocks / smock makers   -made smocks, but the words smock / slop / frock are all related and have a confusing history. A smock might have been everyday outerwear, or a woman's linen undergarment, or a long-skirted coat worn only by men or an elaborately embroidered Sunday-best worn by country folk. Whatever they were and whomever made them, they were less constrained by the tailor's guild.

smoking jacket   -a jacket a man would wear while slouching about the house and smoking. It served to keep ashes off his real jacket and also serves to illustrate what to American would view as crazy British formality. A man would still be fully dressed with shirt and tie, and wearing his smoking jacket, but if an important guest arrived, he would take it off and put on a proper coat.

snooker   -not quite like pool or billiards. The army brought it home from India about 1884. It's played with a white cue ball and 21 other balls to be knocked into the standard 6 pockets of a pool table, but the snooker table is much larger -70 by 140 inches vs. a pool table of 52 by 84 inches. Snooker players look down on mere pool players.

snug / snuggery   -either a cozy back room in a pub, or a private room in a men's club.

soccer -see *football*

Social Democrats   -splintered off from the Liberal Party in 1981 because some *MP*s thought the party had become a little too liberal. see ***political parties***

social security   -not retirement, but public assistance and what Yanks would think of as welfare.

sod   -a general purpose expletive. It's used in things like *Sod it!, sod-off, sodding mess,* etc. It is interchangeable with the American eff word -but less vulgar. An *old sod* may be a good guy, but the word does derive from sodomy.

Soho   A neighborhood in the City of Westminster and part of London's West End. It was the center of various sex trades for more than 200 years until the

1980's when the neighborhood began to gentrify. In addition to the sex industry, Soho was also England's center of the pop-music scene -first the beatniks of the 50's, then the rock and roll crowd in the 60's & 70's. Eric Clapton, Brian Jones, Elton John, Queen, Jimmy Hendrix, the Beatles, the Rolling Stones, and David Bowie all recorded or performed in Soho.

Solent c the channel between the ***Isle of Wright*** and ***Portsmouth***. It shows up in sea stories a lot.

Solicitor the public side of the law profession. These are the chaps you go to when you need a contract sorted out, or to sue your landlord, or– heaven forbid–need to be defended in a criminal trial. In this last case, the solicitor will hire a ***barrister*** who will put on a wig and stand up before the justices on your behalf. see ***barrister***

Barristers	Solicitors
Advocate (in the courtroom)	Legal advice
Hired and instructed by solicitors	The client's point-man
Wear the silly wig and gown, and work in the higher levels of courts.	Business law, children / family law, divorce, criminal, wills & probate, and general ambulance chasers. In general -the same specialties we see in America
EDUCATION: After undergraduate work, both do a year of Common Professional Exam or Post Graduate Diploma, then...	
1 year Bar Professional Training course	1 year Legal Practice Course
1 year 'pupillage'	2 year training contract

Somerset House -a magnificent neo-classic palace in London started in 1776. A variety of important institutions have been at home there over the years, but it is currently houses Inland Revenue–  England's IRS. In literature, it shows up as either the home of the ***Admiralty*** or the ***Registry*** where the records of all wills etc. must be recorded. It also shows up in movies when they need a magnificent English-looking government building.

Sotheby's -an important auction house for art and other very expensive things. It was founded in London in 1744, but is now a multi-national business with 90 locations and headquarters in New York. Its stock even trades on the New York Stock Exchange.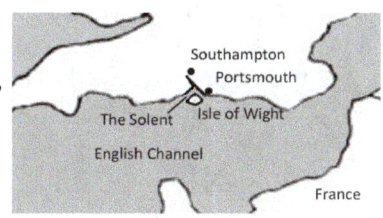

Southampton -a city in the south of England and an important harbor. It is important as the nominal home port for as number of cruise lines (including the Titanic) the birthplace of the WWII fighter plane the Spitfire, and as a staging point for D-Day. It is somewhat less important to the Royal Navy than Portsmouth, but appears more in literature as the place of embarkation for passengers.

sovereigns -a gold coin wort one pound (of silver) until 1971 when they changed it to a coin worth Ł1 and not at all the same thing as 16 ounces of silver. see ***money.***

Special Branch -a crack team in Scotland Yard (The London Metropolitan Police) set up to deal with terrorism and political criminals. But not what you think; it was started in 1887 to deal with the Irish.

spend a penny -take a leak.

spliff -a marijuana joint

spotted dick -desert ***pudding*** with raisins.

sportsman -a hunter or fisherman, as well as an athlete.

squadron In the navy, a squadron is a variable number of ships sent off on a specific task and usually commanded by a Rear Admiral, In the RAF, it is 10 to 20 aircraft also with a specific mission, and in the cavalry, 100 to 200 men. From the Italian *squadra* -a square. see ***military***

squire One of those useful flexible words that has changed so much as to have no specific meaning anymore. Originally it meant a knight's personal servant and / or young knight in training. A knight might be given non-inheritable land that he could not ordinarily pass on to his heirs, but gradually a squire came to mean a land owner and by the middle of the 1600's, a country gentleman -one who both came from a good family and owned enough land. Even then, it was flexible, but he was probably the richest guy in the neighborhood who lived in a ***manor*** and didn't seem to do any work. Squires, or their wives, were the source of second sons who went off to the army, clergy, colonies, or Her Majesties Service. Such sons were very useful to period writers. After about 1800, the squire evolved into a literary character who was generally well-meaning but none-to-bright gentleman more interested in hunting, his dogs, and whatnot than in running the farm. He had an estate steward to do this. see ***gentry, manor,***

squash -a fruit soft drink. In times past, it was made from fruit. Now it is made from powder.

stargazey pie   -a pastie / pastry made with fish heads sticking out and gazing at the stars.

starters -appetizers

steeplechase   - a long distance horse race going back as far as far as 1752 from a wager in Ireland. They involve jumps, hedges, and water filled ditches. The word comes from a combination of the fox hunt which was similarly long and cross-country, and the tradition of running from one church steeple to another church steeple.

stationers   -made pens (dre4ssed quills), pencils, ink & stands, seal wafers, and in short, everything *but* paper. Stationers were also involved in much of the book making & selling process, but *not* the actual printing. The first *Stationers Company* was formed in 1556 under the rule of the church it had more or less a monopoly on literacy. see ***religion***

staymakers   -used whalebone (baleen) to make corsets from the 18th century till 1905.

steak & kidney pie   -a pie, no great surprise here, but it used to be oyster and kidney pie, but oysters got expensive. Nowadays it probably doesn't have kidney either but just beaf and 'taters

stew   -thick soup or a sauna / steam bath. Deriving from this second meaning, a stew in England would be what Yanks would think of as the red-light district.

steward   -originally a butler-like servant, and later an employee of a nobleman to supervise household matters and perhaps the finances. Only in the 20th century, did stewards become waiters on ships and later still, on commercial planes.

sticky wicket   -a difficult situation. In cricket, something like baseball's home plate is actually three wickets –sticks about 30 inches high and three inches apart. Two bails (little wooden do-hickeys) are set to span the top of the wickets. When the bowler (the English equivalent of the American pitcher) hits the wicket and knocks off a bail, the batsman is retired–he's out. If a bail does not fall when the wicket is hit by the ball, it's said to be a "sticky wicket."

stile   -a little stairway / step ladder over a fence instead of a gate which might be mistakenly left open.

stoat   -a little mink-like animal that's brown in summer and white in winter. White stoat fir is ermine and just the thing for king's robes.

stocks   -bonds in America. American stocks are *shares* in England, so while an American stock broker handles stocks and bonds, the English chap handles shares and stocks.

   Stocks were also the punishment device from the medieval to the early 1700's wherein the feet were fastened between two timbers. The pillory was the one with the head, wrists, and sometimes feet being immobilized. Humiliation was part of the punishment, but depending on the time of year and the length of the punishment, either could be fatal. It must be said that such punishments were practiced in the colonies longer than in England.

stock jobber   -the initial underwriter of a stock offering. A *stock broker* in England is much the same person as in America.

stone   -14 pounds or 6.35 kg. The use of stone as a measure of weight goes back to biblical times and varied both from place to place throughout Europe and varied based upon the commodity it was to measure. It's very confusing, so it was standardized in 1814. It is only ever used in the singular -i.e. *twenty stone*.

Stonehenge   -a prehistoric monument and a primitive observatory carefully laid out to mark the solstices. It is the most popular monument among hundreds of other trillionths and burial mounds in the area. Each stone is 13 feet high, 7 feet wide and weighs about 25 tons, Construction began about 3000 BC  and was finished a thousand years later. This would put late it in Neolithic era or the beginning of the Iron Age. Its builders left no written records, so other than archaeological evidence, very little is known about Stonehenge or its builders. A 12th century edgend claims the wizard Merlin and a cooperative giant built Stonehenge.

stoppage   -a labor union strike.

Strand   More often *the Strand. F*rom old English *stroud* -the river's edge. Basically, it's a road from *Trafalgar Square* to the east where it becomes *Fleet Street*. In the medieval era, it was a trading street that ran from the City of London to the Palace of *Westminster*. It was also where rich courtiers put their houses. Later, from about the 1600's to the 1750s', is became a very fashionable shopping neighborhood. In the 1800's it was theaters and restaurants, and today they have added expensive hotels and offices. It shows up in the writing of Virginia Wolf, T. S. Eliot and of perhaps greater renown, in the English version of the game Monopoly.

Stratford (Stratford-on-Avon) -an ordinary little bridge town, (to cross the River Avon), and farming community (lots of potatoes) till Shakespeare came along. There are actually about four Stratfords in England so it's necessary to add  the *at Avon* to make it Shakespearean. Now it is second only to London as a tourists attraction.

subaltern -an obsolete and generic word for junior officers like lieutenants and ensigns.

subjects   England has no citizens, only subjects. This might be more than a semantic subtlety when considering the difference between the Brits and the Yanks. Or not. Ask a sematics professor.

subway   -a passageway for pedestrians. America's subway is England's *underground*.

succession   The question of who will be the monarch next is endlessly fascinating to the English; it's also complicated. As late as 2013 and 2015, Parliament amended a 1701 law (the Act of Settlement) to codify the idea that queens were every bit as good as kings, but Catholics simply will still not do. (But a monarch marrying one is permissible.) Given that next in line is Charles, who has two sons, Elizabethher grand-kids, and now a male great-grandson, it's all a little moot, at least for the next few generations.

Otherwise, and thru most of English history and literature, the order of succession runs as follows: eldest male son, next oldest etc., grandsons etc., and then if there are no male sons or grandsons, the daughters are in line. Failing this, brothers of the monarch are next and then sisters. Then it moves on to cousins. There are examples of all of these succession in England's history.

This is only for royalty. The nobles are far more chauvinistic; only men could inherit titles. This makes sense, if only a little. All the land that nobles historically *owned, the king* technically lent to them in order to extract value from the countryside. Even more than this, the nobility (amnd to a lseer degreee, the knights) were all about their ability and willingness to raise armies for the monarch should he find himself in need. These are tasks best suited to men.

Suez Canal   -a shortcut from the Mediterranean to the Red Sea and on to the Indian Ocean. It was built by the French, and the English bought a partial interest in it in 1875 because of the importance of trade with India. The Brits took care of it up until 1956 when the Egyptian government nationalized it. There followed a very complicated scene involving diplomats & paratroopers, France, Israel, Egypt, and even the US. The final result was England being labeled "imperialist" and withdrawing. To the English, the whole thing is a little distasteful. It's all a little like America's Vietnam.

Sun, the   This newspaper started as a serious unbiased paper and lost money. Ownership changed in 1969 and it became a tabloid with celebrity gossip, UFO stories, and naked women. It quickly came to have the largest circulation of any paper in England. see *page three*

Sunday   The English take Sundays pretty seriously indeed. Everything is closed. They don't go to church necessarily, but they do do the big family mid-afternoon dinner thing. With the coming of big-box stores and multi-screen theaters, this may be changing. see *weekend*

> **Sunday performance / Sunday show**   -because the theaters are closed, this is when amateur theater clubs give their performances.
> **Sunday School**   -late in the 1700's, the local parish taught reading and writing to worker's children. Other that reading the bible, such schools were not religious, but by the early 20th century, they had become primarily for religious instruction.
> **Sunday Times**   -sober, investigative, and international in reach. This paper gives people something to do on Sundays.
> **Sunday Trading Act**   It was only in 1994 did Parliament gave shops the option of opening on Sunday if they wanted.
> **Sunday tripper**   -someone out on a driving jaunt cluttering up the roads like an American *Sunday driver.*

superannuated   -an old fashioned word for old-fashioned. A *superannuation scheme* is a pension plan

supper -usually a late light meal. see *meals*

Supreme Court of the United Kingdom   12 justices appointed from and by the *House of Lords* who act as the last court of appeals for all of the United Kingdom except for criminal matters in Scotland. They have been around since 2005 when they took over from the *Law Lords.* It's impotent to remember that the separation of powers Yanks are so proud of doesn't attain in England. All England's courts are under Parliament.

surgeon   Up until late in the 19th century, surgeons were sort of the laborers of the profession who were instructed by the doctor. They were addressed as Mr., not Dr. This follows a long history beginning with the medieval barbers who extracted teeth, incised boils, applied leeches etc. The red and white stripes on the barber pole are symbolic of bandages and blood. (Striped poles were also symbolic of barber shops in Asia which often fronted for brothels!) In 1163 the Catholic church forbade clergy from performing surgery and so medicine and surgery were separate practices until science began sorting out anatomy, anesthesia, germs &

infection, etc. A *surgery* is a doctor's office even is no surgery is performed there.

surplice -the ceremonial loose white vestment worn by clergy over the *cassock*. The word comes from the Latin super *-over*. Lately it a woman's fashion.

surveyors -someone who does surveys or appraisals. A *chartered surveyor* measured land with transit and chain in the past and now computers and lasers. A surveyor may also be something like America's building contractors.

suss -slang for suspicion or more recently, to **suss out** something is to consider it carefully before deciding about it.

Sussex A county on the coast south of London. Historically, important for iron from even before the industrial revolution. Now it is mostly a bedroom community with some agriculture.

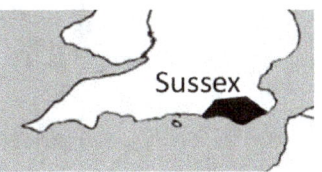

sweater Yes, a knitted top, but Brits wear sweaters only when sporting. Otherwise, a knitted top may be a pull-over, a jumper, or a jersey. see **clothing**

sweet	-candy.
sweets	-as a part of a meal it's desert of any type. see **pudding**
sweetmeats	-candied fruit often in fruitcake.
sweet shop	-candy store, a *sweet kiosk* is smaller and temporary.
boiled sweets	-hard candy like lemon drops etc.
sweetbreads	-the pancreas and thymus. The English eat more of them than Americans

swell / swells From old English, the contraction of 'tis well' -later, 'the swells' refers sarcastically to the posh. Later it came to mean something that is so yesterday and completely-over-with.

Swiss-roll -jelly roll

swings & roundabouts What you loose here, you gain there. Literally, a swing is a child's swing and roundabouts are the little merry-go-rounds you also find in kid's playgrounds. What the children lose when the swing-set tipped over, they gained on the marry-go-round.

Everybody likes *T*. In English, it's the most popular consonant and second only to **e** in the whole alphabet. In some of the oldest languages, it is the last letter; too bad for *U* thru *Z*. It has also been left pretty much alone from the Greek *tau* on to today.

table   In English meetings, to table an issue is to pull it out and talk about it. This is the opposite of the American meaning; which is to set it aside for another time –if at all.

take away   -take out food like curry or fish and chips etc.

tartan   -the woven wool pattern Yanks call *plaid*, but plaid is actually the tartan cloth thrown over the shoulder as part of a *kilt*. Many Scots clans have one or more tartans with distinctive and identifiable patterns.

TD   Territorial Decoration -an award for long service in the Territorial Army which is the all volunteer reserve looking after things at home

tea   To understand the Brit's fascination with tea, begin by boiling some tap water. Let it cool and slurp it down. Tastes filthy doesn't it? Having boiled it, it will not give you cholera so that's a good thing. Now imagine it's not tap water you start with, but pond water, or perhaps worse, water from a well in the wrong part of a crowded city surrounded by a sketchy sanitation system. The boiling part is to kill the wee bugs, and steeping some leaves in it just to make it palatable. Add to this understanding the fact that tea comes from places England colonized. It's not clear they colonized these places to get tea, but it is clear that once they colonized them, they discovered tea to be a very good and profitable thing.

These days, Americans can make tea out of anything that grows: mint, chamomile, seeds, roots, rose petals, and many other varieties of flowers for that matter. The Brits insist proper tea can only be made from a certain evergreen plant with a Latin name that no one cares about. But it comes from China and has been used there literally from before the time of Christ. The Europeans, the Portuguese actually, discovered it only after they got to India in the 1500's when they were looking for pepper.

Tea was sold in London coffee houses as early as 1657. Coffee and tea were neck-in-neck till the next century. This had to do with the price of sugar having come down. The restorative effects of tea were essentially from a generous sugar jolt. To put some dates on it for Yanks, the various Townsend Acts began in 1767 to raise money for the crown. The Tea Act of 1773 was to raise more money as well as an attempt to monopolize the colonist's supply of tea.* The Yanks threw their famous Boston Tea Party later that same year.

Yet more political and financial hi-jinks ensued in 1841 when the Brits tried to break China's monopoly on tea by bringing it to India. The plants they smuggled out of China died, but they shortly discovered a local variety that worked very well. The price of tea continued to drop thru the 1800's and its popularity increased apace. An advertising campaign in India in 1950 left some hundreds of millions of Indians as mad for tea as were the Chinese, the Brits, and most of the rest of the world. Today it is second in popularity only to water as a beverage.

*The British East India Company had attempted to corner the market for tea, failed, and wound up with way too much tea in its warehouses. Prices were taking a beating so the lobbied for, and got a tea monopoly in the colonies. In a very real way, the American Revolution started in part because some businessmen drastically over estimated the demand for some dried leaves.

teacake -yeast raised bread with dried fruit, usually served toasted and buttered.

technical school / college -a secondary school or almost-a-college analogous with America's vocational-technical school.

Teddy-boy -a fashion fad in the 50's involving young men wearing Edwardian era clothing and rock-and-roll hair styles like Elvis Presley. They were not necessarily hoodlums, but frightened the establishment. This was undoubtedly part of the appeal to the lads. see **chavs**

telegram Distances in America are so great that a telegram was the fastest way to communicate between cities back in the day, but in England, they were often used for quick communication across town. Faster than even England's excellent mail. At least until the telephone came along.

Telegraph, the   -technically, the *Daily Telegraph*, but it is only ever called the *Telegraph*. It goes back to 1855 and is now considered the paper of record for the conservative middle-class.

telephone   Alexander G. Bell brought the phone to England in 1878. It was something of an expensive novelty at the time, but would become pretty widespread by the time of WW II. The post office ran things till the phone company was privatized in stages from 1969 to 1981.

term   Like in America, sessions at university come in terms, but unlike America's fall, winter, spring, summer etc., various schools in England have very old traditional names like Michaelmass, Hilary, Lent, Eastern, and Trinity terms. It depends on the school and the length of a term like American school's quarters or semesters.

terrace   -*row houses* in America with common walls, along an entire block. They are typically two or more stories tall, and comparatively narrow. In certain parts of London they are on snooty elegant streets but  by the 1900's they were being built for the working class. They may or may not have *terraces* (balconies in America) nor level or raised terraces in the back yard (patios in America), but they are called terrace houses nonetheless.

Territorials   Like America's National Guard. They stay at home (unlike the expeditionary forces), and help out with emergencies.
test -a cricket match

Thames, River   The most important river in England. It flows thru London, and is navigable all the way there. It's 215 miles long and drops 115 feet. It empties into the North Sea where tides run 20 feet from high to low and tidal effects extend 55 miles upstream. Thames is Celtic for *river* so it's really the River River. BTW -it's pronounced to rhyme with *gems*.

thatchers   -roofers who used straw, reed, heather etc, to cover and waterproof a roof. Thatch is very picturesque, but also very flammable, and was outlawed in various places in the 17th and 18th century. Today it can still be seen either in rural areas, or trendy little cottages built for eccentrics. Thatchers are actually still around, but their work is more for historic preservation than any practical part of modern construction.

Threadneedle Street   In London this is where they keep the Bank of England. It's called the *Old Lady of Threadneedle Street* for its conservative practices.

tie   An Englishman might choose between his school tie, regimental tie, or club tie. It depended on whom he expected he might encounter that day and thereby identify himself accordingly.

toff   -a derogatory term for an upper class git or a swell.

Times, the   A London daily paper going back to 1788. It is considered the most authoritative paper in England and also the dullest. It's primary market is the upper class and government bureaucracy.

tithe   The word derives from the same Germanic root that gives us *ten*. Historically, one tenth of agricultural product paid to the church and stored in *tithe barns,* but it is a moving target thru history. Tithing goes back to the old testament and later was expected of European Christians from the late 400's, and codified in England in 855. The English crown got involved in 1188, and in 1285 wrote a bunch of laws involving tithes, transfers of property, inheritance, etc. The crown got even more involved, with **Henry VIII**'s help when the Catholic monasteries fell apart and some tithes came to be payable directly to the crown. After 1836 tithes–rents actually–were payable in cash rather than rutabagas. They were still fiddling about with it all as late as 1936, and only in 1970 were tithe-like rents abolished. For the American reader, it's all a part of the historic movement of power from the nobility and church, to an increasingly 'democratic' monarch, and finally, to a secular government.

toad in a hole   -sausage baked in batter. Think of a *pig-in-a-blanket*.

toilet   -from the French *toilette*, beaning to get dressed, so a woman at her toilet was doing her hair, makeup and getting dressed. Toilet soap, table, and cover would be bath soap, a make-up table and the cloth covering that table, but all are old fashioned terms. The porcelain plumbing fixture is a *lavatory* in England today.

Tommy   -an army private soldier. It derived from *Thomas Adkins* in about 1815 as England's equivalent to America's *John Doe.* By WW I it was shorthand to just *Tommy* for the British enlisted man. **Tommy-rot** was originally army rations and came to mean worthless junk from the low quality food and tobacco etc. used to pau laborers instead of money.

ton   -in England it's 2240 pounds and a tonne is 1000 kilograms or 2204 pounds. A ton may also be a whole lot, often 100 of something i.e., *going a ton* is going 100 miles per hour.

toolmakers   -made relatively simple–usually agricultural–tools with wood handles and blacksmithed metal at the business ends. As the industrial revolution got underway, the more complicated tool making chores were done by **machinists**.

torch -a flashlight

Torries This political proto-party goes back to about the 1670's. The Tories were largely Catholic and entirely landed-gentry who supported the Stuart kings as absolute monarchs. They fell apart in about 1832 when Parliament was reformed (to give more voice to the little guy) and resurfaced as Conservatives. see *political parties*

The etymology of the word *Torie* is interesting and telling. When the English came to 'colonize' Ireland, the Irish farmers who were kicked off their land took up crime. The Irish word for robber or highwayman is *toraidhe.* In an ironic twist, the aristocratic English who dispossessed the Irish also came to be called *Tories,* and the title stuck to the conservative or rich-guy side of the political divide.

tosspot -an old expression (before Shakespeare) for a drunk. It may also refer to someone with other bad and/or self destructive habits.

Tower of London At various times, the Tower was a palace, residence, fortified castle, armory, torture / execution chamber, administration building, and prison. It is actually a set of four rather squaty towers surrounded by a castle. This is to say, and big tallish building surrounded by shorter fortified walls surrounded by other fortified walls with smaller buildings scattered around. They started building it in 1078, expanded it in 1190, and rebuilt it in 1285. It's most important use was as a prison but generally a smallish prison for important people who lived in comparative comfort while the king decided what to do with them. Perhaps the most famous person sent to the Tower, was *Anne Boleyn*. She stayed there for about two weeks before the king decided how to solve his problem with the pope. It ended very badly for Anne. Today the Tower is one of England's most popular tourist attractions.

Tower Bridge -just east of the Tower and with a draw bridge. It was built in 1896. It is not the old *London Bridge* which is in Lake Havasu City, Arizona now.

toymakers Toys give us a better picture of what was important to people that might appear to be the case at first glance. While dolls in burial practices show up in any number of ancient civilizations, so do dolls as toys. Dolls that survive till today say a

lot about fashion. Doll houses toy carriages, and model ships add to the picture. Toy soldiers go back as far as 1133; consider toy drums & trumpets, pop-guns, rocking horses, etc.
(While stuffed animals show up throughout, Teddy Bears started in America.)

Before toys may be dismissed, a little history in on order. The Enlightenment was about the view that people were important and alongside this view, came the notion that children might also be important and their childhood deserved some enjoyment. Add the industrial revolution and we see a huge flowering of toys for children including intricate mechanized or *clock-work* toys, magic-lanterns, and toy trains etc., if more for the rich than working-class. What might surprise the modern reader, is that as early as the late 1700's, toys were often educational. Board games and jig-saw puzzles were designed to teach children geography. Victorian rectitude of a hundred years later faced the quandary of children having toys and fun on Sunday. In some homes the solution was to only allow children to play with their Noah's Ark and animal figurenes after church.

Trafalgar Square   A public square in the city of Westminster in Central London that commemorates Neslon's victory over 23 French and Spanish ships in the **Battle of Trafalgar** off the coast of Trafalgar Spain. It was pretty much the end of any plans Napoleon had to invade England. It is also the site of **Nelson's Column**

transported / transportation   The idea of rehabilitating criminals didn't occur to the English until well into the 1800's. Up until then, the best thing to do with bad people was to hang them. For minor crimes, and to the modern mind, these were very minor indeed; about 50,000 people were shipped off to Georgia. The American Revolution put an end to using America as a dumping ground so they shipped them off to Botany Bay in Australia. About 160,000 men, women, and children were shipped off to down-under before the practice ended in 1868.

traveler   -or *commercial traveler.* In America this would be a traveling salesman. When a sign in the pub says 'No Travelers', it means no gypsies / Romani / Roma. Salesmen were still welcomed.

treacle   a by-product of sugar making that is like corn syrup. It might be golden or dark syrup which is almost molasses. American *Shoo-Fly Pie* is much like…

Treacle Tart:
- 9" pie crust A crushed graham cracker crust is very nice and easy but thoroughly American
- 1 cup golden syrup (or a 50/50 mixture of corn syrup and

molasses)
- ¼ cup whipping cream
- 1 cup bread crumbs (or ground almonds, or some of both)
- 1 lemon's worth of zest
Oven to 375
1. Press the crust firmly into the bottom of a pie tin.
2. Mix all the other ingredients and pour into the crust.
3. Bake for 25 to 40 minutes till the filling is set.
4. Allow to cool slightly. Serve with **clotted cream** or whipping cream.

trench / trencher   -before the common man had plates, food was served in a flattish loaf of bread that was eaten once it soaked up the good gravy and fat. Today's expression for someone who is a good and copious eater, a *trencherman,* derives from this old practice.

Troubles, the   Begenning in about 1968, the Catholic Irish in Northern Ireland (part of the UK), wanted the six counties to rejoin the 26 counties of the **Republic of Ireland** to the south. The Protestants wanted to stay English subjects. The following guerrilla or 'low-level' war killed about 3500 people–slightly more that half of whom were civilians–by the time it ended with the *Good Friday Belfast Agreement* in 1998.

trunk makers   -worked in both wood and leather, (horse, seal, or shark skin), and made not only luggage, but buckets and fancy cases for silverware and knives.

troop   In the cavalry, a troop was roughly equivalent to an infantry company, but with prettier uniforms. Troopers were more glamorous so *swearing like a trouper* was to do so more expressively and skillfully than the mere infantry. see **military** & **commissions**

truncheon   -a constable's billy-club.

trunk call   -long distance phone call.

try   -in rugby, running across the goal-line didn't count till the ball carrier touches the ball to the ground. This is a *try* and worth four points, or three in professional games. The extra point is worth two points and is called the *kick after a try.* It must be attempted by the scorer. There is none of this silliness involving trotting specialty teams out onto the field like in America football.

tube / underground   London's subway. It actually got started in 1863 and ran on electricity. It sill runs on electricity, but has been improved and expanded repeatedly. In 2014 it carried 1.305 billion passengers. That's about five times the population of the US. Even so, it's only the worlds 11th busiest. A tube may also be a soda-straw.

Tudor, House of   *Henry VIII*'s family–half English and half Welsh. It started with Henry II in 1485 and ended when Elizabeth I died in 1603 without an heir and the Stuart family took over.

Turk   -someone rude and bad tempered. This is not at all PC by today's standards as it is thought that all people from Turkey were so. In the 1800's it meant juvenile delinquents, but has nothing to do with the *Young Turks* political movement in Turkey early in the 20th century.

Turkish   An expensive cigarette made from tobacco grown and sun-cured in countries that had been part of the Ottoman Empire but not necessarily Turkey.

Turkish Delight   After sugar got cheap enough for the commoners, England had something of a candy craze. This candy was the first popular brand of candy to hit England. It's made from sugar, starch , and flavorings and actually came from Arabia thru Turkey and the Ottomans.

turning   -a side street
turn off   -to fire an employee
turn out   -a thorough cleaning -often of a room
turn over   -to search so completely that everything is turned over.
                      -or to start a car's engine
turn up   -a surprise
turn-ups   -trouser's cuffs. (TurnIps are the root vegetable.)

turners   -made wooden kitchen do-dads. Originally they used primitive lathes to make platters. Today, the verb for using a lathe is to turn in England and America both.

turnpike   -a toll road with barred entrances with a heavy spear-like *pike* crossing the road that would be *turned* out of the way when the toll was paid. They go back to the medieval, but became a major growth industry before the industrial revolution and trains came along. There is only one toll road in England today, but there are still a few toll bridges.

Tussauds, Madam (1761–1850)   Marie Tussaud was a skillful wax sculptor from France. She moved to London and opened her museum in 1835. It has been a major tourist attraction ever since. Its exhibits involving murder and torture show up most often in the movies, but are only a part of it all. Today there are about 25 Madam Tussauds all over the world.

tweeny   -a servant of all-help working between any and all of the floors as necessary.

Twelfth Night   -the last of the twelve days of Christmas end January 5. It was sort of a mid-winter's Mardi Graw until the Victorians re-invented Christmas and *Twelfth Night* came to be just one of Shakespeare's comedies. It is also the last day of the *Twelve Days of Christmas* which first appears in print in 1780 as a memory game in a little book for children. The meme that occasionally goes around explaining that the partridges, doves, hens, maids, lords etc are symbolic of Christianity is without historic basis

twit   an exceedingly stupid person. It sounds like a very bad word in America but is actually not a bad word in England. Nor is 'twatwaffel' which means about the same thing as *twit* and is fun to say.

two-fisted   -not manly like in America, but clumsy and inept or *ham-fisted*.

tylers   -roofers in wood shingles or slate up till the 19th century when they also tiled walls with glazed ceramic tiles. (***Thatchers*** were roofers who used thatch.)

U has a confusing ancestry. In Phoenician, it comes from *Y,* but by the late Middle Ages, it descended from *V.* Old buildings with what seems to be a *V* where you would expect a *U* to be, are actually following spelling rules as old as King Author. The *V* shape of *U* was to be used at the beginning of a word and the *U* went anywhere else. What is more, the Enghlish like to stick a *u* in words like *colour* and *labour.*

Ugandan Affair / Discussing Ugandan Affairs   -a popular modern euphemism for illicit sex. From a fairly well documented incident at a party in 1973 when a female journalist was discovered to be upstairs getting it on with a cabinet minister. They claimed they were having a scholarly discussion about Uganda.

Ulster   -an ancient kingdom in Northern Ireland and the last place to be conquered by the Protestant English in 1690. In theory, it is the six counties of Northern Ireland, but the borders and meanings have shifted throughout. see ***Ireland*** and the ***Troubles.***

up the duff -pregnant

up the wooden hill to Bedfordshire   -going to bed

university   Technically, students study at colleges but sit for exams at university from where they are granted degrees. Up until the Victoria era, there were only Oxford and Cambridge in England, Trinity in Dublin, and Edinburgh in Scotland. It was during the Victorian, and in no small part because of the need for people educated in science and engineering (rather than Latin and Greek) that a number of other universities started and often did so in red brick buildings that were the architectural fashion of the day. These *Red-Brick-Universities* had less status, but taught more modern subjects and, after 1960, even did it for comparatively less wealthy students. Now they do so more along the lines the way America's universities do things.

up and up   -not honest and forthright like in America, but moving up and up in one's career or society.

upper class   -an impossibly subjective term and furthermore, one that changes with time. When it is encountered in English writing, it may have many implications, but almost universally, it at least suggests more than one generation of a good education.

up-sticks   -to move domiciles and sometimes in the middle of the night to avoid uncomfortable situation with the landlord involving overdue rent.

U. S. / US   -abbreviation for *unserviceable* from the RAF.

V is hugely important if only to the alphabet archaeologists. It's the father of *F, U, V,* and *Y. V* comes to Latin by way of *Y* but without *Y*'s stem. Consider the word for *W–double-ue*–or two *ues.* But W looks like a double *V.* The first written use of a pointy *U*–a *V*–in England was in 1386. But despite it's name, W isn't even part of the whole *F, U, V,* and *Y* thing. It's not the fault of the French, but in this case, it has more to do with Old German.

V for Victory   Winston Churchill's invention during WW II, with the palm outward, but turned around it is an insult possibly going back as far as the **Battle of Agincourt** wherein English longbow archers used the first and second finger to shoot arrows at the enemy.

valet   -a gentleman's personal servant sometimes refereed to as a *gentleman's gentleman* who was largely responsible for the wardrobe, but he may have covered other duties as well. see *servants*

van   -any truck of a size up to what Yanks call a *semi.* Also the luggage car on a train, or a *caravan.*

V & A   -short for the Victorian and Albert Museum. It goes back to 1853 and covers 12.5 acres with 145 galleries, It is technically a museum of decorative arts, but not an art museum per se. What ever it is, it has at least one of everything. EVERYTHING !

VAT   -Value added tax and essentially a high sales tax. Depending on the economy, it runs between 15% and 17% and is good for about 30% of the inland revenue.

vassals   -a large part of the glue that held feudalism together. A vassal was obligated to a lord or monarch usually in exchange for farmland.

vestry   -a little room off the side of a church where the priest vested or got dressed. Given that it not part of the church proper, it is also where the lay *vestrymen* met to deal with non-religious issues effecting the parish. A bastard whose parents hadn't had a church wedding, was said to be *born in the vestry* or outside the church.

vet -either to do as background check, or veterinarian. A veteran is an *ex-serviceman* in England.

verger -an official caretaker or attendant to a church. In the past, he was a layperson who assists in religious ceremonies by carrying a ceremonial rod, the *verge*. The Catholic Church as no vergers, but rather ushers who do not carry rods, but collection baskets on long handles

vicar It depends on the religion; a Catholic vicar is the representative or deputy of a bishop and an Episcopal vicar is a clergyman in charge of a chapel. In the Church of England, he would be a parish priest supported by local tithes. Vicars, viceroys, and, vice-presidents are derived from the Latin *vicariou* -a deputy or representative.
     In each case, the parish priest, parson, rector etc, might enjoy the income of the parish without the bother of living in the neighborhood or doing anything other than receiving the money, but he did need to appoint a substitute who lived in the *vicarage* which was the center of the parish social network. In much of English writing, a Vicar is poor, but devout, and often has a wife who was the very model of common sense and community involvement. see *clergy*

viceroy -a local representative of the monarch or vice-royal. When the English Crown decided the sub-continent of India was too valuable to leave in the hands of the private stock company (the **East India Company)** in 1858, they took over and installed a Governor General or Viceroy. (A vicereine can be either a female viceroy or the viceroy's wife.) Louis Mountbatten was the last viceroy of **India** when Indian gained its independence in 1947.

Vickers -the manufacturer of the Vickers machine gun used in WW I

Victoria, Queen (1819-1901) -crowned in 1837 at age 18. She was the last of the house of Hanover. Her mother was a German Princess. She had nine children who married into royal families all over Europe. Her oldest daughter, Victoria, would marry Kaiser Wilhelm of Germany and of WWI fame. Most Americans picture her a sour dumpy old women, but in her youth, she was considered beautiful, if in a Betty Davis sort of way.
     England was on top of the world during her reign, but it was also firmly a constitutional monarchy. None the less, she tried to influence Parliament from time to time, but usually unsuccessfully. Her popularity with the public varied. But after the death of her husband -consort Albert and her long widowhood, her popularity increased. The Victorian Morality

(sexual restraint, low tolerance of crime, strict social conduct, and rabid elitism) may not be entirely a consequence of Victoria, but she certainly exemplified these values. It has been suggested that it was equally a reaction to previous ribald excess of the previous king. It has also been observed that despite the Victorian era's self-imagined rectitude, prostitution and child labor were quite widespread.

Victoria Station   It's actually the London Victoria Station, but everyone calls it simply Victoria. It started in 1860 and while it's not the biggest in London, (London Waterloo is a bit bigger), 80+ million people pass thru it every year on their way to the southern end of the country often on holiday. Sherlock Holmes, several Oscar Wilde characters, and many movies deal with Victoria with some regularity.

Vikings   The Vikings were Norwegians and Danes or actually seafaring tribesmen from what would come to be Norway and Denmark. They raided all over northern Europe and well into the Mediterranean. None the less, England was the favorite target of the Danish Vikings. A particularly nasty raid of the monks of Lindisfarne in 793 was recorded in the chronicles and Christian prayer, "Deliver us from the Northmen, oh Lord." This lead to the somewhat undeserved reputation of the Vikings in Christendom. Norwegian Vikings actually settled Cork and Dublin in Ireland. The Vikings were big on raiding monasteries not because they were particularly anti-religious bullies, but because this was where portable gold was! Not stupid these Vikings. In the end, the Vikings were responsible for fortified cities on the coast of England. The Norman Conquest pretty much put an end to the Vikings.

village   the mallest division of England's political entities usually with a church, but with no more than 1000 residents. In the earliest history, the village was pretty standard for anyplace smaller than a market town. People living there walked off to work in the commons, or the fields surrounding the village. As the ***Enclosure Act***s unfolded along with industrialization, people left the villages for the city, and the village became little more that a bedroom community for the manor's workers who lived in marginal pocervy (The squire's servants lived in the manor house, or surrounding out-buildings and were better paid and of higher status.)

During the Victorian era, the urban middle-class came to idealized the village as a pastoral escape from the bustle and pollution of London and other industrializes cities. Early in the 20th century, there were a number of experiments at building utopian villages. (Most were failures and none survive today as planned.) The notion of a village–utopian or otherwise–proved to have had more in common with Disneyland than reality. First the trains, and then the automobile, flooded villages with developers and built-communities with all the charm of America's Levitt Towns.

In English writing, the village still holds forth as a nice quiet place to live in a snug little cottage, read, and potter about in the garden. Curiously, it is rarely viewed as a good place to raise children the way Americans tend to view their own white-picker-fence suburbs.

Viscount   The fourth level of the peerage. There are very few pure Viscounts, but about 250 who for whom Viscount is a secondary titles. Lord Mountbatten (1900 - 1979), the last Viceroy of India was a Viscount and a Lord.

vole   -a rodent a little bigger than a mouse and smaller that a rat.

Volunteers   -originally a volunteer local militia presumably for defense of the homeland, like the Yeomanry, but more attractive to weekend warrior types of the 18th and 19th century. Shortly before WW I, it was subsumed into the army as a reserve force. When encountered in writing, and depending on the period, it is likely that it refers to something quite different from the pretty uniform wearing regular regiments, and later, even more different from the disciplined and highly professional 20th century army.

Vote   The right to vote evolved gradually in England as follows:

1432	Only men who owned a *40 shilling freehold.* They were pretty rich.
1832	Men who rented valuable land, about 1 in 7.
1867	Men who owned valuable property in the city.
1884	Legislation to balance city and town voters, but still covered only 60% of men. see **Reform Bill of 1832**
1895 - 1918	The woman's suffrage movement was active at this time, but more or less set aside during WW I.
1918	All men who fought in the war, all men over 21 and women over 30 who worked in the war effort.
1928	Universal suffrage for all citizens over 21 years of age.
1967	Suffrage for everyone over 18.

vote of no confidence   Given that the majority party in Parliament IS the government, the prime minister must have the confidence of Parliament to function. To put it in different words, the various secretaries, ministries, and departments are led–at least politically lead–by members of Parliament, and when the greater part of Parliament has doubts about the prime minister, his appointees must also be suspect. This has happened only twice in the 20th century. The rules now are that after a vote of no confidence the government has 14 days to get it together, or a general election is held. On a couple of occasions, the issue was resolved by combining two parties into a **coalition government**. Ordinarily, elections are held every five years.

Maybe the only letter in English that does not come form people living thousands of years ago around the southeast corner of the Mediterranean, *W* is Germanic. This does not, however, make it a simple matter. It's all tangled up with *V, U,* and *Y.* Being as there is no Latin W and Latin was about the extent of literacy in England up until after the Protestant Reformation, *W* was considered barbaric, or at least Germanic, which amounted to about the same thing. In the 16th century, a German grammarian by the name of Valentin Ickelshamer wrote, "Poor *w* is so infamous and unknown that many barely know either its name or its shape, not those who aspire to being Latinists, as they have no need of it, nor do the Germans, not even the schoolmasters, know what to do with it or how to call it; some call it *we*, others call it *uu*, and the Swabians call it *auwawau.*" You can't make this stuff up and I am not going to even try to untangle it further.

WAAC -*Women's Auxiliary Army Corps* during WW I, It was changed to *ATS -Auxiliary Territorial Service* during WW II **WAAF** -*Women's Auxiliary Air Force* during WW II and **WRAF**, *Women's Royal Air Force* after the war. see *voting*

wainwrights -made wagons with four wheels and steering mechanisms. They were considerably larger and more complicated than a carts with a single axle and two wheels that were made by *cartwrights*.

waistcoat -like a vest, but stuffier and older.

Wales Wales is a wee country tucked into the western belly of the England. It is mountainous and has a long rugged coastline. The

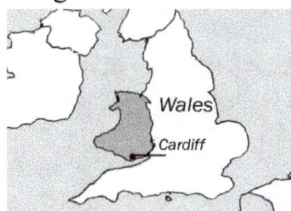

important thing to remember about Wales is that they resisted the Romans more successfully than the English, and today the Welsh speak a derivation of the original Celtic language, which has the distinction of having the most unpronounceable words and some of the longest words of any know language living or dead. The Welsh were also successful at resisting the Franks and even resisting the

English up until about 1485 when the Tudor family with Welsh roots, took over the crown. After that, the Welsh and English started getting along. This accelerated with the Industrial Revolution when England needed Welsh coal, iron, and copper. Today Wales has both agriculture and metals but sadly no oil. It's population is just north of three million people and where you will find the village of Llanfairpwillgwynglyllgoogerychwyrndrobwyllllartysiliogogogoch. This translates roughly as *The Church of Mary in the hollow of the white hazel near a rapid whilrpool and the Church of St. Tysillo near the red cave*.

walk   The English love to hike about, but they are not so keen on camping like the Americans. An English walking holiday probably involves a meal at pub after the day's walk and a nice comfy bed upstairs.

wallah   A word imported from India meaning a minor authority or what an American might call a *tin god*. For example, a *desk wallah* is a bureaucrat, and possibly a **wanker.**

wallet -a briefcase or note case.

wall safe   -kitchen cupboard. (An old-fashioned American *pie-safe* is a cupboard for pies.)

wank   modern slang for self abuse. Enough said. A **wanker** is a useless or incompetent person who is perhaps given overmuch to wanking.

War of the Roses   -a series of smallish wars, (1455 - 1487), fought between the Houses of Lancaster & York on one side and the House of Plantagenet on the other. It's complicated, but the House of Tudor came out on top and the Tudors weren't even in it.

War Office   -the ministry supervising the army till 1964 when it was combined with the **Admiralty** to look after the **Royal Navy** as well.

washing powder   -laundry soap
washing up   -doing the dishes
washing up liquid / powder
                        -dish soap

Waterloo   In 1815 a coalition of English, German (Prussian actually) and forces from pretty much all of Europe, defeated Napoleon in Waterloo. It had been a long time coming and the English were so enthused by Wellington's Victory that they named a bunch of things like bridges, streets, and railroad stations after this otherwise unimportant small Belgian town.
    An interesting aside arises. Beethoven was a fan of Napoleon until Beethoven recognized Napoleon's imperial ambitions. He was composing

his Third Symphony at the time, and had named this work after Napoleon. When Napoleon invaded Beethoven's hometown, the composer renamed ths work the *Sinfonia Eroica* -the *Heroic Symphony.* In 1813 Napoleon's brother Joseph was defeated in Spain by the same Wellington who would defeat Napoleon himself at Waterloo two years later. Beethoven was so pleased with this first victory, that he wrote *Wellington's Victory,* a great rousing composition performed with actual cannon and musket fire.

If this were not enough, in 1880 Ilyich Tchaikovsky wrote the *1812 Overture* to celebrate Napoleon's frozen retreat from Russia in 1812. This is an even more rousing bit of music that has nothing to do with America and their *War of 1812* against Britain. Nonetheless, is often heard as accompaniment to fire-works shows in America on the Forth of July which celebrates America's independence from England involving a completely different war in a completely different century in a completely different part of the world. Americans are often confused by history.

watermen -sailors but not necessarily with sails. They moved boats and barges around inland rivers, lakes, and canals. *Wherrymen* rowed passengers around in *wherrys or* water taxis.

wattle and daub For a good bit of England's history, this was how the common man built things like houses, barns, shops etc. A timber frame was put up, wattle was woven between the timbers and daubed, a stone fireplace and chimney was built, and the roof was thatched. The floor was packed dirt

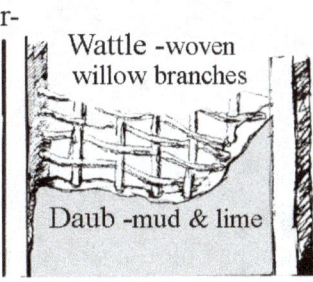

possibly glued together with cow blood. Windows made of oiled paper or linen were put in, but there were not many of them and they were small. see ***houses*** and ***architecture***

wazzock -not merely an idiot, but a crazy idiot.

wedding Marriage was hugely important to the nobility, and even more so to royalty. This had to do with carefully negotiated unification of estates and property for the nobility and unification of entire kingdoms for royalty. In no small way, it also had to do with whose son would be the next king. But for the common man without property, it was somewhat optional because weddings were often heavily taxed. From 1753 to 1827 all weddings had to be performed by the ***Church of England***. Thereafter, what Yanks would call a civil wedding could be done in the local registrar's office. Most of England's wedding ceremonies and traditions are faithfully copied in America with the exception of the multilayer wedding cake. England's wedding cakes are fruitcake while Yanks go with white or sponge cake. This is one of the rare areas where the Yanks are more faithful to the medieval tradition of serving wheaten cakes at wedding feasts. Such cakes were made with white flour rather than other less expensive grains. see *marriage, women, bhans*

weekend   -a comparatively modern notion, at least for working people. For the **middle class** and nobility, the week was *six Saturdays and a Sunday.* Working professionals enjoyed something like a weekend after 1870 when economic conditions lead at least some of them to have a place in the city usually for Dad, and another one in the country where he kept the wife and kids. This involved commuting and to make the trip worthwhile, they simply had themselves a weekend. The working class, on the other hand, had only a single home close to their jobs, had to soldier on. see *Saturday*

webster   -a female weaver. In fact, jobs ending in ...*ster* indicate a woman practitioner. Consider names like *Brewster* and *Dempster,* or for that matter, *spinster* who was a female spinner of thread.

Welsh rarebit / rabbit   A gourmet version of cheese on toast. The name is something of an English joke, coined in the 18th century when many Welsh were so poor they could not even afford a cheap meat like rabbit. Given that it's often made with beer–and some of the English beers are not to be trifled with–cheese and toast could be a substantial meal–with or without the rabbit.

Abby

West End   -the largest central business district in all of the UK and the most expensive. As far back as Roman times, it was a wealthy neighborhood and remains so to this day. *Picadilly Circus, Covent Garden, Trafalger Square,* and *Soho* are all in the West End.

Westminster Abby   -a very old church west of *The City* that has long been church of the royalty for weddings, coronation, and burials etc.

Westminster Cathedral

-a Catholic cathedral and home of the Catholic Archbishop. It is in no way related to Westminster Abby or the Church of England. By the standards of the day, it is a baby; construction began in 1884. What is more, its architecture is Byzantine rather than Gothic. In 1977 Queen Elizabeth

Cathedral

attended a flower show there. This was the first time since the Restoration that a reigning monarch had set foot in a Catholic Church -officialy anyway.

Westminster, City of

The center of government for the United Kingdom. Technically, Westminster and London are separate and equal cities. Westminster began as the center of royalty and was therefor content with

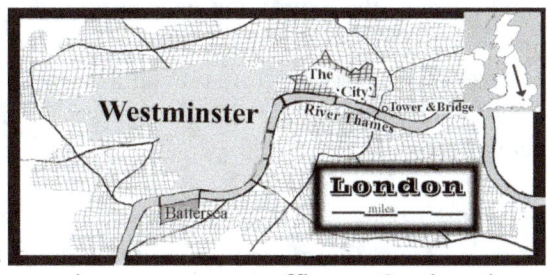

assorted palaces that were converted to government offices . On the other hand, London grew commercially and geographically. Westminster has maintained its independence with its own government and traditions.

Westminster Palace / Palace of

Palace

Westminster.   -a Gothic revival palace in London and the site of the House of Parliament. Construction started in 1016, it burned down in 1512. and again in 1834. From 1332 on some form of Parliament has gathered there. It is also the home of **Big Ben**.

wheelwrights   -made wheels after the blacksmith made the iron rim, but also repaired wheels which was more often necessary in the day than flat tires are now.

Whigs   A political party popular between the 1680's and the 1850's. They were originally constitutional monarchists–as apposed to an absolute monarchy–and therefore concerned with aristocratic families and Protestantism. By the 19th century they supported the Parliament over the king, free trade, tolerance of Catholics, women's suffrage, and the abolition of slavery. They were comparatively progressive by the standards of the time. They would in fact morph into the Liberal party by 1870. After that, they would variously merge and split with the aristocratic Conservatives, and Unions. It's very confusing to Americans.   see *political parties*

As far as word-origins goes, the word *whig* has two possibilities. First, it is old-fashion slang for moving forward in a slow steady pace like on a walking horse, and the *Whigs* were in favor of reform and change, but presumably done gradually. Or the word could be a shortened insult from the word *wiggamore*, (also having to do with draft horses), and refers to a bunch of Scottish Presbyterians who did a clownish job of opposing *Charles I*, They came to be called w*higs* which came then to mean something like country bumpkins.

whist   -a predecessor of the card came bridge. It was played in the 1700 & 1800's with some passion in the military and by the leisure class. Like bridge, it is played by two teams, with the goal of taking trumps, but without bidding. No talking; in fact *whist* is slang for hush. The scoring is, however, so complicated that it prompted Edmund Hoyle to write his book and gives us the expression *according to Hoyle*.

white tie   -more formal even than mere *black tie*. White tie involved tails, stiff shirt and boiled collar. *Black tie* means dinner jacket and cummerbund.

Whitehall   -England's Washington DC. It's a road in London running from ***Trafalgar Square*** to ***Chelsea,*** and considered the center of Her Majesty's Government as the street is lined with government departments, ministries, and memorials.

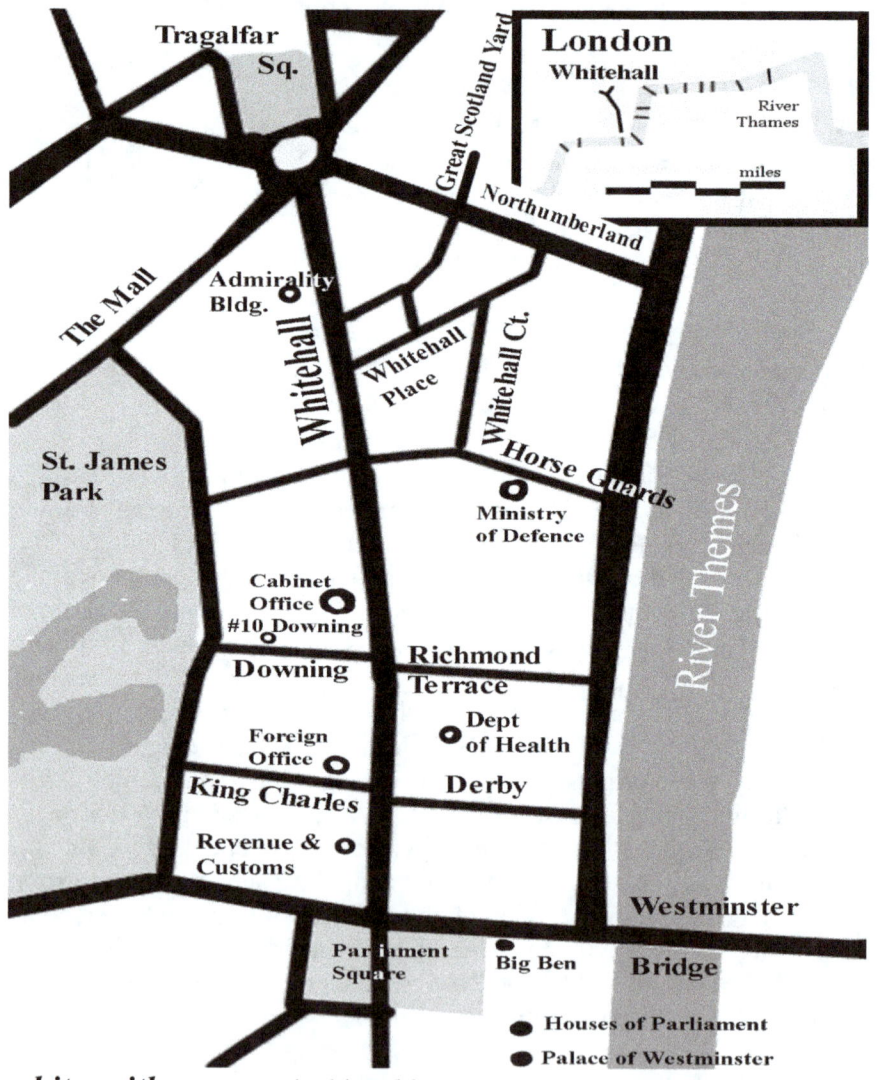

whitesmiths   -worked in white metals alloys like pewter but not tin, silver, copper, or brass

widdershins   -anti-clockwise or going about things the wrong way around. The right way is the way the sun goes in the northern hemisphere.

wigs   -the silly things worn by *barristers.* Everyone who was anyone back in the 17th century wore wigs as a fashion statement. Judges and Barristers (the English lawyers who appear in court) still wear wigs and robes because it lends solemnity to the proceedings. It also disguises an impoverished poorly dressed advocate so as not to influence jurors, and further disguises the various players so criminals would have a harder time finding them and taking revenge. If all these explanations strike you as a doubtful tradition and the wish to be seen as snooty and as 'lawyerly' as possible, this is as good an explanation as the previous. One law professor wrote that "They continue to wear them because no one has ever told them to stop."

wilderness, in the -of politicians, it is the time spent out of office.

William the Conqueror   William the Bastard was born in France in 1028, but after the Norman Conquest in 1066 he became William the Conqueror, at least in England. (While in France, he still owed fealty to the French / Frank King). First he had to fight to keep control of Normandy on the continent after his father died, and then he fought equally hard to keep things under control in England, but he was a descendent of Vikings so it came easily.

William was forced to build castles all over the place to stay in control. England's feudal government—and by now, the conquered government—was arguably more sophisticated than that back home in Normandy at the time, and therefore a greater threat, so William replaced all the Anglo Saxon aristocracy with Norman families. He also had to sort out who he could tax and how much he could tax them. To this end, be sent assessors out to assemble what would come to be called the *Doomsday Book*. The knights employed by the rich Norman families would later evolve into the backbone of the English Feudal system.

William's maturity was spent shuttling back and forth between England and France. One gets the impression he was not so much majestic king as he was a harried business executive who would much rather have been fishing,

The Saxon rich-guys (we can call them the 'nobility' but 'thugs' might be more accurate) were the big losers when William took over. For the little guy, slavery went away. It was replaced with serfdom, which was only marginally better, but it was progress.

Wimbleton   -a wealthy town on the south-west edge of London there they have been playing tennis since at least 1877 when they did their first championship.

Winchester   -the capital of Saxon England before the Franks came along. Its cathedral is one of the oldest and largest in England, and was the center of education until Cambridge opened for business. In literature, Winchester is the center of the Arthurian Legends like Camelot and all, and in the 1800's, it was the source of various educated and enlightened characters like Sherlock Holmes. Perhaps the best book set in Winchester is Ken Follett's <u>Pillars of the Earth</u> which traces history from 1123 to 1174 with a good deal of accuracy and a great deal of vivid storytelling.

Winchester Cathedral   A huge Church of England cathedral about 70 miles southeast of London. It was begun in 1079 and various sorts of construction have continued ever sense. In 1966 Geoff Stephens of the *New Vaudeviloloe Band* wrote populr song blaming it for neglecting to ring its bell when his baby left town.

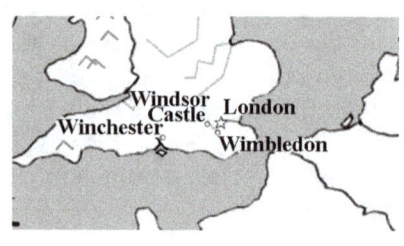

Windsor Castle: -one of six *royal residences*. William the Conqueror first built a fortress a little ways west of London during the 1200's. It actually served a military function; it withstood a siege or two back then and more recently, sheltered the royal family during the German bombing. It and has three

concentric walls with actual crenelations (note the fiddly bits on the roof in the picture.) and had a *mote and bailey*. The showy *palace* part of the castle was started by Henry II and has been added to, plumbed, wired, remodeled and just generally improved regularly ever since. Today it is the Queen's favorite weekend home; but she usually spends the week in London.   see *castle*, *royal residences,* and *architecture.*

Windsor, House of   -the last and current family home of the monarchy. It had been the House of Saxe-Coburg & Gotha until about half way thru the First World War when German things were not popular. It started in 1901 with Edward VII followed by George V, then Edward VIII who hung it up to marry an American divorcee (Oh! The horrors!), another Edward -this one the 6th, and finally the current Queen Elizabeth II.

Wolsey, Thomas   *Henry VIII*'s advisor and Lord Chancellor and the guy who failed to get the pope to give Henry a divorce from Catherine of Aragon so he could marry Anne Boleyn. He fell out of favor and retired, but was recalled to court to face charges of treason and probably be beheaded, but died on the way to London.

women in England   To write about women and their role in society without either having a long string of letters behind one's name, or without being equipped with the proper chromosomes, is apt to be fraught with all manner of danger and opportunity to offend. The issue is simplified only a little in consideration of the fact the American women and

English women were much the same, at least for as long as there have been American women. It is therefore reasonable in this work to speak to the subject of women in England before the English (and the other Europeans) came to America and in due course, fetched along European women to become colonists. After 1776 or so, they become *American* women. As has been mentioned throughout, England has a lot more history than America does and this provides fertile ground for discussion of the topic.

For the American reader a brief study of the history of women and their place in society[12] might as well begin with the Roman occupation up until 410 or so. The Celts, whom the Romans overran, left no written records, so discussing the role of women then would be pure archaeological guesswork.

As to role of women during the Roman Occupation, reading about the intrigues by the wives of various Roman Emperors, senators, and generals might be useful at least for the rich people; for the common man, particularly in Britannia, not so much.

When the Roman left, the Angels, Saxons and Jutes came. Consider Anglo-Saxon women. Think of then as great tall blonds as tough as their husbands rather than pale tea-sipping more modern WASPs. They had it better in many ways than the women who came later. An Anglo Saxon woman could own land in her own name. (This right would be denied *modern* English women until 1882 with passage of the Married Woman's Property Act.) Make no mistake, Anglo-Saxon women ran the household and raised children but men cooked or at least roasted game and they evidently ate a lot of game being as they were more inclined to hunting than farming, The proper role of a wife and hostess in those days was to serve mead. Even before they were married, the man had to give a gift to her father as opposed to later dowries when dad had to give the potential husband some value to get him to take her off dad's hands. Divorce was even a possibility among the Anglo Saxons.

Marriage may or may not have been for love, but it was at least a matter of individual choice with one exception. An Anglo-Saxon *peace-weaver* was a woman who was married off to the son or brother of the next king down the road to keep the peace between the two tribes. Per one contemporary chronicler, "It is believed that, through birth, a woman wove peace by mixing her blood with the blood of another tribe." While this is an admirable end, it also hints at future dynastic marriages arranged to gain or maintain political power. It is also the beginning of two ways of doing things—one way for the rich and another for the poor.

With the Norman invasion, William the Conqueror took property from the Anglo Saxon rich-guys and gave it to Norman rich-guys. The good news was that slavery was much reduced under Norman law, not eliminated, but reduced, and the Catholic Church was becoming a bigger and bigger thing. This last would come to be a mixed blessing. As for

---

[12] The words 'woman's role in society' may have already have offended. What is meant is women's unique role in history, society, politics, the economy, the arts & sciences, and even in the home.

women, they didn't have it quite as good as their Anglo-Saxon ancestors. For starters, they couldn't own property unless they were widows. Their children technically and legally belonged to their husbands. They couldn't marry with out their parents consent, nor own a business without various guild and church permissions. They could not inherit from their parents if there was a surviving brother. They couldn't divorce, but in fairness, nor could men. This is about time we begin to see 'damsels' showing up in literature, but damsels–in distress or otherwise–were rich men's wives and daughters. Otherwise, life was "nasty, brutish, and short.[13]" The common man -or women- didn't see much change with the arrival and subsequent exit of the Normans. We might call this period the Anglo-Norman period to sound all academic, or just call it the *medieval* or even the *dark ages*.

The time from the Norman Conquest in 1066, until the Protestant Reformation in 1517, is a big chunk of history with lots of war and world exploration and Renaissance-ing and such, but a conveniently homogenous period for women. It is necessary first to slice and dice the domestic history into smaller chunks. First and most obvious division is between men & women, then the aristocracy & commoners, and finally, between city and countryside. It turns out that this last one is by no means trivial. It must be stressed that the few records that survive on these matters concern the rich towns-people to a far greater degree than poor country folk.

Let's deal with rich town women first because they are easy. Their job was to bear male heirs and that's about all. They didn't even have to bother with raising them. There were wet-nurses, governesses (for girls) or boarding schools (for boys but a bit later in the chronology) to deal with these bothersome details. The only bad news was they often had to marry fat ugly old farts whom their fathers picked out for them, and had to do so at appallingly young ages; 14 and 15 years of age was about average[14]. Much literature about women in this era shows them with nothing much else to do but relentlessly scheme to get someone off the throne and their son onto the throne or otherwise in power. This was accomplished by hook or by crook, by assignation, seduction, betrayal, murder (often with poison) and all manner of nefarious deeds that make for great stories. This brings us back to Roman women, but the Roman intrigues are pretty well nailed by historic records. It is not clear the medieval women were quite so handy with intrigue, murder, and such. Even so, such plots show up in a lot of Shakespeare's work as well.

In one real-life example, Elizabeth Countess of Shrewsbury (1518 - 1608) married three times explicitly to consolidate her holdings. She buried

---

[13] The political philosopher Thomas Hobbes wrote this to describe things in 1651 during and about the English civil war. It has, however, often been used to describe the dark ages. The quote runs... 'continual fear, danger, of violent death; and the life of man, solitary, nasty, brutish, and short."

[14] There are records of marriage for girls as young as twelve. In one case, they 'were seen abed' together, as was tradition after the wedding feast, but no one expected them to do the deed till they were at least little older.

three husbands and fought with two of the surviving families over inheritance. She finally married her fourth husband only after negotiating for one of her daughters to marry one of his sons, as well as one of her sons to marry one of his daughters. (Today's much divorced and blended family is simple by comparison.) Perhaps some of these women deserve just a little sympathy given the rules they had to follow particularly when viewed by the modern liberal reader.

Among the ordinary folk, things were quite a little different. Everyone worked. Often from the age of eight or nine. Eleven and twelve year-olds were considered adults. BUT, and this is surprising, the average age for marriage among the common folk as twenty five and this is among people who were apt to be dead at forty. Women were paid less, and getting paid at all was likely only to happen during harvest season. A day spent reaping would pay a man eight pence, but a woman would earn only five.

Aside from farm work, the guilds controlled who did what we might think of as skilled middle-class work and women who did such work, did so only under the supervision of their husbands. There are rare court records of cases wherein the husband died and his wife was accepted into the guild and was able to continue doing the work, but the fact that these records are from court proceedings suggests that it only happened as a consequence of what probably was a pretty contentious litigation. What we would think of factory work would come along much later and manufacturing of the day was done in the home or in a workshop in the back yard.

The picture of Sleeping Beauty pricking her finger while spinning wool is accurate. Women were active in the fabric industry, but only under their husband's supervision and she wasn't paid.[15] The *Grimm's Fairy Tale*[16] Rumplestiltskin is perhaps more revealing. The heroin didn't know how to spin straw into gold for the king, but Rumplestiltskin–a man–did and saved her if only to blackmail her later.

Much is made of the fact that women had no role in politics or society at large, but nor did men. The medieval household was a considerably larger more complicated thing than the 20th century family with its 2.3 children. If it was a freeman guild-member's home it was also a factory with servants, apprentices, workers, and step children. [17] (It's harder to draw comparisons between the village guild household and the farm because farms were usually large and owned and managed by rich people but the farm had many workers and the manor house had many servants as well.) So a woman who played a large role in the household, arguably played a larger role in medieval life as a whole; far more than did the

---

[15] Lace-making was an important exception. This was ever a woman's specialty from 1600 to about 1750. It is interesting to note that the average age for these comparatively well paid independent contractors was older than among women in general.

[16] The Grimm brothers were German and published Grimm's Fairy Tales in 1812 -considerably later than the period in question, but the analogy is apt.

[17] Given the mortality rates–particularly in childbirth–remarriage with step-children was far more common then than today, at least until the high rate of modern divorce and blended families is considered. As anecdotal illustration, consider all the evil step-mothers and step-fathers that figure in fairy tales -*Cinderella* and her evil stepmother being but one.

aristocratic brood-mare.

Here are some revealing statistics from the period and once again, it must be stressed that they are sketchy given the level of literacy and record keeping of the day. In 1520 only 25% of men (and probably their wives, but these numbers are even harder to pin down) were wage laborers, and 75% were employers, guilds-men, or otherwise self-employed. By 1650, money was necessary even in the most self-supporting farm; even more so in the village among the guild shops making things. This is to say that serfs were increasingly paid in money rather than turnips. By 1850, the ratio of self-employed to employees had been more than reversed and everyone received a monetary wage. This was chiefly because of the industrial revolution and the factory. But we are ahead of ourselves.

In the early middle ages, a woman's' status was almost entirely a function of her husband. At the top were wives and daughters of the nobility like dukes and earls and such. A bit lower were *gentle-women*, who were the wives of non-hereditary aristocrats like knights. Some small number of women held these titles independent of husbands and there was a degree of blurring between a noblewoman and a gentlewoman.

A *lady* was a married woman who was the head of a large household that had servants. She was probably the wife of a successful merchant or master guilds-man. A bit lower were *citizen's wives* whose husband was a freeman or master of his craft and who had some standing in the community, but without apprentices, employees, or servants. There seems to be more opportunity to improve one's status in society than there would be later, but for women, it was done by either advancing her husbands status, or becoming the mistress of a rich nobleman.

At the bottom were women who were widowed or had been abandoned, spinsters, and aged women. Atypically good records from 1570 in Norwich indicate that 62% of the citizens over 16 were women, and 68% of those on parish poor relief were women over 60 years of age. These numbers are probably low because women were less likely to attract the attention of courts in one way or another.

 Women have always lived longer than men, but less than might be expected if warfare and violent death is factored in (or *out* as the case may be). This came down to childbirth. Between the age of 25 (marriage age for common folk) and 35, a woman was four times more likely to die than a man of the same age. She was twice as likely between age 35 and 45. To put it differently, if she survived the birth of her first child's birth and subsequent childbirths up thru the age of 45, she was likely to live to 60 or more. Mortality apparently rose and fell equally for men and women with all the usual causes like famine, disease, and so forth. Turning one again to the good Norwich records of 1570, there were two men and five women aged between 95 and 100 in a community of 1,400, and about 15% of the poor were over 60. In general, mortality among both sexes, for all ages, and between the classes would not surprise the modern reader. Fewer car wrecks obviously, but more boys doing dumb things and getting killed. High infant mortality, horrible medical practices, and epidemic diseases

killed people across the board. Diseases resulting from poor nutrition etc. killed more poor people. War killed more men. What's interesting during the middle ages is that excluding famine and war, wealth or poverty didn't have much of an effect on mortality. This was because medical treatments of the day were often worse than no treatment at all. Drowning was a popular way to die among women who fetched water from open wells and rocky creeks. Fire in wooden houses with fireplaces killed both sexes about equally. And so it went.

Marriage among the common folk is another area that might not hold many surprises for the modern reader -other than perhaps the fact that people worked and saved up in order to set up housekeeping till their mid-twenties. Economics explains much of the delay both because of the need to save up for a house and household as well as a steep marriage tax. Marriage among regular people was usually 'affective rather than dynastic' which is to say out of affection rather than to preserve or grow political power. Husbands and wives were about the same age -usually no more than a few years apart. When there was a large difference, it was usually a (rich) old widower marrying a younger woman, occasionally a rich widow marrying a younger man. A large portion of the population never married. One inclusive study of demographics finds that only 33% of the whole population was married[18], about 6% widowed, and whopping 61% single. Very few women over 40 lived independently, most unmarried women of this age lived with her parents. Those women who did have their own household were almost always widows.

A medieval woman might expect six or more live births in her lifetime but it was not uncommon for only two to make it to adulthood. Nor was it uncommon for the first child to be born less than nine months after the marriage, but teenage pregnancy and illegitimate births were very rare. This is perhaps misleading because illegitimate babies were not baptized and therefore did not make it into the record books. On the other hand, there were –at various times and in various places– taxes on marriage, so these babies might have been born to a committed loving couple that simply hadn't gotten around to the paperwork, tax payment, and the church ceremony.

Given late marriages and life expectancy, it was unusual for more than two generation to live in a given household. Four or five was the usual size of a family, (mom, dad, and the kids -not counting servants and apprentices), but because it was at twelve years of age when kids went out on their own, the youngest child might have many older brothers and sisters who he or she only saw on feast days–if at all. Add to this migration and from the 16th century onward and it is easy to see how an otherwise large blended family might only have two kids at home. Do not think of these people as cold-hearted toward their children. While they sent their own kids off to learn a craft, they often took in other children as orphans, (for which the parish paid them), or took in apprentices to the household craft.

---

[18] Except the Irish. They got married more often and at younger ages than the English, even the English Catholics.

Migration within England during the late Medieval was mostly about leaving the farm and coming to the city. London, for example was as much as 70% immigrants. Men tended to migrate in their teens, and women do so in their twenties. More domestic servants, (women), migrated than farm workers, (men), and so in a middling large market town the ratio of unmarried women to unmarried men might be as high as ten women to seven men.

In general, a thoughtful reading about life for the common woman would not surprise the modern reader. Less divorce, less opportunity, and earlier death not-with standing, women–then as now–act in their own best interest but with what must be called Christian Charity. They loved their children, and often even their husbands. Even then it was recognized that a woman's work was never done. A book of advice to women in 1580 said, "Some respite to husbands the weather sends, but housewives affairs have never an end." But it is also clear that they had time for gossip, shopping, and a little recreation & travel.

Before we finish up with the middle ages and bump along to the Protestant Reformation, we need to stir the Catholic Church into the mix. There were various religious communities for women. Hamlet's advice to Ophelia to 'get thee to a nunnery' was all well and good, but usually only useful to rich families who needed to store an inconvenient daughter or spinster aunt. They were refuges from the world as well as being centers for learning, one of the few places where women actually could learn something besides a craft, but the number of nuns and almost-nuns had been dropping from about 1500 onward.

So how did things shake out for women with the Protestant Revolution? Hard to say one way or the other. On one hand, people got to worship the way the wanted to, and some of these people were women. On the other hand, the flavor of Protestantism called Puritanism was virulently repressive and intolerant of sin of all sorts, particularly carnal sin. Oddly enough, women were seen as temptresses more than the victims, at least in the eyes of the old, the self-appointed, and the self-righteous. One of the things that the Pilgrims felt was contrary to their religion were new rules that forbade them to exact corporeal punishment on people the felt needed a little whipping or a good long spell in the *stocks*. This increasingly fell to the crown–or local secular authorities–so they set off to the colonies where they could torture people as they saw fit. (About forty years after they got there, the Puritans hanged fourteen women and six men between 1692 &1693 in Salem Massachusetts.) On the other hand, this was a drop in the bucket compared to what the Catholic Church and assorted Inquisitions had done somewhat earlier all up and down Europe.

In general terms, Protestantism reduced the possible roles of women in church activities. A Catholic wife could go out and about, do things for the church, celebrate various Saint's Days, or even enter the convent if she were that devout. A good Protestant wife on the other hand, was expected to stay home, educate the children in religious matters, defer to her husband, and read her prayer-book.

From the Reformation forward, it's all about economics. The industrial revolution was still a little ways off, but as food became more plentiful, England turned to manufacturing. To say about the same thing backwards, as England got better making things, they could afford to import more food that someone else grew somewhere else. This manufacturing was different from that done in the earlier times of the craftsmen and his workers and apprentices working in his home-shop producing for local consumption. These products would also be sold by the craftsman, or his wife if he were busy out in the shop. As things got more industrialized the *putting-out*[19] system came along. It would be used for many forms of making, but fabric will serve as an example. Someone–typically a merchant of some sort– would bring a pile of wool to the home shop to be cleaned and come by later to pick it up and drop off another batch. At this time he would do some quality control and pay for the work done. He would then take the clean wool to another shop to be carded, and yet another shop to be spun, and on thru the other necessary specialized processes to achieve what ever end-product was sought. Specialization is more efficient, but it also reduces the need for craftsmanship and thereby reduced wages. What is more, this sort of arrangement required something approaching our modern notions of formal agreements and contracts. Such things were thought to be outside of the proper place for women. So the trend for women as the putting-out system grew was lower wages and they were removed further from participation in the economy. This also meant fewer employers and more employees.

There is some small good news for women about now. The tiny germ of the idea that maybe women had rights equal to those of men just barely begin appear. This idea would grow as the industrial revolution hit its stride toward the beginnings of the 1800's. Now at last, women were coming to have plenty of work opportunities outside the home. This work was in huge factories. The problem was that this work was done under pretty deplorable conditions, and some of the worst job–those needing the least skill and that paid the least–were being done by children.

It was these factories that WERE the industrial revolution. Both cause and effect attains. Factories had to be big because they were full of expensive machines. Expensive machines had to be run day and night if they were to be profitable, therefore people had to work around the clock. (Except Sunday. England was still a Christian The machines first ran on running water, and water runs only where there are hills and hills are not good for farming nor for cities. It was easier to get workers to come to factories on hillsides that it was to move hills to cities, so they had to build better roads and railroads to get food to the workers and get the finished product to big city markets. Beyond water power, even bigger machines ran on steam which came from burning coal. Air-quality?

---

[19] The putting-out system continued to work in the manufacturing of small arms for the English military thru the 19th century. In fact, a modern form of the system was quickly set up to provided England with the bits and pieces to be assembled into fighter planes during the *Battle of Britain* during WWII.

Forget it. Various lung diseases were responsible for one quarter of all deaths in industrialized England during all of Queen Victoria's reign. These big expensive machines also needed to be paid for and England's financial markets came to be the biggest most important in the world. (This might be a good thing or a bad thing depending on your views of capitalism.)

We have wondered a bit far afield from our topic of women. During the 1700's, a woman's choices came down to coming from a very rich family, marrying a moderately rich professional man, being a wage earner on the farm or in the factory, or going into domestic service. In the later case, she had to hope to meet a husband by the time spinsterhood descended on her -about age 25 to 30. Not all of them succeeded.

Fast-forward now to the 1800's and the Victorian era. One more opportunity presented itself to women during this stern and upright period, that being prostitution. This was not actually illegal in England, and while they had fewer brothels than Paris for example, rooming houses wherein they did their work were common and tolerant. Some fairly rigorous scholarship in this area suggests that there was one prostitute for every

 twelve adult men in London in 1841. There is, however some debate as to the real numbers. There are also problems surrounding how a prostitute be defined. Was she a casual prostitute, typically someone's domestic servant doing a little moonlighting, or a full time professional who was likely a women with children, legitimate or otherwise. What is known is that they enjoyed a better standard of living than women in legitimate jobs, and had generally better health. This could be explained by noting domestic servants put in a 14 hour work day. Prostitution is a fascinating–if morbidly fascinating–part of Victorian English history, but perhaps outside the scope of this work.

Much beyond the Victorian era (Queen Victoria died in 1901) the differences between American women and English women is of trivial importance. They are pretty much the same in terms of all the things people with fancy degrees study, measure, and natter on about. There were a couple of world Wars that changed the Brits far more than the Yanks. America arguably gave women more political power sooner than did the Brits. Wyoming, being a wild and woolly wilderness, gave women the vote in 1869 just to attract more of them. (It didn't work.) The rest of America got around to this in 1920, but the Brits dawdled around till 1928 before they gave women full suffrage.

Worcester / Worcestershire   Worchester is the town in Worchestershire County. *Worcestershire Sauce* was invented in the town of Worcester despite its spelling, but it is pronounced *woster sauce, Woster* being the shortened slang for Worcester. No one is entirely sure why this is so, but it may have had to do with 19th century trademark law.

What is rather better known is that a couple of chemists, John Lea and Bill Perrins were trying to come up with a curry sauce. One batch was a failure so they set a barrel of it aside, but happened to taste it again about a year and a half later. Lea and Perrins was born in 1830.

words, have   -to *have words* is to argue, but *have words with* is to advise or chat with.

work   In your reading, you will come across job titles, most of which are obvious to the American reader -farmer and teacher, for example, but some will be confusing or utterly impenetrable -consider *loriner* or *costermonger*. Furthermore, some of these occupations will sound like common last names: Fletcher, Sawyer, Cartwright, etc. but were in fact occupations, occupations that no longer exist, but the surnames live on. From the middle ages, people had the first names their parents gave them, and the family name which was often the family's occupation. Some occupation names sound familiar, but describe jobs that have changed considerably over the years; *engineers, milliners* and *poachers* for example do not mean now what they meant back in the day.

Up until the repeal of the ***Articles of Artificers*** in 1653, the **guild** and **apprentice** systems very strictly prescribed who could do what, labor unions times ten. In the bustling economies of the 16th and 17th century London for example, shoe makers, bootmakers, and clog makers were permitted to make only shoes, boots, or clogs, and even clogs had both the guy who made the wooden sole -the *clogger*, and the *clogmaker* who made the upper leather part. This explains all the X-makers, Y-makers, and Z-workers that would all seem to be doing much the same thing.

working class   When the peasantry left the farm for the factory as the industrial revolution unfolded, they became the working class, but the term is from rather later in the game, actually, the late 1800's.

For the American reader to understand what an English writer means when he used the term, he must remember two things: first, the *middle class* was very rich, but they were just not nobility, and the working class had the very un-American view that being in the working class was just fine thank you. There was no burning desire to work one's way up. In general terms, the working-class had their own religion -Methodist, entertainment -music halls, social places -pubs, and eventually, even their own ***political party -Labor***.

Towards the end of the 20th century the term became synonymous with unemployment, but only because manufacturing jobs were becoming increasingly scarce.

Not much to be said about *X*. It's Greek in origin and pronounced in various ways. The Yanks and the Brits use *X* pretty much the same way. There are some minor fussy spelling differences though: the Brits favor ending certain words *-xion* and the Yanks use *-ction*.

x-factor   -a union contract stipulation regarding special circumstances and usually extra pay. Also a contemporary reality TV show involving singing.

Y goes back to the Semitic, but the Romans only used it for foreign words. The English Great Vowel Shift made it a vowel. Sometimes. It's also part of the whole *U, V, Y* controversy. When printing first came to England, there was no way to do a *Þ*, (called a thorn and meant *th)*, so they used a **Y** to get to *ye* in place of *the*. This gives us silly things like *Ye Olde Shoppe* trying to be clever and archaic.

yellow lines   Yellow lines are painted on the side of the road to indicate parking restrictions.

Yeoman / Yeomanry   Originally the word meant small land-owning farmers. During the French Revolution and later Napoleonic Wars, there was fear England would be invaded. Yeoman officers were recruited from the nobility and they in turn recruited soldiers from among their tenants and other locals. These soldiers could not be sent offshore to fight; they were strictly for home defense.

Yoeman of the Guard   The bodyguard of the monarch and the oldest military corps in continuous existence in the realm. They were created by Henry Seven way back in 1485. They still dress that way, all red and gold, and carry a *partizan* which was a long ornamental spear. They are nicknamed the *Beefeaters* and not to be confused with the **Queen's Guard** .

York   Founded by the Romans at the confluence of the Rivers Ouse and Foss. It is in the far north east of England with a population of a little over 200,000. In the Middle ages, it was the wool trading center and capitol of the Church of England. In the 19th century it was a railroad hub and manufacturing center.

Yorkshire   The largest county in England -so large that it has been subdivided into confusing boroughs, districts, regions, and authorities. It is to the northeast corner of the country and is flat, green, and has lots of sheep. It was about as far north as the Romans got. It's also where the Romans first brought Christianity to England. The Celts re-emerged when the Romans left, and while they weren't exactly Christian, nor were they entirely opposed to Christianity. Then an early Viking, Eric the Bloodaxe showed up and things went downhill fast. They didn't get much better when the Normans came, followed by the Black Death, followed by the War of the Roses -between the House of York and the House of Lancaster, followed by the English Civil War. The 19th century was fairly calm and Yorkshire went about mining coal, making steel, and weaving wool. Today the heavy dirty industries have gone down and service & tourism have taken their places.

Yorkshire pudding   In America, this dish might be considered a giant popover or a Dutch Baby. Essentially, a thin batter is made from flour, eggs, and milk or water and poured into oily drippings from a beef roast in a hot pan and baked. As the batter cooks, it creeps up and over the oil and soaks it up. Delicious! Not healthy, but delicious. This dish got started way back when starvation was a far more likely cause of death than congestive heart failure, so nothing was wasted, and fat is a very nutritiously dense food.

Yankee Yorkshire Pudding (Americanized -simple and fast.)
- a pound or two of your favorite hamburger (extra lean may not be the best way to go.)
- boxed biscuit mix
-or-
- canned dough -the things that pop open. Buttermilk or Country Style are good, but any of them will work except the sweet cinnamon ones.
  1. Arrange two oven racks in the middle of an oven and set it to 350.
  2. Follow the instructions on the side of the box of biscuit mix for a few servings of biscuits. Or pop open one of those fresh poppy-dough tubes.
  3. Prep a shallow baking dish with grease or spray oil.
  4. Spread the biscuit dough in a single layer or arrange the poppy-dough blobs close together on a baking sheet or dish in the middle of the pan.
  5. Make four or six hamburger patties and arrange them on a grilling rack. The idea is to arrange them so that as the fat oozes out, it drips down onto the biscuits as they bake.
  6. Put the biscuits on the lower rack and the burger on the higher rack. Bake until the burgers are done and the biscuits have browned.
  7. Serve the burgers on top of the biscuits. You really don't need

---

ketchup or other sauce.

Real Yorkshire Pudding (The way the Brits do it.)
- a three-bone standing rib roast baked in a 9 x 12 pan. (You are really looking for about a quarter cup of the fat drippings in the bottom of the pan.)
- 2 cups of flour
- 1 ½ teaspoons of salt
- 4 large eggs -best at room temperature
- 2 cups milk
- ¼ cup drippings -divided

1. Remove the roast from the oven and from the pan. Tent it in aluminum foil and let it rest.
2. Turn the oven up to 400.
3. Let the fat cool a bit.
4. Place the flour, salt, eggs, milk, and all but 1 tablespoon of the oil into a blender.
5. Whiz it up for 30 seconds.
6. Pour the reserved oil back into the roasting pan and pour in the batter.
7. Bake for 35 or 40 minutes until it's puffy and golden.

Your Grace -proper form of address for a duke, duchess, or archbishop.

Your Ladyship   -considerably more complicated than *Your Grace*. Before the early 1700's, Your Ladyship was for wives of mere barons and bishops and *My Lady was* for wives of **vicounts, earls, marques,** and **dukes**. After then *My Lady* became more common, and by the 20th century it didn't make much difference one way or the other. If a Yank finds himself in a situation where it does matter, he might expect to be carefully briefed in the anti-chamber. The English are a thoughtful this way.

Your Lordship   -proper address for a lord (Barron), judge, or woman sheriff, but like *Your Ladyship / My Lady*, the distinction between *My Lord* and *Your Lordship* blurred after about 1750.

Your Worship   -a magistrate or mayor. It's little like *Your Honor* in America.

Z's history is pretty normal among the letters. First it was the Semitic letter-picture for sword or weapon, then Phoenician, and then Greek, but Z is unique in that it came from Etruscan before it got to Latin. It has been a part of the European alphabets for a comparatively long time. Except in England. They used *G* or *J* until the French came along. *Jealous* and *zealous* actually used to be the same word. *Z* has not always been the last letter in the alphabet; up until the 19th century, English school children finished the alphabet ...*x y x &*. The letter is the least used on both sides of the Atlantic, but more used in America with words like *extemporize and eulogize* that end in ...*ize*. In England, the same words end in *ise*. Finally, it's called *zed* in England.

zebra crossing   -crosswalk

Z-car / Zulu car   -police car from the radio call sign for *Z -Zulu*

zimmer   -a walker

zip   -a zipper for clothing

Acronyms

Shortening expressions with a string of first letters is largely—but not entirely—a 20th Century thing. If your reading is staged before WWI, you probably don't need any of this, UNLESS it involves knights, decorations, military orders, and medals etc.

A

AA	Automobile Association
AC	Assistant Commissioner
ADC	Amateur Dramatic Club (at Cambridge)

AFM	Air Force Medal
AoNB	Area of Natural Beauty
APS	Acting Police Sargent
ATS	Auxiliary Territorial Service

B

BAA	British Airports Authority
BEF	British Expeditionary Force

BMA	British Medical Association
BSI	British Standards Institute
BST	British Summer Time

C

C of E	Church of England
CAD	Catholic Anti-Discrimination
CB	Order / Companion of the Order of the Bath
CBE	Order / Commander of the British Empire
CID	Criminal Investigation Department

CMC	Crime Management Center
CMG	Commander of the Order of St. Michael
CND	Campaign for Nuclear Disarmament
CPO	Compulsory Purchase Order
CSC	Conspicuous Service Cross
CSE	Certificate of Secondary Education
DHSS	Department of Health and Social Security

D

DBE	Dame of the British Empire
DC	Detective Constable
DCA	Due Care and Attention
DCB	Dame Commander of the Order of the Bath
DCC	Detective Chief Constable
DCI	Detective Chief Inspector

DL	Democratic Left
DOE	Department of Energy
DoH	Department of Health
DPP	Director of Public Prosecutors
DSM	Distinguished Service Medal
DSO	Distinguished Service Order

DCM	Distinguished Conduct Metal	DSS	Department of Social Security
DCMC	Dame Commander of the Order of St. Michael and St. George	DULC	Democratic Unionist Loyalist Party
DED	Department of Economic Development	DUP	Democratic Unionist Party
DFM	Distinguished Flying Medal	DVLA	Driver and Vehicle Licensing Agency

F

		FEC	Fair Employment Commission
FCO	Foreign and Commonwealth Office	FSQ	F___ing Silly Question

G

GATSO	Gobby and Totally Silly Officer	GCMC	Order of St. Michael & St. George
GBE	Order of the British Empire	GCSE	General Certificate of Secondary Education
GBH	grievous bodily harm	GM	George Medal
GC	George Cross	GMT	Greenwich Mean Time
GCB	Order of the Bath	GPO	General Post Office

H

HM	His / Her Majesty's anything	HMS	His / Her Majesty's Ship

I

		IPLO	Irish People's Liberation Organization
INC	Irish national Conference	IRA	Irish Republic Army
INLA	Irish National Liberation Army	ITN	Independent Television News ./ Network

K

		KCMG	Knight Commander of St. Michael and St. George
KB	Knight / Order of the Bath	KG	Knight / Order of the Garter
KBE	Knight / Order of the British Empire	KT	Knight / Order of the Thistle

L

		LMF	Lack of Moral Fiber
LDP	Liberal Democratic Party	LP	Labor Party
LLD	Doctor of Law	LSE	London School of Economics

M

MC	Military Cross	MO	Medical Officer
MEP	Member of the European Parliament	MOT	Ministry of Transportation
MisPer	Missing Person	MP	Member of Parliament
MM	Military Medal	MV	Member of Royal Victorian Order

N

NAS/ UWT	National Association of Schoolmasters / Union of Women Teachers	NSPCC	National Society for Prevention of Cruelty to Children
NBG	no bloody good	NUGMW	National Union of General and Municipal Workers
NDP	National Democratic Party	NUJ	National Union of Journalists
NFI	No F___ing Interest	NUM	National Union of Mineworkers
NF	National Front	NUR	National Union of Railway Workers
NI	National Insurance Northern Ireland	NUT	National Union of Teachers
NP	Nationalist Party		

O

OAP	Old Age Pensioner	OO	Orange Order
OBE	Order of the British Empire	OU	Oxford (or Open) University
OC	Officer Commanding	OV	Orange Volunteers
OM	Order of Merit		

P

		PPE	philosophy, politics, & economics (an old degree)
PA	Personal Assistant	PPP	psychology, philosophy, & physiology
PC	Police Constable	PPP	People's Progressive Party
PD	People's Democracy	PPS	Principal / Parliamentary Private Secretary
PG	Paying Guest	PR	Proportional Representation
PLC	Public Limited Company	PSF	Provisional Sinn Fein

PLR	Public Lending Library	PYO	Persistent Youth Offender

Q

QB	Queen's Bench	QC	Queen's Council
		RIR	Royal Irish Regiment

R

RA	Royal Academy or Royal Artillery	RL	Rugby League
RAC	Royal Automobile Club	RLP	Republican Labor Party
RAF	Royal Air Force	RM	Royal Mint
RAM	Royal Academy of Music	RM	Royal Marines
RAMC	Royal Army Medical Corps	RMC/A	Royal Military College / Academy
RC	Roman Catholic	RN	Royal Navy
RCA	Royal College of the Arts	RoSPA	Royal Society for Prevention of Accidents
RCM	Royal College of Music	RP	Received Pronunciation
RCP	Royal College of Physicians	RS	Royal Society
RCS	Royal College of Surgeons	RSA	Royal Society of the Arts
RD	refer to drawer (a bounced check)	RSC	Royal Shakespeare Company
RDC	Royal District Council	RSM	Regimental Sergeant Major
RE	Royal Engineers	RSPB	Royal Society for the Protection of Birds
RFC	Royal Flying Corps	RSPCA	Royal Society for the Prevention of Cruelty to Animals
RGS	Royal Geographical Society	RTA	road traffic accident
RHG	Royal Horse Guards	RU	Rugby Union
RHS	Royal Historic Society	RUC	Royal Ulster Constabulary
RIBA	Royal Institute of British Architects	RWV	robbery with violence

S

SAE	Self Addressed Envelope or Society of Automotive Engineers	SDP	Social Democratic Party

SAS	Special Air Services	SF	Sinn Fein
SAYE	Save As You Earn	SIS	Secrete Intelligence Service
SB	Special Branch	SLD	Social and Liberal Democrats
SC	Special Constable	SO	Special Operations

T

TA	Territorial Army	TT	Teetotaler
TGWU	Transportation and General Workers Union	TUC	Trades Union Congress

U

UCA	Ulster Citizen's Army	UDR	Ulster Defense Regiment
UDA	Ulster Defense Association	UFF	Ulster Freedom Fighters
UDC	Urban District Council	UIP	Ulster Independence Party
UDP	Ulster Democratic Party	US	Unserviceable

V

VAT	Value added Tax	VO	Victorian Order
VC	Victory Cross	WP	Workers Party

W

WAAC	Women's Auxiliary Army Corps	WReN	Women's Royal Navy
WAAF	Women's Auxiliary Air Force	WRVS	Women's Royal Volunteer Service

Y

YHA	Youth Hostels Association

Bill Harvey grew up in Colorado which is a state poorly equipped with oceans. Because of this, he read all of C. S. Forester's ***Horatio Hornblower*** novels by the time he finished middle school. (He was a bookish lad.) From there it was a fairly straight line from maritime history, to the industrial revolution and its Victorian 'high-technology,' and finally, the history of economics and finance. England was the center of it all.

In order to support his reading, Harvey taught various things to various people, mostly adult people; including a stint teaching GED subjects to people in jail. (As an employee, NOT an inmate.) Along the way, he got very good at explaining complicated things to people. For example, factoring polynomials in the morning and the English Civil War in the afternoon.

American readers, particularly those who enjoy any era of English writing, can often take meaning from context when they stumble across something the British reader takes for granted, but for Harvey, there was a need understand these Briticisms and explain them–to himself or otherwise –and have a little fun along the way. What you are holding in your hands now is the consequence of this obsession.

Harvey currently makes his home in San Francisco and supports his reading habit with a little fancy woodwork on the side.

Any comments, questions, criticisms, or recipes would be welcomed.
wharvey904@hotmail.com